Public Policies and
Household Saving

A National Bureau
of Economic Research
Project Report

Public Policies and Household Saving

Edited by James M. Poterba

The University of Chicago Press

Chicago and London

JAMES M. POTERBA is professor of economics at the Massachusetts
Institute of Technology and director of the Public Economics Research
Program at the National Bureau of Economic Research.

The University of Chicago Press, Chicago 60637
The University of Chicago Press, Ltd., London
© 1994 by the National Bureau of Economic Research
All rights reserved. Published 1994
Printed in the United States of America
03 02 01 00 99 98 97 96 95 94   1 2 3 4 5
ISBN: 0–226–67618–8 (cloth)

Library of Congress Cataloging-in-Publication Data

Public policies and household saving / edited by James M. Poterba.
        p.   cm. — (National Bureau of Economic Research project
    report)
      Includes bibliographical references and index.
      1. Saving and thrift—Government policy.   2. Saving and
    investment—Government policy.   3. Taxation.   I. Poterba, James.
    II. Series.
    HG7920.P83   1994
    339.4'3—dc20   93-42088
                                                                CIP

Relation of the Directors to the
Work and Publications of the
National Bureau of Economic Research

1. The object of the National Bureau of Economic Research is to ascertain and to present to the public important economic facts and their interpretation in a scientific and impartial manner. The board of Directors is charged with the responsibility of ensuring that the work of the National Bureau is carried on in strict conformity with this object.

2. The President of the National Bureau shall submit to the Board of Directors, or to its Executive Committee, for their formal adoption all specific proposals for research to be instituted.

3. No research report shall be published by the National Bureau until the President has sent each member of the Board a notice that a manuscript is recommended for publication and that in the President's opinion it is suitable for publication in accordance with the principles of the National Bureau. Such notification will include an abstract or summary of the manuscript's content and a response form for use by those Directors who desire a copy of the manuscript for review. Each manuscript shall contain a summary drawing attention to the nature and treatment of the problem studied, the character of the data and their utilization in the report, and the main conclusions reached.

4. For each manuscript so submitted, a special committee of the Directors (including Directors Emeriti) shall be appointed by majority agreement of the President and Vice Presidents (or by the Executive Committee in case of inability to decide on the part of the President and Vice Presidents), consisting of three Directors selected as nearly as may be one from each general division of the Board. The names of the special manuscript committee shall be stated to each Director when notice of the proposed publication is submitted to him. It shall be the duty of each member of the special manuscript committee to read the manuscript. If each member of the manuscript committee signifies his approval within thirty days of the transmittal of the manuscript, the report may be published. If at the end of that period any member of the manuscript committee withholds his approval, the President shall then notify each member of the Board, requesting approval or disapproval of publication, and thirty days additional shall be granted for this purpose. The manuscript shall then not be published unless at least a majority of the entire Board who shall have voted on the proposal within the time fixed for the receipt of votes shall have approved.

5. No manuscript may be published, though approved by each member of the special manuscript committee, until forty-five days have elapsed from the transmittal of the report in manuscript form. The interval is allowed for the receipt of any memorandum of dissent or reservation, together with a brief statement of his reasons, that any member may wish to express; and such memorandum of dissent or reservation shall be published with the manuscript if he so desires. Publication does not, however, imply that each member of the Board has read the manuscript, or that either members of the Board in general or the special committee have passed on its validity in every detail.

6. Publications of the National Bureau issued for informational purposes concerning the work of the Bureau and its staff, or issued to inform the public of activities of Bureau staff, and volumes issued as a result of various conferences involving the National Bureau shall contain a specific disclaimer noting that such publication has not passed through the normal review procedures required in this resolution. The Executive Committee of the Board is charged with review of all such publications from time to time to ensure that they do not take on the character of formal research reports of the National Bureau, requiring formal Board approval.

7. Unless otherwise determined by the Board or exempted by the terms of paragraph 6, a copy of this resolution shall be printed in each National Bureau publication.

(Resolution adopted October 25, 1926, as revised through September 30, 1974)

Contents

Acknowledgments

This volume is part of a multiyear research program on International Comparisons of Household Saving that is being conducted under the auspices of the National Bureau of Economic Research (NBER). I am grateful to Martin Feldstein, president of the NBER, for his help in formulating the project and his constant interest and advice regarding research strategy. I am also grateful to the John M. Olin Foundation and the Dean Witter Foundation for financial support of this research.

Organizing a conference with participants from three continents is not a simple task, and the NBER conference department staff provided outstanding logistical support for the meeting at which these papers were presented. I am particularly grateful to Carl Skinner, who served as conference coordinator, and would like to thank Kirsten Davis, director of the NBER Conference Department, for ongoing help in planning and organizing the meeting. My administrative assistant at MIT, Marie Myers, played a critical role in preserving smooth lines of communication between me and the other authors throughout the project.

My final debt is to Deborah Kiernan of the NBER Publications Department, who has carefully guided the manuscript through the tortuous editorial process and into print.

Acknowledgments

Introduction

James M. Poterba

The declining rate of national saving in the United States has stimulated seemingly endless debate on whether government policy should seek to reverse this trend, and if so, how it should achieve this objective. Much of this discussion has centered on policy options for raising household saving. In the early 1980s, the United States experimented with a program of universal retirement saving accounts, individual retirement accounts (IRAs), that relied on tax incentives to encourage household saving. In part because the institution of these accounts coincided with a decline in the private saving rate as measured in the national income accounts, and in part because of fiscal pressures associated with the Tax Reform Act of 1986, IRAs were partially phased out in 1986. The low private saving rate in the United States has persisted, however, and led to an ongoing search for new ways to encourage personal saving.

One reason policymakers suspect that personal saving rates can be influenced by government policy is the wide range of such rates across countries. Table 1 presents personal saving rates in a set of seven industrialized nations during the period from 1970 to 1988. The data show that the low-saving countries are the United States and the United Kingdom, with household saving rates of 5 percent of disposable income in the late 1980s. France and Germany report household saving rates twice as high, and the saving rates in Japan and Italy are three times as high as that in the United States.

The striking differences in the level of household saving across countries are matched by differences in government policies toward saving. While the United States has tried to increase private saving, some other nations, notably Japan, have tried to do the opposite. During the late 1980s, Japan curtailed the system of postal saving accounts that had for decades attracted substantial

James M. Poterba is professor of economics at the Massachusetts Institute of Technology and director of the Public Economics Research Program at the National Bureau of Economic Research.

Table 1   **Personal Saving Rates in Industrial Nations (%)**

Country	1970	1980	1988
Canada	5.6	13.6	9.4
France	18.7	17.6	12.4
Germany	13.8	12.7	12.6
Italy	38.2	29.1	22.7
Japan	17.7	17.9	15.2
United Kingdom	9.3	13.5	4.4
United States	8.3	7.3	4.3

Source: Dean et al. 1990.

flows of household saving. Other policies, such as credit liberalization, were also adopted in an attempt to reduce private saving and stimulate consumption.

International comparisons of household saving incentives frequently focus on individual policy instruments, such as IRAs or postal saving accounts, even though personal saving incentives are affected by a wide range of government policies. Many of these policies operate through the tax system. They include income tax policies that drive a wedge between the pretax and posttax return to saving, as well as specialized tax policies that encourage households to save in particular institutional forms (such as IRAs in the United States) or particular assets (such as the tax exemption for capital gains on corporate stock in some nations). Household saving incentives can also be affected by the tax treatment of private pension plans and other retirement saving arrangements, by tax rules and credit market institutions that affect the after-tax cost of borrowing, and by a range of other policies.

The chapters in this book describe the array of policies that affect saving incentives in seven industrialized nations. Systematic study of the experience in different countries can yield important insights for both policymakers and academics whose knowledge is largely confined to their home country. International comparison can both expand the set of policy options that can be considered when discussion turns to private saving, and also provide potentially valuable information on the likely effects of various policy reforms.

The authors of each of the seven chapters in this volume are experts on the idiosyncratic features of their country's policies. Yet each chapter is written in a format that systematizes the description of institutions in different nations. Each of these chapters was presented and discussed at a conference held at the NBER offices in Cambridge, Massachusetts, in June 1992. The result is a collection of papers that provides a wealth of detailed information about saving incentives in a comparable and accessible fashion.

Each paper is divided into five major sections. The first provides an overview of the household balance sheet in each country, describing the relative importance of different assets and liabilities. This is important background information for analyzing tax policies and other public policies that affect private saving incentives. Although comparable data is not available for all seven nations in this study, the authors have tried to provide similar information where possible and to direct readers to primary sources for further data on household wealth holdings.

The second section in each paper focuses on tax policies toward capital income. Each paper summarizes the tax treatment of dividends, interest income, capital gains, and household interest payments to creditors. The papers also note the range of specialized tax policies, such as wealth and estate taxes, that apply to capital in some countries. The chapters describe the structure of the tax system as well as the effective tax rates that face households in different income and wealth strata.

The third section of each paper describes the system of employment-linked retirement saving. In many countries, pension saving accounts for a large fraction of total personal saving. One goal of this project is to provide detailed data on the structure of pension saving and the policy instruments that encourage or discourage it in various nations. The papers also include information on government retirement pensions, such as Social Security, and discuss any specialized provisions that may apply to saving for health expenditures late in life.

The next section in each chapter focuses on targeted saving programs. These are the specialized programs that typically operate through the tax system and provide higher returns if households save through specialized accounts or in particular assets. One of the central findings of this study is that there is substantial heterogeneity across countries in the terms of these programs. In some cases funds are locked away until retirement (IRA's and 401(k) plans in the United States); in other cases they can be withdrawn at the saver's discretion (registered retirement saving programs in Canada). In some cases the tax incentive for saving is provided when the contribution is made; in other cases it is delayed until funds are withdrawn from the saving account.

The fifth and final section of each chapter focuses on saving through insurance contracts. In some of the nations in this study, insurance contracts are one of the most important means of wealth accumulation. The tax treatment of insurance saving and the institutional structure of the insurance market are thus important influences on private saving behavior.

The country-specific analyses display a wide range of policies both across countries and within countries over the past few decades. It is difficult to generalize from the studies, except to say that there is great diversity. In Germany, for example, saving through employer-provided pensions is relatively unimportant, while in the United States and Canada pensions are a tax-favored form of saving that accounts for a substantial share of retirement income. The Japanese analysis provides important information on the relative importance of tax-subsidized saving, with the authors estimating that roughly half of all household saving in the mid-1980s was channeled to tax-favored saving plans. This finding suggests that to understand saving in Japan, it is not sufficient to analyze only contributions to the specialized saving programs.

The studies also show important differences in households' access to credit and suggest that this can affect the saving rate. High-saving countries, such as Japan and Germany, have tax systems that discourage consumer borrowing. These incentives are reinforced by relatively restrictive credit market conditions for individuals. Credit institutions and tax rules have also been subject to substantial change during the past decade. In the United States, for example, consumer interest was tax-deductible until 1986 but is no longer deductible. It is more difficult to describe the effects of changes in financial structure, in both the United States and other countries, that may have increased consumer access to various debt instruments.

The papers in this volume describe the saving policies and incentives in various nations, but they do not analyze their effects on private saving. To convincingly assess the impact of each program on saving would have resulted in a volume many times the size of this one, and in many cases the findings would be subject to criticism and dispute. This volume is therefore limited to cataloging the structure of policies in different nations. The second-stage research projects designed to identify the effects of various policies are left to readers whose interest in this subject may be encouraged by reading the chapters in this volume.

Reference

Dean, Andrew, and Martine Durand, John Fallon, and Peter Hoeller. 1990. Saving Trends and Behavior in OECD Countries. *OECD Economic Studies* 14 (Spring): 40–41.

1   Government Saving Incentives in the United States

James M. Poterba

Public policies in the United States affect incentives for household saving in many ways. While income from capital is included in the federal income tax base, investments through private pension plans, individual retirement accounts (IRAs), some types of life insurance policies, and various other special programs receive favorable tax treatment. Public policy toward saving has been unstable during the past two decades. IRAs were introduced in 1981 to encourage household saving, but they were significantly restricted in the 1986 Tax Reform Act. Major changes in marginal tax rates affected the incentives for households to save through traditional saving vehicles, and coincident changes in the technology of financial services affected opportunities for both borrowing and investing.

This paper provides an overview of government policies that affect household saving incentives. It is divided into five sections. The first provides background information on saving in the United States, including information on the asset composition of household net worth. Section 1.2 describes the tax treatment of capital income and outlines the changes in capital taxation that have taken place during the last two decades. Section 1.3 focuses on saving through private pension plans, which is the single most important channel for tax-favored saving. Assets in pension plans account for more than one-sixth of household net worth. It also includes a brief discussion of the U.S. Social Security system. The fourth section describes several specialized policies which raise the return to private saving: IRAs, 401(k) pension plans, tax-favored life insurance policies, and related saving vehicles. There is a brief concluding section.

James M. Poterba is professor of economics at the Massachusetts Institute of Technology and director of the Public Economics Research Program at the National Bureau of Economic Research.

The author is grateful to Daniel Feenberg for assistance with the NBER TAXSIM model and to the National Science Foundation, the John M. Olin Foundation, and the Dean Witter Foundation for research support.

Table 1.1   Distribution of Household Net Worth, 1989 (thousand 1989 $)

	Family Income (thousand 1989 $)				
	<10	10–20	20–30	30–50	>50
Net worth					
Mean	30.1	63.1	89.6	150.2	586.7
Median	2.3	27.1	37.0	69.2	185.6
Share of:					
Households	20	20	17	23	20
Total wealth	3.2	6.8	8.2	18.6	63.2
	Age of Family Head				
	<35	35–44	45–54	55–64	>65
Net worth					
Mean	46.9	148.3	286.4	292.5	244.0
Median	6.8	52.8	86.7	91.3	71.9
Share of:					
Households	26	23	14	14	22
Total wealth	6.6	18.5	21.8	23.9	29.1

Sources: Kennickell and Shack-Marquez (1992) and author's calculations.

1.1   The Household Balance Sheet

Table 1.1 presents summary statistics on the distribution of wealth holdings from the Survey of Consumer Finances, the single best source of information on the wealth and income of households with capital assets. The table shows that the vast majority of all nonhuman wealth is concentrated in a small group of high-wealth households. Nearly two-thirds of the household sector's wealth is held by the one-fifth of the households with the highest net worth; even this wealth is highly concentrated within this population subgroup. In contrast, the bottom 40 percent of households account for less than 10 percent of the household sector's net worth. Table 1.1 also shows the pattern of net worth across households of different ages and demonstrates some concentration of net worth among older households.

Table 1.2 shows the composition of net worth by asset types and reveals several simple patterns. First, owner-occupied housing is a crucial component of household wealth, accounting for nearly one-quarter of total assets. When home mortgages are subtracted from the total, *net* owner-occupied housing equity accounts for just over 10 percent of net worth. Second, pension reserves account for nearly one-sixth of net worth. Although the table does not show this, for many households, owner-occupied housing and pension reserves account for virtually all of their net worth. Direct holdings of financial assets are near zero for the majority of U.S. households. Third, households have substantial holdings of corporate equities, both traded equities and nontraded equity

Table 1.2   **Composition of Household Wealth, 1991 (trillion $)**

Asset or Liability	Amount
Tangible assets	7.27
Owner-occupied residences and land	4.72
Consumer durables	2.07
Other	0.48
Marketed financial assets	8.57
Checkable deposits and currency	0.55
Other deposits (including money market fund shares)	2.94
U.S. government securities	1.09
Tax-exempt bonds	0.34
Corporate bonds and open market paper	0.63
Corporate equities	2.64
Life insurance reserves	0.40
Pension fund reserves	3.14
Equity in noncorporate business	2.66
Miscellaneous assets	0.28
Total assets	21.92
Home mortgages	2.73
Installment consumer debt	0.73
Other loans and debts	0.58
Total liabilities	4.04
Net worth	17.88

Source: Board of Governors of the Federal Reserve System, *Private Sector Net Worth* (Washington, D.C., September 1991).

shares in unincorporated businesses. Each of these categories accounts for nearly one-eighth of household net worth.

Household debt is small in comparison to the stock of household assets, with a liability-to-asset ratio of less than 20 percent. By far the most important household debt is the home mortgage, followed by consumer installment debt (typically to finance durables). Households have relatively little debt that does not fall into one of these categories. Tax and other policy incentives for households *to borrow* can have important effects on the personal saving rate. The 1986 Tax Reform Act eliminated the income tax deduction for consumer installment interest on all types of borrowing except home mortgages. While this may have raised the cost of borrowing for some liquidity-constrained households, for many with built-up equity in their homes, it probably induced a reallocation of borrowing from credit cards or auto loans to home mortgages or home-equity lines of credit (see Manchester and Poterba [1989] for further discussion). The ratio of mortgage debt to housing equity in 1991, 58 percent, was higher than at any previous time in the postwar period.

Table 1.3 provides a broad overview of the most important government policies that affect saving and guides the remainder of the paper. The next section considers the taxation of capital income when households save through tradi-

Table 1.3   Overview of Saving Incentives

1. Tax Burdens on Capital Income
  Dividends: Top marginal tax rate = 31% (+ state tax)
  Interest income: Top marginal tax rate = 31% (+ state tax)
  Capital gains: Taxed at top marginal rate of 28% on realization, basis step-up at death

2. Pension and Life Insurance Provisions
  Employer pension contributions: No tax on contributions, taxed when paid out as income
  Pension funds untaxed
  401(k) plans: Additional individual retirement saving vehicle, contributions limited to $7,000
    (1986 dollars)
  Life insurance: "Inside build-up" untaxed

3. Government Incentive Programs: IRAs
  Eligibility: Universal for tax-deductible IRA if not covered by employer pension plan, income-
    conditioned eligibility if have pension coverage (alternative is IRA from after-tax dollars)
  Contribution limit: $2,000/year
  Asset restrictions: None
  Withdrawal provisions: 10% penalty tax if withdrawn before age 59 and a half, afterwards
    ordinary income tax on withdrawals; must withdraw beginning at age 70 and a half

4. Other Special Provisions
  403(b) plans: Similar to 401(k) plans for employees of tax-exempt institutions
  Keogh plans: Similar to private pensions for self-employed individuals

tional channels—for example, by holding corporate stock or buying shares in a money-market mutual fund backed by short-term credit instruments. Section 1.3 considers private pension plans, and section 1.4 analyzes special incentive programs such as IRAs.

1.2   The Taxation of Capital Income

There are three types of capital income: interest payments, dividends, and capital gains. Interest and dividends are taxed in similar fashion, while a number of special provisions apply to capital gains income. Capital income is taxed by the federal, state, and, in some cases, local government; my analysis will focus on federal and state taxes.

The current U.S. federal tax code is structured around three basic income tax brackets, with marginal tax rates of 15, 28, and 31 percent, respectively. Table 1.4 shows the levels of taxable income that place different types of tax filers into each of these categories. There are also a number of tax code provisions that make it possible for some households to face tax rates above the "top rate" of 31 percent. Phase-out provisions on both personal exemptions and itemized deductions can raise the marginal tax rate on some high-income households to 35 percent.[1]

1. The phase-out provisions introduce substantial heterogeneity in marginal tax rates across households, due for example to different numbers of dependents in different households.

Table 1.4   **Marginal Tax Brackets in the Federal Income Tax, 1991**

Marginal Tax Rate (%)	Single Filer ($)	Married Joint Filer ($)
15	0–20,350	0–34,000
28	20,530–49,300	34,000–82,150
31	>49,300	>82,150

Source: Internal Revenue Service, *1991 Form 1040 Forms and Instructions.*

The rate structure of the federal income tax, particularly with respect to capital income, was changed substantially by the Economic Recovery Tax Act of 1981 and the Tax Reform Act of 1986. Prior to 1981, the highest marginal tax rate applicable to dividend and interest income was 70 percent. The 1981 reform reduced this rate to 50 percent, and the 1986 reform in turn lowered the marginal rate for very high income households to 28 percent. In less than a decade, the highest statutory marginal tax rate on capital income was therefore reduced by nearly two-thirds. Minor tax changes enacted since the 1986 Tax Reform Act have raised the top marginal tax rate from 28 percent to the current constellation of rates above 31 percent.

Weighted average marginal federal tax rates on dividend and interest income, with weights proportional to these income flows, are shown in table 1.5. The sharp changes in higher-income tax rates as a result of the 1981 and 1986 tax reforms are particularly important for the taxation of dividend income. The weighted average marginal tax rate on dividend income fell from 44.2 percent in 1980 to 24.9 percent in 1988. The change in the tax burden on interest income is less pronounced, since interest income is less concentrated in high income brackets than dividend income.

Table 1.5   **Weighted Average Marginal Tax Rates on Dividend and Interest Income**

	Weighted Average Marginal Tax Rate (%)		
Year	Dividends	Interest	Wages
1979	42.7	29.7	28.6
1980	44.2	31.9	30.2
1981	41.1	32.1	31.2
1982	35.0	27.9	28.2
1983	32.8	25.3	26.3
1984	31.1	25.5	25.8
1985	30.7	25.4	26.0
1986	28.4	23.8	25.9
1987	30.5	23.9	24.2
1988	24.9	22.1	22.5

Source: NBER TAXSIM program.
Note: Each column shows the ratio of increased taxes to increased income flow, when all dividends, interest receipts, or wages are increased by one percent of their reported value.

State tax rates on dividends and interest income differ substantially across jurisdictions. In many cases, state taxes add significantly to the tax burden on capital income. In California, for example, the top state tax rate is 11 percent. Even after allowing for the deductibility of state taxes from federal taxable income, this adds $(1 - .34) \times 11 = 7.3$ percent to the marginal tax burden. While most states follow the federal practice of applying equal tax rates to labor and capital income, a few states, such as Massachusetts, tax capital income at rates substantially above the tax rate on wages and salaries (12 percent vs. 6 percent). The average state marginal tax rate on dividends is approximately 5 percent. Recognizing state tax payments for those taxpayers who itemize reduces these net marginal tax rates to between 3 and 4 percent.

The taxation of capital gains is more complicated than the taxation of other capital income for three reasons. First, gains are taxed at realization rather than accrual, so there can be important differences between statutory and effective tax rates. Because deferral amounts, in effect, to the government granting the taxpayer an interest-free loan, it reduces the effective tax burden on capital gains. Second, the maximum statutory tax rate on capital gains is currently 28 percent. This is a smaller differential between the marginal tax rates on capital gains and dividends than during most of the postwar period, when the statutory tax rate on long-term capital gains was often less than half that on interest or dividends. Proposals to reduce the tax burden on capital gains have been debated almost continuously since the Tax Reform Act of 1986 eliminated the historical capital gains exclusion provision. Third, capital losses can be offset without limit against realized capital gains, and up to $3,000 of losses in excess of gains can be offset against other taxable income. Losses that cannot be offset against current income can be carried back, or carried forward, to offset taxable income in other years. Finally, the tax code includes special provisions for the taxation of gains on assets that are transferred from one taxpayer to another as part of an estate. The "basis step-up rule" allows the recipient of a bequest to increase the tax basis of an asset to the value when it was bequeathed, in effect extinguishing all capital gains tax liability on gains during the decedent's lifetime.

Deferral and basis step-up at death combine to reduce the effective tax burden on accruing capital gains below the tax burden that would be associated with accrual taxation. Bailey (1969) and Feldstein and Summers (1979) estimate that these provisions combine to make the effective accrual rate roughly one-quarter of the statutory rate. There is great heterogeneity across investors, with higher effective accrual rates on investors who are unable to defer realization or to structure their financial affairs in a way that takes advantage of the basis step-up provisions. Most capital gains are realized by households with high taxable incomes, so the average marginal tax rate *conditional on realization* is near the statutory maximum.

1.3   Employment-linked Retirement Saving

Favorable tax treatment of employee pension plans is the single most important public policy incentive for household saving in the United States. The revenue loss in fiscal year 1992 from excluding pension contributions and earnings from taxable income is $51.2 billion, compared with $7.3 billion of lost revenue from IRAs, $8.0 billion from generous taxation of life insurance savings, and $1.8 billion from the existence of Keogh accounts (U.S. Congress, Joint Committee on Taxation 1991). Pension plan assets totaled nearly $3 trillion in 1990 and accounted for roughly one-sixth of household net worth.

There are two tax incentives for accumulating wealth through private pensions. First, pension contributions can be made before tax. Rather than earning one dollar and investing $(1 - \tau)$ dollars in a traditional saving vehicle, an individual can contribute one dollar before tax to a pension plan. Second, pension accumulation is not taxed. If an individual is investing in an asset with a return of i percent per year, the after-tax return on a traditional saving vehicle will be $(1 - \tau)i$, while the same asset held in a pension fund will yield a return of i. When assets are withdrawn from a pension fund, they are taxed as ordinary income.

The tax benefits associated with pensions can substantially increase the return to saving. Assuming that an individual faces the same tax rate throughout his lifetime, the after-tax proceeds from investing one dollar in a pension fund T years before withdrawal is

(1) $$V_{\text{pension}} = (1 - \tau)e^{iT},$$

compared with

(2) $$V_{\text{traditional}} = (1 - \tau)e^{(1 - \tau)iT}$$

in a traditional taxable saving vehicle. The difference between these two expressions can be large, especially when the time horizon is long. The table below shows the ratio $V_{\text{pension}}/V_{\text{traditional}}$ for an individual with a marginal tax rate of 28 percent:

	Time Horizon		
Nominal Return(%)	10 Years	20 Years	40 Years
5	1.15	1.32	1.75
10	1.32	1.75	3.06

The benefit of untaxed accumulation is larger for taxpayers facing high marginal tax rates.

The tax benefits of saving through pension funds explain their importance for U.S. households. Table 1.6 presents information on the prevalence of private pensions. Half of all full-time workers are currently covered by private

Table 1.6   Private Pension Plan Coverage Rates (%)

	Private Wage and Salary Workers	Private Full-Time Wage and Salary Workers
1950	25	29
1960	41	47
1970	45	52
1980	46	53
1987	46	52

Source: Beller and Lawrence (1992).

pension plans; another substantial group receives coverage through government pensions. The fraction of workers covered by private pensions rose sharply in the two decades after World War II but has not increased substantially since then. Table 1.7 provides some information on the composition of pension plans. Until the early 1980s, most private pension plans were defined-benefit (DB) plans: the worker was eligible for benefits equal to a prespecified function of his age, years of service, and lifetime earnings profile with the firm. In 1980, for example, DB plans covered 80 percent of the workers with private pension coverage.

A variety of legislative changes during the 1980s reduced the appeal of DB plans relative to the alternative type of pension arrangement, defined-contribution (DC) plans. In DC plans, there is an account for each participant, recording his or her contributions. Upon retirement, each participant is entitled to the current market value of the account; this can be annuitized or withdrawn in other ways. The number of participants in DC plans nearly tripled during the 1980s. In 1988, the last year of data availability, one-third of pension plan participants were in DC plans.

There is an important distinction between DB and DC plans from the standpoint of household saving. A DB plan consists of corporate liabilities and associated corporate contributions to accounts that prefund these liabilities. These contributions can be viewed as corporate, rather than household, saving. Contributions to DC plans, however, are the property of the account beneficiaries, and as such should be viewed as household saving. The switch from DB to DC

Table 1.7   Numbers of Pension Plan Participants, 1975–88 (millions)

	Defined-Benefit Plan Participants	Defined-Contribution Plan Participants
1975	26.8	3.9
1980	29.7	5.8
1985	28.9	11.6
1988	28.0	14.3

Sources: Employee Benefit Research Institute, *EBRI Issue Brief* (Washington, D.C., April 1989), and idem, *Trends in Pensions 1992.*

Table 1.8   **Pension Assets and Household Net Worth (billion $)**

	1982	1985	1988	1990
Single-employer plans				
Defined benefit	399	545	680	757
Defined contribution	196	325	427	437
Multiemployer plans	61	98	130	144
Private insured plans	211	343	517	580[a]
Federal government plan	98	149	208	251
State/local government plans	262	404	605	756
Total pension plan assets	1,227	1,864	2,567	2,925
(% of household net worth)	(12.1)	(14.7)	(16.4)	(17.1)

Source: Employee Benefit Research Institute, Issue Briefs 97 and 116 (Washington, D.C., December 1989 and July 1991).
[a]Value for 1989, not 1990.

plans may therefore affect the allocation of private saving between households and corporations, but probably has little effect on total private saving.[2] There is an important behavioral issue about the extent to which individuals perceive corporate pension contributions as part of their own saving; there is little satisfactory empirical work on this issue.

Table 1.8 describes the importance of private pensions in household net worth. Pension plan assets totaled $2.9 trillion in 1990, or 17 percent of household wealth. A substantial component of this wealth is accounted for by various government pension plans, most of which are DB plans.

Table 1.9 examines the role of pension plans in providing for retirement living. Pensions are an income source for more than 40 percent of households with someone aged 65 or older. Despite their wide distribution, however, pensions account for a relatively small share of *income*. The third and fourth columns show that the fraction of retirement *income* from private pensions is less than 10 percent. This reflects the presence of many small income flows from private pensions and relatively large income flows from Social Security, earnings for those in households with someone still in the labor force, and asset income, which is highly concentrated among high-wealth elderly households.

The U.S. government also operates an important retirement saving program, the Social Security system. This is a pay-as-you-go system.[3] In 1992, the payroll tax was 15.3 percent, equally divided between an employer and an employee component. Social Security benefits are a function of an individual's work history, with the broad structure involving a minimum benefit, rising benefits for workers with higher lifetime earnings, and a maximum monthly benefit cap. For each worker, the Social Security Administration computes Average

---

2. Poterba (1987) discusses the interaction between corporate and household saving in more detail.

3. There is a separate system of retirement benefits for government workers.

Table 1.9   Sources of Retirement Income, 1980 and 1988 (%)

Income Source	Share of Over-65 Households Receiving		Share of Over-65 Households' Income	
	1980	1988	1980	1988
Social Security	90	92	39	38
Asset income	66	68	22	25
Earnings	23	22	19	17
Private pension/annuity	22	29	7	8
Government pension	12	14	7	9
Public assistance	10	7	1	1

Source: Chen (1992).

Indexed Monthly Earnings, a constant-dollar index of the worker's average wage in jobs covered by Social Security. This amount is used to compute a primary insurance amount, which is the benefit the worker would be entitled to if she retired at the Social Security retirement age. For all workers who have retired to date, this age was 65, but current law calls for a gradual increase to 67 by the year 2030. The Social Security system allows early retirement at ages above 62, and early retirees are eligible for lower benefits per month than those who retire at 65. Workers who do not retire by age 65 also receive a monthly benefit adjustment that increases their benefit once they retire.

Social Security benefits are a central contributor to the retirement income of currently aged Americans. Table 1.9 shows that Social Security is received by more than 90 percent of elderly households and accounts for nearly 40 percent of their income. Social Security represents a smaller share of the retirement income for high-income or high-wealth elderly than for their low-income counterparts.

There have been important changes over time in the generosity of the Social Security system. Until the early 1970s, Social Security benefits did not include an automatic cost-of-living adjustment. This made the level of benefits an outcome of the political process, and several years of real benefit increase significantly increased the level of real Social Security benefits. Since the mid-1970s, benefits have been indexed to the consumer price index.

1.4   Targeted Incentives for Saving Promotion

This section considers a range of specialized tax policies that are designed to encourage saving by particular subgroups in the population. It begins with a discussion of IRAs, then turns to 401(k) plans, which are becoming increasingly important, and concludes with a discussion of several more limited programs.

1.4.1   Individual Retirement Accounts

A number of specialized programs designed to encourage household saving were introduced during the 1980s. Individual retirement accounts (IRAs), which were created by the 1981 Economic Recovery Tax Act, are the most widely discussed. As originally enacted, taxpayers could make tax-deductible contributions to IRAs subject to a limit of $2,000 per earner per year and $250 for a nonworking spouse. Withdrawals could be made without penalty, any time after the account holder turned age 59 and a half; early withdrawals were subject to a 10 percent tax penalty. Withdrawals are taxed as ordinary income.

The power of compound interest makes the IRA an important vehicle for long-term saving. The return to investing through an IRA is similar to that for pension plans, as described in the preceding section. In part because of this high return, IRAs became very popular investment vehicles in the early 1980s. To reduce the current revenue cost of this program, the 1986 Tax Reform Act limited access to tax-deductible IRAs by imposing income tests on the use of tax-deductible IRA contributions. In 1991, single taxpayers with incomes of $25,000 or less and joint filers with taxable incomes of $40,000 or less could make fully deductible contributions. Single filers with incomes above $35,000 and joint filers with incomes above $50,000 could not make tax-deductible contributions if they were covered by an employer-provided pension plan.[4] They could still make after-tax contributions, which will generate tax-free withdrawals from the IRA. For these higher-income taxpayers, the value of the IRA contribution is

(3) $$V_{\text{nondeductible}} = (1 - \tau)(e^{iT} - \tau(e^{iT} - 1)).$$

The second term in this expression reflects the tax liability that is due when the value of the account *in excess of the original contribution* is included in taxable income.

Even nondeductible IRA contributions accumulate tax free, so these accounts yield a higher return than traditional saving vehicles. Individual retirement accounts are nevertheless less liquid than traditional, more heavily taxed, saving vehicles, which may account in part for their limited appeal. Table 1.10 shows the number of taxpayers making IRA contributions in each year since the early 1980s. These accounts became quite popular almost immediately after they were introduced, and at their peak in 1985, more than 16 million taxpayers contributed nearly $40 billion to them. The changes of the 1986 Tax Reform Act reduced the incentives for households to contribute, both by eliminating deductible contributions for some taxpayers and by reducing marginal tax rates on capital income accruing through traditional channels. There was also a substantial decline in IRA promotion by financial institutions in the post-

---

4. Taxpayers with incomes between the thresholds for tax-deductible and taxable IRAs are eligible for partially deductible IRAs.

Table 1.10   Number of Tax Returns Claiming IRA Contributions, 1982–90

Year	Number of IRA Contributor Returns (millions)	Total IRA Contributions (billion $)
1984	15.232	35.374
1985	16.205	38.211
1986	15.535	37.758
1987	7.318	14.065
1988	6.361	11.882
1989	5.882	10.960

Source: U.S. Department of the Treasury, *Statistics of Income: Individual Tax Returns* (Washington, D.C., various issues).

1986 period, and this may have affected the level of contributions. Many taxpayers who could have made tax-deductible contributions in the post-1986 period also appear to have been confused about the IRA program and, therefore, erroneously concluded that they were not eligible for it. Table 1.10 shows that the number of contributors fell by half between 1986 and 1987 and that, by 1990, fewer than 6 million taxpayers reported contributions of just over $10 billion.

The political decision to limit IRAs as part of the 1986 Tax Reform Act reflected two factors. First, the U.S. personal saving rate fell during the early 1980s, although the proponents of IRAs had argued that this program would raise private saving. Many other factors changed during this time period, but the simple correlation between the falling saving rate and the introduction of IRAs had a powerful effect on policymakers. Second, the IRA program spawned an ongoing debate about the effect of targeted saving programs on household saving. This debate centers on the extent to which IRA-like programs encourage new household saving, rather than simply providing an opportunity for households with existing assets or who would have saved otherwise to place their wealth in tax-favored accounts.

Table 1.11 presents an important set of background facts for evaluating this literature. The table shows the distribution of IRA contributions for one of the peak program years, 1983, by taxable income classes. It demonstrates that contributions are more concentrated at high income levels than are contributors. While only 31.6 percent of all contributors had taxable incomes of more than $50,000, they accounted for 39.7 percent of all contributions. The concentration of IRA contributions is lower than for many other types of capital income, because the $2,000 contribution limit prevents a few wealthy households from accumulating large amounts in these accounts. Similarly, the effect of the contribution limit varies over the income distribution. While roughly half of the IRA contributors in middle-income brackets made limit contributions, more than 80 percent of IRA contributors with incomes of $100,000 or more made limit contributions. This distributional pattern played an important

Table 1.11   **Distribution of IRA Participants and Contributions, 1983**

1983 Taxable Income	% of:			Probability of Contributing	Probability of a Limit Contribution, Given a Contribution
	Returns	Contributors	Contributions		
< 5	18.5	0.3	0.2	0.3	7.6
5–10	17.5	2.2	1.3	2.0	41.1
10–15	14.4	4.6	2.9	4.8	48.6
15–20	11.2	6.9	5.1	8.8	51.2
20–30	16.8	17.9	14.6	15.4	55.5
30–50	16.2	36.5	36.3	31.1	56.9
50–100	4.6	25.1	31.4	61.1	73.9
100–200	0.6	4.8	6.2	75.7	84.0
>200	0.2	1.7	2.1	74.6	82.9

Source: Galper and Byce (1986).

role in discussions of whether the IRA limit should be raised, since high-income taxpayers would be more likely to take advantage of the tax saving permitted by such a reform. The simple arithmetic of the income distribution, however, still implies that most of the benefits from such a change would accrue to lower-income households, because their greater numbers more than offset their lower probability of making limit contributions.[5]

Table 1.12 presents summary information on the median financial asset balances of all households ($2,849), as well as of all households who made IRA contributions in 1987 ($22,300, including IRAs and other tax-deferred, hence possibly illiquid, accounts, and $10,025, excluding these accounts).

1.4.2   401(k) Plans

While IRAs have been the most widely discussed tax incentive for household saving in the United States, they are not the only targeted saving program. A second program, known as the 401(k) plan after the section of the Internal Revenue Code which established it, has become an increasingly important saving incentive. The 401(k) plans were established by legislation in 1978, but their use expanded rapidly after the Treasury Department clarified their operation in 1981. These plans, which are established by employers, allow employees to contribute before-tax dollars to qualified retirement plans. Participants in 401(k) plans can defer income tax liability on the income they contribute to

---

5. There are several strands of empirical work on how IRAs affect personal saving. The most substantial research program, described in Venti and Wise (1990,1992), has used household survey data to analyze the saving behavior of IRA contributors and noncontributors. Contributors do not appear to run down their holdings of non-IRA assets when they make IRA contributions. This contradicts the simplest asset-switching explanation of how IRAs could reduce tax revenue without encouraging additional saving. In fact, the majority of IRA contributors have relatively few non-IRA financial assets, which makes it difficult for them to engage in asset switching. Gale and Scholz (1990) present some evidence that suggests that limit contributors could engage in asset switching to a greater extent than nonlimit contributors.

Table 1.12   **Asset Balances for Participants in Tax-deferred Saving Plans, 1987 ($)**

	All Households	IRA Households	401(k) Households
Mean holdings of:			
Financial assets	16,299	40,456	36,693
Non-IRA, 401(k) assets	12,227	27,901	26,614
IRA assets	2,836	9,841	5,186
401(k) assets	1,237	2,714	9,862
Median holdings of:			
Financial assets	2,849	22,300	17,100
Non-IRA, 401(k) assets	2,250	18,600	14,300
IRA assets	0	8,000	0
401(k) assets	0	0	4,000

Source: Poterba, Venti, and Wise (1992).

the plan. Assets in 401(k) plans accumulate tax free, and just as with IRAs, income from these plans is taxed when the funds are withdrawn. An individual can currently contribute up $8,475 per year to a 401(k), making these plans potentially more powerful saving vehicles than IRAs.[6] In addition, the plans are often made still more attractive by employer matching of employee contributions. A General Accounting Office (1988) survey found that three-quarters of employers offering 401(k) plans matched at least some of their employees' contributions to these plans.

The number of employees making 401(k) contributions is now substantially larger than the number of IRA contributors. In 1988, 15.7 million workers participated in 401(k) plans, up from only 2.7 million in 1983. These plans are now available at virtually all large firms and are currently diffusing through smaller firms as well. Participation in a plan indicates only that an employee has a 401(k) account, not that he made a contribution in a given year. The probability of contributing, given 401(k) eligibility, however, is more than 60 percent.

Table 1.13 reports summary information on both 401(k) and IRA participation rates in 1987. The tabulations are based on information from the Survey of Income and Program Participation, a random sample of U.S. households. The table shows that while both the IRA and the 401(k) participation rates rise with income, the 401(k) participation rate *conditional on being eligible for such a plan* is much higher than the IRA participation rate. This general pattern suggests that some features of the 401(k) program—for example, the often-generous employer matching rate or the link to the workplace, which can encourage all workers to participate together—are important aspects of the plan. The high 401(k) participation rates also suggest that as these plans diffuse

6. Prior to 1986, individuals could contribute up to $30,000 per year to their 401(k) plan. The 1986 Tax Reform Act reduced this limit to $7,000 per year and indexed this amount for inflation, yielding the $8,475 limit in 1991.

across firms, and more workers become eligible, there will be increased use of 401(k) plans for retirement saving.

Table 1.13 also suggests that 401(k) participants are spread more equally across the income distribution than are post-1986 IRA contributors. This pattern is confirmed by the statistics reported in table 1.12. That table shows that median holding of all financial assets by 401(k) participants was $17,100 in 1987, compared with $22,300 for IRA participants. The average balance in 401(k) accounts, just under $10,000, is comparable to the balance IRA contributors have in their IRA accounts. Table 1.14 tracks the growth of total assets

Table 1.13   **Participation in IRA and 401(k) Saving Plans, 1987**

Age or Income Group	IRA Participation Rate (%)	401(k) Plan	
		Eligibility Rate (%)	Participation Rate (%)
All	28.8	20.0	12.5
Income (thousands)			
<10	8.3	3.9	1.9
10–20	12.3	10.3	5.1
20–30	22.7	16.7	9.2
30–40	31.9	24.1	14.9
40–50	41.1	31.9	20.6
50–75	56.1	35.8	24.3
>75	66.6	33.2	27.8
Age			
25–35	16.3	18.3	9.7
35–45	25.1	22.2	14.1
45–55	37.4	21.3	14.3
55–65	48.1	17.6	12.7

Source: Poterba, Venti, and Wise (1992).

Table 1.14   **Asset Balances in IRAs and Keogh Plans, 1981–90**

Year	Asset Balance (billion $)	Asset Balance/ Net Worth (%)
1981	38.6	0.4
1982	68.0	0.7
1983	113.0	1.0
1984	163.1	1.4
1985	230.4	1.8
1986	304.9	2.2
1987	366.2	2.5
1988	426.8	2.7
1989	501.7	2.9
1990	563.9	3.3

Source: Employee Benefit Research Institute, Issue Brief 119 (Washington, D.C., October 1991).

Table 1.15   **Growth of 401(k) Plans**

Year	Number of Plans (millions)	Number of Participants (millions)	Contributions (billion $)	Assets (billion $)
1984	17.3	7.5	16.3	91.8
1985	29.9	10.4	24.3	143.9
1986	37.4	11.6	29.2	182.8
1987	45.1	13.1	33.2	215.4
1988	68.1	15.5	39.4	277.0

Source: Turner and Beller (1992).

in IRAs and Keogh plans. While these assets accounted for less than one-half of one percent of household net worth at the beginning of the 1980s, they represented more than 3 percent of net worth by 1990. If 401(k) balances were included as well, this share would be substantially greater.

Table 1.15 charts the rapid growth of 401(k) plan assets during the past decade. Between 1984 and 1988, the number of plans more than tripled, and the number of participants more than doubled. Contributions increased even more than the number of participants, even though the 1986 Tax Reform Act limited the maximum contribution. Despite this rapid growth, 401(k) plans still account for a relatively small share of household net worth—in 1988, roughly 1.8 percent.

1.4.3   Other Special Plans

IRAs and 401(k) plans are the two most significant incentive plans for personal saving. A partial listing of other programs and their provisions follows.

403(b) Tax-sheltered Annuity Plans

These plans are available to employees of educational institutions and some other nonprofit institutions. These plans allow taxpayers to make contributions from before-tax dollars, and they function in the same way as 401(k) plans in allowing tax-free accumulation subject to some restrictions on withdrawal. The current limit on contributions to a 403(b) plan is $9,500 per year, but this amount is reduced by any contributions an individual has made to 401(k) retirement plans.[7]

Keogh Plans

These are retirement plans for self-employed individuals. They are effectively substitutes for the employer-provided defined-benefit and defined-contribution plans that wage and salary workers can participate in, and they offer the same tax treatment and the same favorable opportunities for invest-

---

7. Contributions to 403(b) plans may not exceed 25 percent of a taxpayer's "reduced salary," defined as salary excluding 403(b) and other contributions to tax-deferred saving plans.

ment. There are limits on contributions. In most cases, an individual cannot contribute more than 20 percent of total earnings or $30,000, whichever is smaller.

1.5 Insurance-based Saving Vehicles

Saving through insurance plans is a relatively uncommon form of asset accumulation in the United States, especially for currently young households. There is effectively no saving through any instrument other than whole life insurance and various hybrid policies.

Most U.S. households that purchase life insurance purchase *term* insurance, in effect paying a premium each year equal to the actuarial estimate of the payoff on their policy, plus additional charges to cover administrative and other expenses. There is another type of insurance, *whole-life* insurance, for which individuals make a payment to the insurance company that is larger than the expected payout on the policy in the next year. The excess contribution is invested by the insurance company, and the investment income receives favorable tax treatment. The accruing investment income is not taxed until the money is withdrawn, often as an annuity when the insured is retired. Saving through whole-life policies is therefore another way to achieve tax-free asset accumulation. Unlike saving through IRAs or Keoghs, however, which enable households to receive the same pretax return that they could earn on taxable investments but to save the tax payment, saving through insurance may not yield the full pretax return. Insurance companies frequently offer returns on whole-life policies that are below the pretax return on the assets that back the policies. The differential is explained by the costs of administering insurance policies. In addition, insurance purchases are made with after-tax rather than before-tax dollars, so they do not offer the opportunity to defer tax liability on earned income. In part because of the complexity of insurance investments, and in part because for many households they do not offer attractive rates of return, the total value of accumulated reserves in life insurance contracts accounted for little more than two percent of household net worth in 1990.

1.6 Conclusion

The analysis in this chapter has focused on the incentives to accumulate financial assets. A critical stylized fact about the distribution of wealth in the U.S. economy is that many households have very little accumulated wealth in financial assets. For a sizable number of households, their home is their principal asset. Investment in housing is encouraged by a variety of provisions in the U.S. tax code, notably the exclusion of imputed income on owner-occupied houses from the definition of taxable income (see Poterba [1992] and the references therein). Another important omission from this analysis is accumulation of wealth in unincorporated businesses. This item is an important component of the household balance sheet, and saving through this form can be affected by some of the tax rules discussed above, for example the capital gains tax, as well as estate and gift taxes that may affect the ultimate disposition of a private business.

References

Bailey, Martin J. 1969. Capital gains and income taxation. In *The taxation of income from capital*, ed. Arnold C. Harberger and Martin J. Bailey, 11–49. Washington, D.C.: Brookings Institution.

Beller, Daniel J., and Helen H. Lawrence. 1992. Trends in private pension plan coverage. In *Trends in pensions 1992*, ed. John A. Turner and Daniel J. Beller, 59–96. Washington, D.C.: U.S. Department of Labor.

Chen, Yung-Ping. 1992. The role of private pensions in the income of older Americans. In *Trends in pensions 1992*, ed. John A. Turner and Daniel J. Beller, 149–76. Washington, D.C.: U.S. Department of Labor.

Feldstein, Martin S., and Lawrence H. Summers. 1979. Inflation and the taxation of capital income in the corporate sector. *National Tax Journal* 32 (December): 445–70.

Gale, William G., and John K. Scholz. 1990. IRAs and household saving. Department of Economics, University of Wisconsin. Mimeograph.

Galper, Harvey, and Charles Byce. 1986. IRAs: Facts and figures. *Tax Notes,* June 2.

Kennickell, Arthur, and Janice Shack-Marquez. 1992. Changes in family finances from 1983 to 1989: Evidence from the Survey of Consumer Finances. *Federal Reserve Bulletin* (January): 1–18.

Manchester, Joyce M., and James M. Poterba. 1989. Second mortgages and household saving. *Regional Science and Urban Economics* 19 (May): 325–46.

Poterba, James M. 1987. Tax policy and corporate saving. *Brookings Papers on Economic Activity,* no. 2: 455–515.

———. 1992. Taxation and housing: Old questions, new answers. *American Economic Review* 82 (May): 237–42.

Poterba, James M., Steven F. Venti, and David A. Wise. 1992. 401(k) plans and tax-deferred saving. In *Topics in the economics of aging*, ed. D. Wise. Chicago: University of Chicago Press.

Turner, John A., and Daniel J. Beller, eds. 1992. *Trends in pensions 1992*. Washington, D.C.: Government Printing Office.

U.S. Congress, Joint Committee on Taxation. 1991. *Estimates of federal tax expenditures for fiscal years 1993–1997*. Washington, D.C.: Government Printing Office.

U.S. General Accounting Office. 1988. *401(k) plans: Incidence, provisions, and benefits*. Washington, D.C.: General Accounting Office.

Venti, Steven F., and David A. Wise. 1990. Have IRAs increased U.S. saving? Evidence from consumer expenditure surveys. *Quarterly Journal of Economics* 105:661–98.

———. 1992. Government policy and personal retirement saving. In *Tax policy and the economy*, vol. 6, ed. James M. Poterba, 1–41. Cambridge: MIT Press.

2 Government Incentives and Household Saving in Canada

John B. Burbidge and James B. Davies

2.1 Introduction

This paper examines tax incentives for personal saving in Canada. It pays particular attention to tax-deferred retirement savings plans and focuses on the period since 1970, during which there have been major changes in the Canadian tax system. These changes have been on such a scale that a discernible impact on saving behavior would not be surprising. It is not our task here to measure these effects. Instead, our purpose is to investigate carefully the structure of incentives, and their changes over time, as groundwork for future attempts at such measurement.

The period studied started with the introduction of capital gains taxation (in 1972), but the tenor of tax developments quickly changed, with the appearance of a whole stable of new shelters for saving in 1974 and the enrichment of previously existing shelters, such as the well-known registered retirement savings plans (RRSPs) and registered pension plans (RPPs) and dividend tax credit. Combined with fairly comprehensive indexation of the personal income tax (PIT), these measures made Canadian income taxes more bearable for many but contributed to a shortfall of revenue which produced very large federal deficits in the early 1980s. Since 1981 there has been a gradual tightening-up of the PIT, which has seen the termination of the majority of the important shelters. Thus, during the period 1970–90 saving incentives first

John Burbidge is professor of economics at McMaster University. James Davies is professor of economics and chair of the Department of Economics at the University of Western Ontario.

The authors would like to acknowledge helpful comments from participants in the NBER International Retirement Savings Comparison Project, Richard Bird, Keith Horner (Department of Finance, Government of Canada), and Jim Pesando, as well as help with data from Keith Horner, and from Preston Poon (of Statistics Canada). The authors are solely responsible for all errors and omissions. The contents of this paper does not represent the views of the Department of Finance, Government of Canada, or of Statistics Canada.

grew and then receded.[1] There was a corresponding hump in Canadian personal saving rates, which peaked in 1982. The extent of the causal relation between these trends is an extremely interesting question. Some light may be thrown on this by the behavior of Canadian saving rates during the 1990s, since a distinct new phase began in 1991. In that year a sweeping reform of the RRSP/RPP system was introduced, and new higher contribution limits and carry-forwards are being phased in over the period 1991–95.

In addition to setting out the important features of Canadian PIT and reviewing recent tax history, this paper assembles a variety of data which provide a foundation for future analysis of the likely effects of the tax system on the level and composition of saving. We look at the national accounts figures on saving, national balance sheet data on household wealth and its composition, consumer survey data on both saving and wealth holding, and data from tax records on contributions to sheltered saving plans.

The paper is organized as follows. Section 2.2 presents an overview of household wealth holding and saving in Canada since 1970, using national accounts, national balance sheet, and sample survey data. In section 2.3 the relevant current features, and recent evolution, of the Canadian tax system are set out. The structure and use of tax-deferred retirement savings plans, and the salient features of social security in Canada, are reviewed in section 2.4. Finally, existing evidence on the impacts of government incentives for saving, on revenue as well as saving, is discussed in Section 2.5.

2.2 Overview of the Household Balance Sheet

One significant contribution of this paper may be to help researchers who may be unfamiliar with Canadian data sources find information on Canada's tax system and household behavior. We begin, therefore, with a brief description of four data sources and then use these to shed some light on the household balance sheet.

2.2.1 A Brief Description of Some Data Sources

One source is the Canadian system of National Accounts. These include the Income and Expenditure Accounts, the Financial Flow Accounts, and the National Balance Sheet Accounts. The Income and Expenditure Accounts provide information on gross domestic product (GDP) income-based, GDP expenditure-based, and their components. They monitor four main sectors—"persons and unincorporated business," "other business enterprises and financial intermediaries," "government," and "transactions with the rest of the world." The difference between income and outlay (excluding capital consumption al-

---

1. While we are confident that this is the right way to summarize the overall trend, as discussed in the body of the paper, the introduction of a lifetime capital gains exemption in 1985 (whose limit grew to $100,000, where it was capped in the 1988 tax year), and a small increase in RRSP contribution limits in 1986, softened the withdrawal of other shelters in the late 1980s.

lowances) for each sector is gross saving. Over any time period, each sector's gross saving plus capital assistance equals its net acquisition of nonfinancial assets (investment) plus the excess of lending over borrowing. The Financial Flow Accounts measure transactions in financial assets that correspond to the saving and investment decisions of each sector. They also provide much more detail, especially on financial intermediaries, as the four sectors of the Income and Expenditure Accounts become 13 sectors in the Financial Flow Accounts. The National Balance Sheet Accounts comprise corresponding estimates of the stocks of physical and financial assets and liabilities.[2] We will use these quite heavily to see what financial and nonfinancial assets Canadian households hold in the aggregate.

Statistics Canada also releases public-use sample tapes which report on individual responses to questionnaires based on subsamples of the Labour Force Survey sampling frame. In carrying out the research for this project, we will employ microdata drawn from various public-use sample tapes—four Family Expenditure (FAMEX) Surveys, two income, asset, and debt surveys by the Survey of Consumer Finances (SCF), and the annual SCFs (income) for economic families and individuals.[3] The FAMEX surveys are conducted in February and March and collect information on each household's income and expenditures during the previous calendar year; we have information for the 1978, 1982, 1984, and 1986 calendar years. The SCFs are conducted in late April and early May every year. About every seven years, the SCF measures family assets and debts as of the date of the survey and, as it always does, income for the previous calendar year. We have SCF asset and debt data for April/May 1977 and 1984. Public-use tapes for surveys of income exist for 1971–81 (biennial) and then 1982–90 (annual).

Two more sources of information are *Taxation Statistics* (annual), which is published by Revenue Canada (Ottawa, Ontario), and *The National Finances* (annual) and *The Provincial and Municipal Finances* (biennial), which are published by the Canadian Tax Foundation (Toronto, Ontario). The first publication contains facsimiles of federal income tax forms as well as descriptions of the tax code and tables based on samples of taxpayers. The other two publications provide succinct summaries of changes to the tax code as well as tables on the costs of various programs and the beneficiaries of these programs.

In the next section, we use some of the macrodata from the Income and Expenditure Accounts and the National Balance Sheet Accounts to initiate our exploration of personal saving and taxation. Thereafter we turn to microdata to focus on the asset and debt-holding behavior of Canadian families.

2. See Statistics Canada (1989) for a careful description of the role of the Income and Expenditure Accounts, the Financial Flow Accounts, and National Balance Sheet Accounts in the Canadian system of National Accounts. Many of the most frequently used data series are available in machine-readable form on CANSIM, a computerized data-retrieval system operated by Statistics Canada.

3. Microdata tapes may be purchased from the Data Dissemination Division, Statistics Canada, Tunney's Pasture, Ottawa, Canada, K1A 0T6.

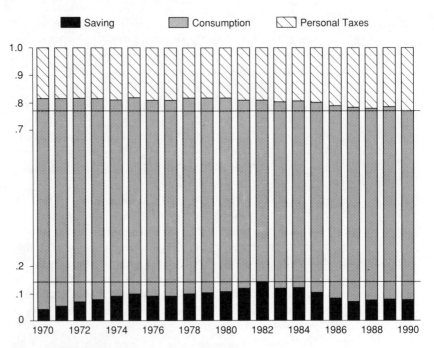

Fig. 2.1   Shares of personal income, 1970–90

Source: Statistics Canada, CANSIM matrix no. 6632.

Note: "Personal income" includes the income of unincorporated businesses as well as persons and excludes capital consumption allowances and any capital assistance provided by the government (1990 personal income of $580 billion may be compared with 1990 GDP at market prices of $670 billion). "Personal taxes" are income and payroll taxes paid by persons and unincorporated businesses less funds transferred from the government to this sector (e.g., interest on the public debt). "Consumption" includes purchases of all new consumer durables (e.g., new cars), except housing.

Evidence from Macrodata

One may obtain some sense of the interaction between taxation and saving by using the Income and Expenditure Accounts to study the distribution of personal income across consumption, personal taxes, and saving, for the years 1970–90, as shown in figure 2.1. Figure 2.1 reveals that, according to the National Accounts measure, saving as a fraction of personal income exhibited a hump-shaped pattern over the 1970–90 period.[4] The saving rate out of personal income peaked at 14 percent in 1982, which represents a saving rate out of disposable income of nearly 18 percent. Figure 2.1 also shows the increase in

4. Personal savings, as measured by the National Accounts, are obtained by subtracting consumption from disposable income. The latter may be adjusted by subtracting the purely inflationary component of interest income. This flattens the personal saving series somewhat, but does not remove the measured rise in saving over the period 1970–81 (Beach et al. 1988, 24–29). A further adjustment to include accruing capital gains in income makes personal saving highly volatile, and makes it difficult to generalize about trends (Dagenais 1992).

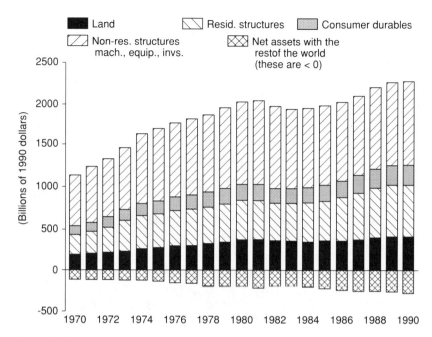

Fig. 2.2   Components of national net worth, 1970–90
Source: Statistics Canada, CANSIM matrix no. 792.

the ratio of personal taxes to personal income after 1985. The increase in the share of personal income taxed away has been associated with a decline in the apparent saving rate out of personal income. In fact, the National Accounts–based saving rate mirrors remarkably the at-first rising, and then declining, generosity of tax incentives for saving over this period.

The 13 sectors monitored in the National Balance Sheet Accounts may be aggregated to yield a picture of the country's net worth. These accounts provide annual estimates of the market value of physical and financial assets and liabilities. Physical assets comprise land, residential structures, consumer durables, nonresidential structures, machinery and equipment, and inventories. Net financial assets from the country's point of view represent its net claims on assets in the rest of the world, if positive, or the rest of the world's net claims on the country, if negative. The sum of the value of physical and net financial assets is the country's net worth.

Figure 2.2 shows the components of national net worth for the period 1970–90. Particularly noteworthy is the decline in real net worth after 1981; the 1981 level was not exceeded until 1987. Increases and declines in net worth are associated with similar movements in its components. The shares of land, residential structures, consumer durables, and so on, are very stable. Even Canada's net foreign indebtedness rose only from 11.2 percent of net worth in 1970 to 12.7 percent of net worth in 1990, which is somewhat surprising in view of

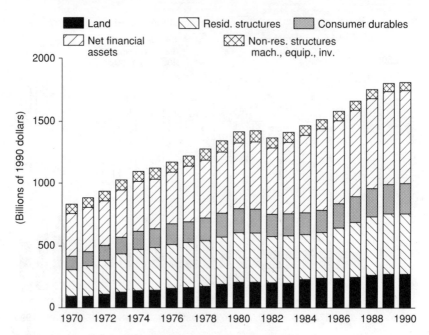

Fig. 2.3   Components of personal net worth, 1970–90
Source: Statistics Canada, CANSIM matrix no. 751.

the very large deficits run over much of this period by the federal government.

Figure 2.3 repeats figure 2.2 for the personal and unincorporated business sector. Like national net worth, personal net worth declined in real terms after 1981, but only for two years. Once again no component appears to have grown out of step with the rest. One interesting feature of figure 2.3 is the size of net financial assets relative to real assets. The major items in net financial assets are currency and bank deposits, deposits in other institutions, bonds, shares, and the assets of private pension funds. For the "average household's" portfolio, real wealth is more important than net financial wealth. It is also worth noting that wealth held in the form of land is about equal to wealth held in the form of consumer durables. Another important implication of figure 2.3 is that about half of personal wealth is held in real assets which attract no personal income tax (PIT): owner-occupied houses (including the value of the land they stand on) and consumer durables.

We have obtained national balance sheet data from Statistics Canada which enable us to examine the components of personal financial assets, including RRSPs, private pension funds, saving through life insurance, bonds, shares, and currency/deposits, for the period 1980–90. The shares of each category are shown in figure 2.4. The share accounted for by RRSPs clearly has the highest growth rate, rising from 4 percent in 1980 to 10 percent in 1990. The

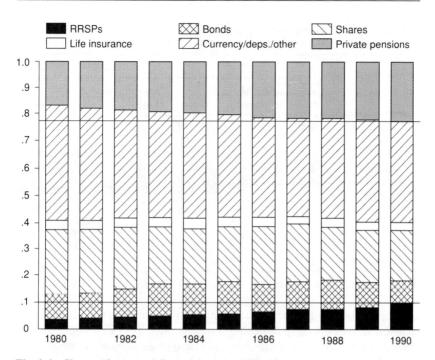

Fig. 2.4 Shares of personal financial assets, 1980–90
Source: Special compilation by Statistics Canada.

share of another tax-sheltered instrument, private pensions, also grew, from 17 percent in 1980 to 22 percent in 1990. Currency/deposits and shares declined in importance over the 1980s. It is reassuring to observe that tax incentives do seem to exert some influence on portfolio composition. Savings have been channeled more and more into the few remaining fully sheltered forms, fleeing assets which are increasingly exposed to income taxation.

We saw above that about one-half of personal net worth is in the form of owner-occupied housing and consumer durables, neither of which is taxable under the PIT. Figure 2.4 indicates that currently about one-third of personal financial assets are in fully sheltered forms—RRSPs or private pensions. Putting these two facts together, about two-thirds of personal wealth is fully sheltered from PIT in the Canadian system. Income on the remaining one-third is in principle fully taxable, but the effective tax rates vary widely, as implied by the discussion in section 2.3.

Evidence from Microdata

The public-use tapes from the 1977 and 1984 SCFs include information on households' financial assets (e.g., deposits, bonds, stocks and shares, and RRSPs) and nonfinancial assets (e.g., market values of cars and owner-occupied homes and equity in businesses). While households were asked to

Table 2.1   **Financial and Nonfinancial Assets and Net Worth of Families and Unattached Individuals: 1977 and 1984 SCFs (1990 $)**

	1977			1984		
	Financial Assets	Nonfinancial Assets	Net Worth	Financial Assets	Nonfinancial Assets	Net Worth
Weighted means	25,557	101,355	107,790	27,724	98,192	110,374
Quantiles:						
.2	694	1,165	2,306	546	1,293	2,768
.5 (median)	5,020	64,758	49,873	6,020	58,457	50,980
.8	26,788	149,084	153,510	34,971	133,209	153,334
Shares of top:						
10%		50.7			51.4	
5%		37.6			37.5	
2%		24.8			23.9	
1%		17.6			16.9	
No. of observations		12,734			14,029	

Source: Authors' calculations using Statistics Canada's SCF public-use microdata tape.

report premiums paid for employer-sponsored pension plans and life insurance policies, it would be very difficult to estimate private-pension wealth or life-insurance wealth from these numbers. Also absent are estimates of wealth held in the form of consumer durables other than vehicles and housing. The reporting of debts is much more comprehensive but it lacks the detail accorded assets. These facts mean that reported net worth is underestimated; for example, if a household had taken out a bank loan to purchase a refrigerator, the liability would have been recorded but not the asset. They also imply that one cannot obtain clean estimates of net worth in financial versus nonfinancial assets; the data do not permit one to determine whether a loan is for the purchase of, say, shares or an automobile. In tables 2.1 and 2.2 we report financial assets and nonfinancial assets (none of the household's debt is attributed to these assets) and net worth (total assets minus total debts).

It is clear from table 2.1 that, while average levels of household assets and net worth are substantial, many households hold little wealth, particularly financial assets. Median holdings of financial assets in 1990 dollars (about $5,000 in 1977 and $6,000 in 1984) may be compared to each survey's estimate of median after-tax income of about $28,000 for both years. Over 60 percent of households have at least some equity in housing, which accounts for the relatively higher numbers for nonfinancial assets and net worth. It is intriguing that .5 (median) and .8 quantiles for nonfinancial assets declined between 1977 and 1984. Since the rise in median financial assets more or less matches the rise in median net worth, households appear to have reduced their debts over this period. This is not surprising since interest rates were extraordinarily high in the early 1980s. Finally, we note that the share of wealth held by the top 5 percent of households was virtually constant across the two surveys but that

Table 2.2 | Financial and Nonfinancial Assets and Net Worth of Urban, Married-Couple Families: 1977 and 1984 SCFs (1990 $)

	1977			1984		
	Financial Assets	Nonfinancial Assets	Net Worth	Financial Assets	Nonfinancial Assets	Net Worth
Weighted means	23,799	114,818	111,323	34,787	123,818	136,275
Quantiles						
.2	1,502	10,948	14,759	1,520	12,933	17,615
.5 (median)	7,540	101,330	78,581	10,139	90,530	81,071
.8	30,679	166,322	165,739	44,489	160,368	185,241
Shares of top						
10%			38.1			45.2
5%			26.1			32.8
2%			16.1			21.5
1%			11.0			15.4
No. of observations			5,317			6,012

Source: Authors' calculations using Statistics Canada's SCF public-use microdata tape.

the share of the top 10 percent rose slightly, and the shares of the top 2 percent and 1 percent fell slightly between 1977 and 1984.[5]

Measuring the assets and debts of any household is difficult, but it is particularly so for those whose income originates primarily from self-employment (e.g., farming or fishing). In addition, it is instructive to focus on a more homogeneous group of households. Table 2.2 repeats table 2.1 for urban households with the following characteristics: married couples, husband's age greater than 25, husband not self-employed, and husband's main occupation not farming or fishing.

As one might expect, means and quantiles are generally higher in table 2.2; median financial and nonfinancial assets and median net worth are about 50 percent higher for both years. Nevertheless, for most households financial assets are still a small proportion of after-tax incomes, which, in 1990 dollars, were about $38,000 in 1977 and $39,000 in 1984. It is also not surprising that wealth is less concentrated within a more homogeneous group of households. All of the percentages reported in table 2.2 are lower than the corresponding numbers in table 2.1. The sharp increase in apparent wealth concentration between 1977 and 1984, however, is surprising, especially since there was little

5. As is the case with most sample surveys, there are major difficulties in using the SCF surveys to estimate inequality in the distribution of wealth (see Davies 1979). The top shares shown in the table are underestimates since, in practice, the surveys do not reach very far into the upper tail. The highest net worth of a family observed in the 1984 SCF, for example, was $6 million. By consulting journalistic sources and work done by private consultants, Davies (1993) concludes that in 1984 the share of the top 1 percent in the Canadian wealth distribution was likely less than in the United States or Britain, but quite a bit higher than indicated by the SCF. A number in the range 25–30 percent is a "best guess." There is insufficient evidence to establish trends over time.

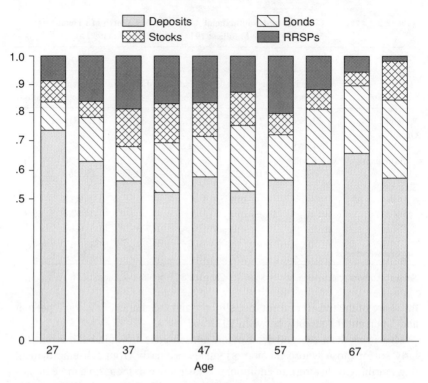

Fig. 2.5   Components of family financial assets by age, 1977
Source: Statistics Canada, 1977 SCF.

change for the full samples in table 2.1 and that was mainly in the opposite direction.[6]

We have used these data to examine the portfolio composition of household financial assets and debt, conditional on husband's age. Figures 2.5 and 2.6 study the four main assets in the average household's portfolio of financial assets, by age, for 1977 and 1984. Two points are worth noting. First, for each year, middle-aged families have more diversified portfolios than either younger or older families. Second, between 1977 and 1984, families at all stages of the life cycle substituted RRSPs for deposits in financial institutions.

Figures 2.7 and 2.8 show the components of household debt. The 1977 and 1984 SCFs group debt into three categories: (i) mortgage outstanding on owner-occupied house; (ii) consumer debt, which includes charge accounts and all credit card debt, loans from chartered banks secured by household goods, certain loans from chartered banks, trust companies, and other financial

6. The increase in apparent inequality is not simply due to outliers. This is indicated by the increasing gap between median and .8 quantile wealth between the two years. In 1977 wealth at the .8 quantile was 110.9 percent higher than the median; in 1984 the gap had increased to 128.5 percent.

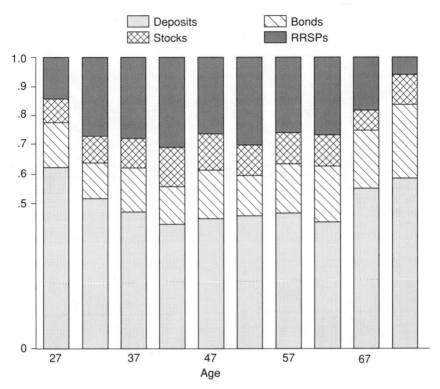

Fig. 2.6   Components of family financial assets by age, 1984
Source: Statistics Canada, 1984 SCF.

intermediaries; and (iii) other debt, which includes loans from chartered banks secured by stocks and bonds, loans for the renovation of residential property, student loans, loans from stock brokers, insurance companies, savings banks, etc., unpaid bills for medical and dental care, and money borrowed from members of other households. Figures 2.7 and 2.8 clearly reveal the predominance of mortgage debt at all stages of the life cycle, with some tendency for mortgage debt to decline in importance with age. The graphs for 1977 and 1984 are very similar except in two respects. First, the 70–75 age group had a much larger share of its debt in mortgages in 1984 than in 1977. Second, "other" debt was more important late in the life cycle in 1984 than in 1977. We now turn to a description of the rules for the taxation of capital income.

2.3   Taxation of Capital Income

This section outlines the general features of the Canadian PIT and its treatment of capital income, other than the provisions for sheltered retirement saving, which are discussed in section 2.4.

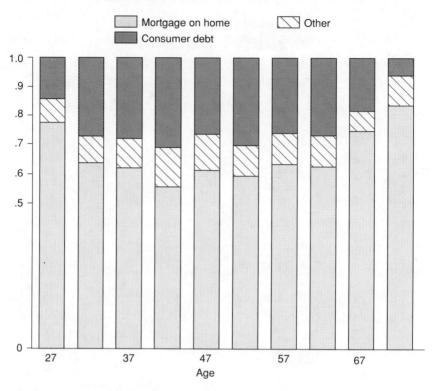

Fig. 2.7   Components of family debt by age, 1977
Source: Statistics Canada, 1977 SCF.

2.3.1   General Features of PIT

The Canadian PIT is levied on an individual basis and, since the 1987 tax reform, has imposed marginal tax rates at the federal level of 17, 26, and 29 percent in three tax brackets. Since 1987 a system of nonrefundable personal credits rather than deductions has been in force. There are also sizable refundable credits—the GST (sales tax) and child tax credits—which introduce an element of negative income tax.[7] Provincial PIT is a flat percentage of the federal tax (although not in Quebec, which has a separate PIT), except for various provincial surtaxes and special credits (e.g., property tax credits for low-income or elderly taxpayers) implemented from time to time.

7. In 1991 the 17, 26, and 29 percent tax rates applied in brackets whose limits were 0–$28,784, $28,785–$57,567, and $57,568+ in terms of taxable income. The personal credits were $1,068 for each taxpayer plus $890 for a dependent spouse, $69 for the first two children, and $138 for additional children. (In single-parent families, the credit for the first child was $890.) The child tax credit was worth $585 per child, and the GST credit $190 per adult and $100 per child. The child tax and GST credits were taxed back at a 5 percent rate on family income in excess of $25,000.

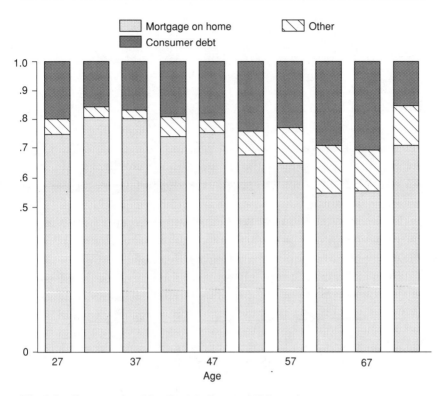

Fig. 2.8   Components of family debt by age, 1984
Source: Statistics Canada, 1984 SCF.

Figure 2.9 summarizes combined federal and Ontario tax brackets and marginal tax rates for the period 1970–90.[8] There have been three significant regime changes over this period. One, the reduction in the top marginal tax rate from 63 to 50 percent in 1982, is not apparent in figure 2.9 since the graph only shows tax rates on income up to $100,000. The other two regime changes are apparent in figure 2.9. First, 1972 saw the PIT base broadened substantially and marginal tax rates on high-income individuals reduced dramatically.[9] This represented a reaction to the recommendations of the Carter Commission, whose "a buck is a buck" philosophy suggested that the income tax base should be as comprehensive as possible. Thus, even most transfer payments have been taxable since 1972. There are, of course, significant exclusions from the tax base. These include, for example, social assistance ("welfare") pay-

8. The interaction of federal and Ontario surtaxes makes these calculations difficult. We have used the basic federal tax brackets and simply reported the highest marginal tax rate possible in each bracket.

9. Prior to 1972, marginal tax rates on high incomes were steeply graduated, actually exceeding 100 percent on taxable income over $1,500,000 (1990 dollars) per annum!

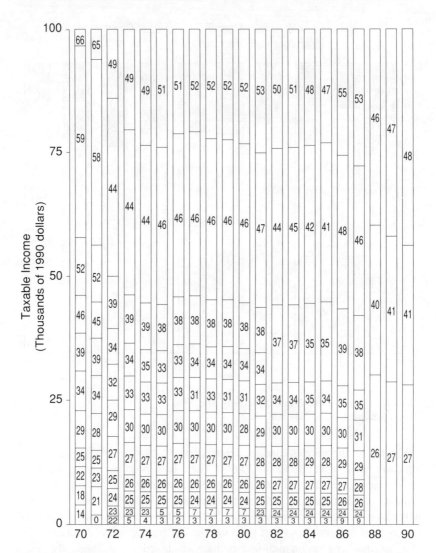

Fig. 2.9   Tax brackets and marginal tax rates for a resident of Ontario earning less than $100,000 (1990 dollars): 1970–90
Source: Revenue Canada, *Taxation Statistics* (Ottawa, various issues).

ments made by municipalities and provinces, imputed income on owner-occupied housing, capital gains on principal residences, and the first $100,000 of otherwise taxable capital gains, under the lifetime capital gains exemption. A second regime change is that, effective January 1, 1988, 10 tax brackets were collapsed to three and combined federal and provincial tax rates were reduced for most people (the exceptions are clear from fig. 2.9).

Even with figure 2.9 much more work would be required to generate careful estimates of weighted average marginal tax rates. One can get some sense of what these rates would be, however, by using data from *Taxation Statistics* to see how individuals are distributed across the tax brackets graphed in figure 2.9. These numbers show for example that, in 1970, less than 1 percent of taxpayers faced marginal tax rates of 66 percent or higher. More important, we find that median total (pretax) income in 1990 dollars is remarkably constant over the 1970–90 period at about $27,000, corresponding to taxable income in the range $15,000–$20,000. Marginal tax rates in this range were very stable around 30 percent until 1988 when they dropped to 26 percent. Looking across incomes, a similar pattern is observed at most levels, although there are particular ranges where, for example, marginal tax rates rose with tax reform in 1988. Summarizing, it seems quite likely that average marginal tax rates in Canada were fairly stable from 1970–87 but declined a few points in 1988.

Although we are not explicitly concerned with the corporate income tax (CIT) in this paper, it is important to have in mind some of its salient features. As under the PIT, most provinces piggyback on the federal CIT, which is levied at a standard rate of 28 percent on "general business." Adding on provincial taxes, the total CIT rate varied from 44 to 46 percent across provinces in 1991. Lower rates apply to manufacturing and processing profits (23 percent federal rate) and the first $200,000 of income for a Canadian-controlled private corporation (CCPC)—the "small business" rate of 12 percent. Including provincial taxes, the total CIT rate for manufacturing and processing varied between 30 and 41 percent in 1991, and the small business rate varied between 16 and 23 percent (see Canadian Tax Foundation 1992, tables 7–18 and 7–20).

2.3.2   Incentives for Saving—General Trends

As mentioned earlier, the period 1970–90 saw at first increasingly generous tax incentives for saving, and then a decline. In contrast, the period 1990–95 will see increasing generosity of such incentives as new, higher RRSP/RPP limits are phased in. The rate of shelter innovations over the last two decades has been high. A complete recounting of this history would be tedious. The following discussion highlights the most important trends.

2.3.3   Interest and Pension Income

From 1974 until 1987 (inclusive) interest received by Canadian taxpayers was partially exempt from tax under the $1,000 investment income deduction.[10] Since this deduction was fixed in nominal terms during years of significant inflation, it became less generous over time. In addition, since it was deduction for *nominal* interest income, in periods of high expected inflation for

---

10. This deduction is perhaps more frequently referred to as the interest and dividend deduction, since in the most recent period that it was in force it applied only to interest and dividends. Older literature, however, refers to it as the investment income deduction, since it extended to domestic capital gains between 1977 and 1984.

many taxpayers it sheltered less of their real interest income. This aspect has, in practice, been quite important since the Canadian inflation rate, and nominal interest rates, have at times been quite high in the last two decades.

A further important preference for interest income was that, until the mid-1980s some major deferrals were available. Interest accruing on a Canada Savings Bond (CSB) or Guaranteed Investment Certificate (GIC), for example, did not have to be taxed until maturity. Now the interest on such assets is computed and taxed every year.

Annuity income received as part of a pension plan has also received special treatment, effectively an incentive to save via such plans. From 1975 until 1987, the first $1,000 of pension income was not taxed. Since then, together with the conversion of personal deductions to credits in the Canadian tax reform, the first $1,000 is creditable for federal taxes at a 17 percent rate (which corresponds to the marginal tax rate in the lowest bracket).

An important feature of the Canadian PIT is that no consumer interest is deductible. Thus, unlike most other countries, Canada does not have mortgage interest deductibility. This puts interest *payments* (as opposed to *receipts*) on a consumption tax basis.[11] This simple provision likely acts as a powerful personal saving incentive. Although Canadians take on considerable mortgage debt, they typically pay it off at a high rate.

In contrast to the probity of the Canadian PIT with regard to consumer debt, there is no effective limit on the deductibility of interest for business or investment purposes. As we shall see below, although the PIT has been tightened up considerably in recent years, there are various ways in which the income produced by assets acquired with debt finance can be sheltered from tax (e.g., via the lifetime capital gains exemption), so that, looking at the PIT in isolation, the unlimited deductibility is "too generous." Rather than simply not penalizing saving, the tax system in such cases actually subsidizes it.

One interesting example of excess interest deductibility for saving or investment purposes in the Canadian system is that prior to November 13, 1981 (budget day), interest on funds borrowed to purchase an RRSP was deductible. Termination of that provision is another example of how incentives for saving were reduced in the 1980s.

2.3.4 Dividends

The Canadian tax system has partially integrated corporate and personal income taxes, via the dividend tax credit. Under this system, dividends paid by taxable Canadian corporations are first "grossed up" by 25 percent, to get back (partially) to the underlying corporate income on which the dividend is based

---

11. Note that while annual income tax advocates would, in principle, be in favor of the deduction of real mortgage interest, their support for such deductibility is conditional on the full income from owner-occupied houses—i.e., both imputed rent and capital gains—being taxed. Thus (thankfully) consumption tax and income tax supporters can agree that mortgage interest deductibility is handled correctly in Canada.

(i.e., to allow for CIT payments). A credit is then allowed which is equal to 13.33 percent of the grossed-up amount. Note that this arrangement creates a bias toward holding shares of domestic rather than foreign companies.

The Canadian dividend tax credit has an obvious shortcoming in comparison to a scheme of full integration of PIT and CIT. This is that the gross-up and credit factors are arbitrary and may differ considerably from what is appropriate for a particular corporation. For full integration the gross-up factor should equal $\tau_c/(1 - \tau_c)$, where τ_c is the actual CIT rate levied, and the credit rate should simply be τ_c. Thus, for a firm facing the general business tax rate of 28 percent, the gross-up factor should be approximately 39 percent and the credit rate 28 percent. For a manufacturing and processing firm the rates should be 30 and 23 percent, and for a small business they should be 14 and 12 percent.

Before jumping to the conclusion that the Canadian dividend tax credit is generally inadequate to achieve CIT/PIT integration, note that the credit is received irrespective of whether the corporation actually paid tax. Although CIT has been tightened up recently, along with the PIT, it is still true that many profitable corporations do not pay tax—as a result of accelerated depreciation, investment tax credits (still available in certain regions), resource sector incentives, and the carry-forward of losses.

The extent of relief under the dividend tax credit can be gauged by comparing the amounts claimed with CIT collections. In 1989, for example, the dividend tax credit reduced PIT burdens by $655 million, which compares with federal CIT revenues of $12.0 billion in that year. Even allowing for the fact that many taxpaying corporations were foreign rather than domestic, it seems clear that overall the dividend tax credit fell short of canceling out the CIT burden of domestic corporations.

As observed earlier, the dividend tax credit has been present throughout the entire period since 1970. However, its generosity has changed substantially over time. In 1970 and 1971 the credit was not yet of the "gross-up and credit" variety. Instead a credit equal simply to 20 percent of the dividend received was allowed. In 1972 a one-third gross-up was introduced, and the credit equaled 20 percent of the *grossed-up* amount. Then, in 1976 the credit was raised to the highest level it has ever taken on, with a 50 percent gross-up and 25 percent credit on the grossed-up amount. This very generous dividend tax credit remained in force until the end of 1986.[12] Since then, the gross-up factor has been reduced in stages—to 33.3 percent in 1987, and 25 percent in 1989.

2.3.5   Capital Gains

Capital gains taxation was introduced in Canada in 1972 as part of the government's response to the recommendations of the Carter Commission. Cana-

---

12. The 25 percent credit was reduced to 22.67 percent in 1982, but the 50 percent gross-up remained in force.

dians are taxed on realized capital gains earned since valuation day in December 1971. Currently, three-quarters of realized gains are taxable. (Prior to the 1987 tax reform only one-half of gains were taxed.) Principal residences are exempt, and each taxpayer has a standard $100,000 lifetime capital gains exemption.[13] The latter can be increased to $500,000 for capital gains on disposition of qualified farm property or the shares of small-business corporations.[14] Benefits of the lifetime exemption are deferred somewhat for those taxpayers who have net investment losses. Such losses, which include interest expense incurred for investment purposes, are cumulated starting in 1987 (in the form of a CNIL—cumulative net investment loss) and must be fully offset by positive investment income before any capital gains are eligible for the lifetime exemption.

An important feature of capital gains treatment in Canada is that gains are deemed to be realized when a taxpayer loses Canadian residence or dies. The latter feature—deemed realization on death—was felt to be sufficiently onerous that federal gift and estate taxes were abolished when capital gains taxes were introduced in 1972. Provincial succession duties remained in force in most provinces initially but have since all been removed. Thus Canada is unique now in having deemed realization of capital gains on death but no wealth transfer taxes.

Whether one counts tax-based savings incentives or looks at their provisions, there is a generally hump-shaped time profile of the generosity of shelters over the period 1970–90. The introduction of the lifetime capital gains exemption in 1985 bucked this trend. How important is this exception? The cumulative amounts that could be sheltered under the exemption were initially fairly small—$10,000 in 1985, $25,000 in 1986, and $50,000 in 1987. And when the exemption hit $100,000 in 1988, a phase-in of the three-fourths taxation of capital gains also began. Thus, while capital gains taxation has clearly become lighter for small investors, for the genuinely wealthy it has become heavier—with the 50 percent increase in the inclusion rate swamping the lifetime exemption.

The effective weight of capital gains taxes was further reduced in the pre-1981 period by the availability of a sophisticated averaging device known as the income averaging annuity contract (IAAC). These annuities could be taken out to average over a lengthy period nonrecurring income, such as that earned by artists or professional athletes and capital gains. Tax would then be charged on the annuity instead of the initial income. Astute investors could make use of the additional flexibility in tax timing afforded by an IAAC to significantly reduce their eventual total tax liability on a capital gain.

13. The lifetime capital gains exemption was introduced in the May 1985 budget. Originally it was to be phased in until it reached the level of $500,000. The 1987 tax reform halted the phase-in at the $100,000 level, except for the two types of gains indicated below.

14. The sum of exempt capital gains of all types cannot exceed $500,000.

2.3.6   Life Insurance

The rules governing the tax treatment of the investment income accruing under life insurance policies were completely revamped in Canada about 12 years ago. Prior to that time, this investment income accumulated tax-free (and disbursements to beneficiaries were tax-free). Now, only policies which pass a fairly rigorous test to assure that they provide only insurance, and not an investment element, are given exempt status. Policies issued before December 2, 1982, however, are "grandfathered." (Income earned as a result of premiums in excess of those fixed prior to December 2, 1982, is, however, taxable. Thus there is no marginal incentive for life insurance saving for the holders of those policies.) Investment income accruing in those policies issued between December 2, 1982, and December 31, 1989 is taxed every three years, and that produced by policies purchased after 1989 must be included in taxable income every year.

2.3.7   Other Tax Shelters

From the mid-1970s to the early 1980s, the Canadian PIT featured a virtual cornucopia of tax shelters. (This was also a period in which a very serious federal deficit emerged, so that the tax shelter proliferation was probably not sustainable.)[15] As under the CIT, generous investment tax credits and accelerated depreciation were available to businesspersons. In addition, a variety of special vehicles had been devised or sanctioned to encourage activity in housing, mining, energy, research and development, and Canadian films. As a result of the general tightening-up of the Canadian income tax system since 1984, most of these tax shelters have been eliminated. The most significant remaining ones are for exploration and development in mining and oil and gas.

While "other tax shelters" are decreasingly important in Canada, in thinking about patterns of saving and investment over the last two decades, it is quite important to bear their features in mind. Here we summarize the history of shelters for housing, exploration and development, and Canadian films since 1970.

A tax shelter for multiple-unit residential buildings (MURBs) was introduced in 1974 at a time of rapidly rising house prices and rents, in order to encourage rental construction. These MURBs allowed losses on approved projects to be deducted against other sources of income and allowed such "soft costs" as interest on construction financing, mortgage fees, and legal and accounting fees, which typically formed about 25 percent of the cost of constructing a building, to be immediately expensed. Concern over revenue losses

---

15. The virtually full indexation of the PIT in this period also contributed to the development of the deficit problem. One could perhaps argue that the proliferation of shelters would have been sustainable with partial indexation. (The May 1985 federal budget introduced partial indexation, effective in the 1986 tax year. This system, which only adjusts brackets for increases in the CPI in excess of 3 percent, is still in force.)

led to the requirement that soft costs be amortized over the life of a building, and to the eventual termination of the shelter in 1981. No new MURBs could be created after 1981, but existing MURBs were allowed to continue fully in force until June 17, 1987. After that date, if a MURB was sold, eligibility for special treatment of rental losses would be lost. Finally, MURBs are now close to being fully phased out. By 1994 they all will have lost their favored treatment.

Another important housing-related incentive was the Registered Home Ownership Savings Plan (RHOSP), also introduced in 1974, but terminated by the May 1985 federal budget. This plan allowed deductible contributions of up to $1,000 per year and $10,000 in total. Interest in the plan accrued tax-free, as in an RRSP. Funds withdrawn to purchase a house were tax-free.

Throughout the period under consideration, there have been very generous incentives for exploration and development in mining and in oil and gas. Mining and energy companies can pass through their exploration and development expenses directly to personal investors via limited partnerships or "flow-through shares." The immediate tax benefits are substantial. Canadian Exploration Expenses are immediately written off;[16] Canadian Development Expenses receive a 30 percent write-off; Canadian Oil and Gas Property Expenses are written off at a 10 percent rate.

One of the most remarkable episodes in Canadian tax history was that of the Scientific Research Tax Credit (SRTC), introduced in 1983 and withdrawn in haste only two years later (by a new government). The SRTC allowed R&D losses to be sold to individuals. It became an unexpectedly popular tax shelter, with much highly questionable "R&D" being performed in order to manufacture the credits. The revenue losses amounted to over $1 billion, despite the short lifespan of the shelter.

Finally, the tax shelter for certified Canadian feature films dates from 1974. This initially allowed the immediate write-off of the depreciable costs of producing a film with specified levels of Canadian inputs. This was replaced by a reduction in the depreciation rate to 50 percent, and then to 30 percent in 1988. The shelter now applies to videotape as well as film. Alongside the decreased tax incentive there has been much less activity in the Canadian feature film industry.

2.3.8   Alternative Minimum Tax

An important feature of the current Canadian PIT is the alternative minimum tax (AMT) introduced in 1986, which may have a dramatic effect on the effective marginal tax rate on personal capital income if an investor has received

---

16. Canadian Exploration Expenses (CEE) are included in the calculation of the cumulative net investment loss (CNIL) referred to above. Thus, making use of these expenses may result in tax being paid on capital gains that otherwise could qualify for the lifetime capital gains exemption. (Note, again, that the taxpayer does not permanently lose access to his lifetime capital gains exemption. It is merely deferred until his CNIL is wiped out by positive investment income.)

large capital gains or made significant investments in tax shelters. In the calculation of AMT, a basic exemption of $40,000 is allowed, and individuals retain their basic personal tax credits (but *not* the dividend tax credit discussed above). The federal minimum tax rate was 17 percent in 1991; adding provincial taxes brings this up to 25–28 percent across the provinces. These rates are applied to "adjusted taxable income," which differs from ordinary taxable income through the addition of the nontaxable quarter of capital gains, RRSP and RPP contributions, deductions for Canadian oil and gas exploration and development expenses, and losses arising from capital cost allowance claims on MURBs or Canadian films (see above).

2.4   Tax-deferred Retirement Savings and Social Security

There are several important forms of deferred retirement saving in Canada: (i) employer- or union-based pensions—known as registered pension plans (RPPs), (ii) individual accounts similar to IRAs in the United States—known as registered retirement savings plans (RRSPs), and (iii) deferred profit sharing plans (DPSPs).[17] The main element is the RRSP/RPP system, which has always been integrated and has recently been rationalized and enhanced (starting in 1991) (see Horner 1987). The enhancement of this system moves contrary to many of the other changes in the Canadian PIT in recent years, which have increased the taxation of capital income.

2.4.1   RRSP/RPP Contribution Limits

As in most countries, Canadians can save via occupational pension plans—RPPs—where contributions are deductible, income accrues tax-free, and pension income is taxed when it is received. Both employer and employee contributions are deductible. There are two major types of RPP: defined-benefit and money-purchase plans. Defined-benefit plans have been the most popular, since until recently it was possible to shelter more saving under these plans than under money-purchase plans.

Under the former RRSP/RPP system, taxpayers who were not members of an RPP could each year contribute to an RRSP the lesser of $5,500 or 20 percent of earnings. Taxpayers covered by an RPP at work, and their employers, could each contribute up to $3,500 to an RPP. In addition, the taxpayer could contribute to an RRSP as long as the combined (nonemployer) contributions

17. Deferred profit sharing plans are similar to money-purchase pension plans, except that they give generally greater flexibility. They are not subject to federal or provincial pension benefits legislation; there is more flexibility in the time pattern of contributions; investments in the shares of the employer corporation are allowed; withdrawal prior to termination of employment and payout in either lump sum or installment form is allowed. The contribution limit is the lesser of (a) 18 percent of salary or (b) 50 percent of the money-purchase RPP contribution limit. The use of DPSPs has declined dramatically since new rules denying a deduction for contributions to plans for the benefit of significant shareholders and related persons were introduced. We have not looked at DPSPs in any detail in this study.

Table 2.3   RRSP Contribution Limits, 1970–94

	Nominal Dollars		1989 Dollars	
Year	Not RPP Eligible	RPP Eligible	Not RPP Eligible	RPP Eligible
1970	2,500	1,500	9,191	5,515
1971	"	"	8,929	5,357
1972	4,000	2,500	13,652	8,532
1973	"	"	12,698	7,937
1974	"	"	11,429	7,143
1975	"	"	10,309	6,443
1976	5,500	3,500	13,189	8,393
1977	"	"	12,222	7,778
1978	"	"	11,224	7,143
1979	"	"	10,280	6,542
1980	"	"	9,338	5,942
1981	"	"	8,308	5,287
1982	"	"	7,493	4,768
1983	"	"	7,088	4,510
1984	"	"	6,782	4,316
1985	"	"	6,532	4,157
1986	7,500	"	8,552	3,991
1987	"	"	8,188	3,821
1988	"	"	7,870	3,673
1989	"	"	7,500	3,500
1990	"	"	7,156	3,340
1991	11,500	11,500 − PA	10,388	10,388 − PA
1992	12,500	12,500 − PA	—	—
1993	13,500	13,500 − PA	—	—
1994	14,500	14,500 − PA	—	—
1995	15,500[a]	15,500 − PA	—	—

Source: Authors' compilation from standard references.

Note: PA = "pension adjustment." The *PA* is the sum of pension credits under DPSPs or RPPs. For money-purchase plans, this is simply the sum of employer and employee contributions. For defined-benefit plans an imputation is made.

[a]Indexed to average wage for subsequent years.

did not exceed the lesser of $3,500 or 20 percent of earnings. These contribution limits were held constant, in nominal dollars, from 1976 to 1985 (inclusive). In 1986 the $5,500 RRSP contribution ceiling was raised to $7,500 and the $3,500 limit on employee contributions to RPPs was removed. The $7,500 limit remained in place from 1986 to 1990 inclusive. (See table 2.3 for a summary of these changing limits.)

A far-reaching reform of the RRSP/RPP system was first proposed in the February 1984 federal budget. The main elements of the reform would be an increase in contribution room for money-purchase plan RPPs to give them treatment equivalent to that of defined-benefit plans, improved portability of plans, a phase-in of increased contribution limits to the lesser of $15,500 or 18 percent of earnings (for all RPP plus RRSP contributions) by 1990, indexation of contribution limits to the average wage after 1990, and a carry-forward of unused contribution room to later tax years (now limited to seven years). These main elements remain in place in the reform, implemented in the 1991 tax year, but with several postponements of the reform, the real steady-state contribution limits will be smaller than originally anticipated, since they will hit $15,500 in nominal terms in 1995, rather than 1990, and thereafter be indexed to the average wage.

In addition to setting out the history of nominal RRSP/RPP contribution limits, table 2.3 reports these numbers in constant 1989 dollars. Until 1991 there was a ratchet effect, with the real value increasing discretely from time to time, with the adjustments in nominal contribution limits, and declining between adjustments. Interestingly, real contribution limits were at their peak in 1972. This peak was almost regained in 1976, but by 1985 half the real value of the limits was gone. If moderate rates of inflation are experienced in the next four years, the $15,500 limit of 1995 should approximately match the real 1972 or 1976 contribution limits. Thus, those who believe that high RRSP contribution limits were behind the historically high Canadian personal saving rates in the 1970s might expect a resurgence of saving in Canada in the 1990s.

2.4.2 Portfolios and Withdrawals

An important aspect of the RRSP/RPP system is that there are restrictions on the portfolios that can be held. As elsewhere, the direction of investment of pension plan assets is closely regulated. One important feature of this regulation in Canada is that only up to 15 percent of the portfolio may be in foreign assets. On the RRSP side, there is a similar restriction on foreign investments. In addition, funds have largely been confined to investment in bonds, shares, mortgages, or life insurance policies. The May 1985 budget, however, introduced a number of features to encourage pension plans to invest in small business, and also allowed RRSPs to be invested in the shares of private Canadian corporations.

Individual control over portfolio composition is relatively rare under the institutional pension (RPP) component of the system but does occur under some money-purchase RPPs. In contrast, RRSP investors have great discretion over the type of assets they choose to hold via their choice of type of plan. Complete control can be achieved using a "self-directed" plan, under which the issuer (a bank or trust company) will adjust the portfolio whenever desired by the saver. Management fees for such plans are modest and they are becoming increasingly popular.[18] Self-administered plans are still chosen by a small minority of

---

18. For example, the Canadian Imperial Bank of Commerce currently offers self-directed mutual fund RRSPs with a $25 annual management fee and a $15 withdrawal fee. These fees are tax-deductible. The portfolio may be adjusted daily.

RRSP holders, however. In the non-self-administered category there are five basic types of plans: (1) "guaranteed" plans, providing a fixed rate of return, (2) "income" plans, with investments in fixed-income securities, (3) "equity" plans, invested in stocks, (4) "mortgage" plans, and (5) registered life insurance policies, under which the savings portion of the policy is treated as equivalent to an RRSP (now a less popular option than in earlier years). Due to increasing competition in the Canadian financial industries, rates of return on these various plans are now generally very attractive. A large variety of products are available, however, and savers must look closely at their fees and provisions. Routine advice is to select a plan without penalty, or with a low penalty, for early withdrawal or transfer of funds to another RRSP. Provided this advice is followed, the saver retains considerable flexibility and discretion in the choice of saving vehicle, even when the plan is not self-directed.

All funds in an RPP must be converted into an annuity before the taxpayer's seventy-first birthday. In contrast, great flexibility is allowed in cashing out an RRSP. First, taxpayers may withdraw all of the funds at any point and include them in taxable income that year. Second, they may purchase an annuity (possibly a joint-survivor annuity with spouses) prior to their seventy-first birthday. The annuity payments would enter taxable income, except for the first $1,000, which would be eligible for the pension income deduction. Third, it is possible to transfer withdrawals from an RRSP to a registered retirement income fund (RRIF), where savings continue to accumulate tax-free, but a series of annual payments must be made from the fund, which will exhaust it by the taxpayer's ninety-first birthday.

Another important aspect is that part or all of an RRSP contribution may actually be made to a spouse's RRSP. This allows an element of income splitting—and not just in retirement, since the amount contributed to the spouse's RRSP may be withdrawn after just two years, being treated as the spouse's income.

The most recent modification of RRSP withdrawal options was the introduction in the February 1992 federal budget of a home buyers' plan, under which up to $20,000 could be withdrawn tax-free from an RRSP in order to buy a house. A couple could therefore withdraw up to $40,000 for this purpose. The $40,000 would have to be restored to the RRSPs over the next 15 years, but the net effect would be a transfer of equity from the RRSP to the home. This plan will of course strengthen the incentive to save via an RRSP for many people, as well as having an effect on portfolio composition.

2.4.3   Participation in RPPs and Use of RRSPs

Flows

Tables 2.4 and 2.5 present summary information on the incidence of employee RPP and RRSP contributions and the amounts contributed in 1981 and 1989, by age and income groups, respectively. These data come from unpub-

Table 2.4   **RRSP and RPP Contributors and Contributions, by Age Group**

Age	1981			1989		
	RPP	RRSP	RPP or RRSP	RPP	RRSP	RPP or RRSP
% of C/QPP Contributors Contributing						
<25	18	3	19	14	9	21
25–34	43	13	49	37	26	53
35–44	51	20	58	50	36	68
45–54	51	29	62	52	44	74
55–64	56	36	68	47	60	83
Total	42	17	49	40	34	60
Average Amount per Contributor (1989 $)						
<25	554	1,220	701	691	1,463	1,151
25–34	898	1,489	1,211	1,212	2,032	1,887
35–44	1,153	1,761	1,644	1,666	2,479	2,510
45–54	1,139	1,991	1,893	1,808	2,700	2,832
55–64	1,056	2,074	1,992	1,571	3,616	3,515
Total	994	1,836	1,551	1,498	2,830	2,644

Source: Unpublished tabulations, Department of Finance, Government of Canada.

Note: C/QPP stands for the Canada and Quebec Pension Plans. Among those of working age, the group of contributors to these plans corresponds closely to the set of individuals who are eligible to make RRSP or RPP contributions.

lished Department of Finance compilations. Tables 2.6 and 2.7 supplement this flow data with information on the stock of RRSP wealth held by families in 1984, according to Statistics Canada's Survey of Consumer Finance (SCF).

Table 2.4 shows the fraction of contributors to the Canada and Quebec Pension Plans (C/QPP) who also contributed to RPPs, RRSPs, or either type of plan, as well as amounts contributed, by age group.[19] Note, first, that the incidence of both RPP and RRSP contributions rises with age, but does so more steadily for RRSPs. There is a plateau of about 50 percent contributing to RPPs from age 35 to age 64. In contrast, the *amount* contributed to an RPP has a hump-shaped profile, with the maximum contribution occurring in the 35–44-year-old group in 1981 and in the 45–54-year-old group in 1989. The incidence pattern of RPP contributions did not change very much from 1981 to 1989, but the average contribution rose by 51 percent, with the rise being especially marked for older groups.

In contrast to RPPs, the incidence, as well as average amount, of RRSP contributions increased dramatically in the 1980s—in part reflecting the disappearance and curtailment of many other tax shelters. While in 1981 only 17

19. It is useful to divide by the number of C/QPP subscribers since they approximate closely the set of eligible RRSP/RPP contributors in the working-age group. Many retirees who are not C/QPP subscribers make RRSP contributions, however. This results in some instances in table 2.5 where the figures for RRSP/RPP contributors as a percentage of C/QPP subscribers exceed 100 percent.

Table 2.5   RRSP and RPP Contributors and Contributions, by Income Group

Income (thousand $)	1981			1989		
	RPP	RRSP	RPP or RRSP	RPP	RRSP	RPP or RRSP
% of C/QPP Contributors Contributing						
0–10	5	2	7	7	6	13
10–20	19	7	25	19	20	36
20–30	48	14	55	47	35	69
30–40	64	23	71	66	47	86
40–50	75	32	82	71	56	92
50–60	82	47	90	70	58	98
60–70	75	51	87	65	62	102[a]
70–80	73	61	88	59	66	101[a]
80–90	62	60	93	52	70	103[a]
90–100	53	65	90	46	74	104[a]
>100	39	71	91	28	83	101[a]
Total	42	17	49	40	34	60
Average Amount per Contributor (1989 $)						
0–10	197	455	275	200	911	614
10–20	376	979	602	490	1,634	1,264
20–30	652	1,247	915	954	2,225	1,865
30–40	960	1,600	1,400	1,490	2,646	2,586
40–50	1,272	1,907	1,917	2,032	2,897	3,235
50–60	1,553	2,042	2,420	2,582	3,539	3,868
60–70	1,907	2,355	2,923	2,866	4,455	4,541
70–80	1,964	2,682	3,321	3,074	5,056	5,084
80–90	2,042	3,087	3,324	3,307	5,820	5,674
90–100	2,103	3,510	3,727	3,659	6,343	6,218
>100	2,136	4,281	4,254	3,571	7,288	7,032
Total	994	1,836	1,551	1,498	2,830	2,644

Source: Unpublished tabulations, Department of Finance, Government of Canada.
[a]See n. 19.

percent of the C/QPP population contributed to RRSPs, by 1989 this fraction had doubled to 34 percent. Amounts contributed also increased sharply (54 percent overall), with the biggest increases again coming for older groups. The relative increase in contributions by older groups likely reflects, in part, their increasing relative prosperity. It also reflects the fact that the rise in the RRSP contribution limit from $5,500 to $7,500 in 1986 would not benefit workers who earned less than $27,500 (since for them the effective limit was 20 percent of earnings). Such lower-income workers are of course more heavily represented among the young than the middle-aged.

Table 2.5 looks at the pattern of RRSP/RPP contributions by income group. The incidence of RPP contributions has a hump-shaped profile as one moves up the income groups, with the largest incidence occurring in the $40,000–$60,000 range. High-income taxpayers are more likely to be independent professionals and businesspeople and therefore not covered by employer/union pension plans. The incidence of RRSP contributions, in contrast, climbs with income throughout.

One interesting change in the 1980s, indicated by table 2.5, is that the incidence of RPP contributions rose slightly in the lower-income groups and fell in all the groups with incomes of $40,000+. The incidence of RRSP contributions, in contrast, rose in all income groups. While overall RRSP contributions went up on average by 54 percent, there was little change in the relative size of contributions across the income groups. On the other hand, the relative contributions of high-income contributors to RPPs increased from 1981 to 1989, likely reflecting the removal of the $3,500 limit on employee RPP contributions in 1986.

In conclusion, amounts contributed to both RPPs and RRSPs rose substantially both in aggregate and per contributor. The pattern of incidence did not change radically for RPPs, but the incidence of RRSP contributions doubled overall, and rose for all age and income groups. Older contributors had the largest increase in RRSP contributions, while the highest-income groups had the biggest increases in RPP contributions per contributor. These changes seem to be adequately explained by a general increase in the desire to use the RPP/RRSP saving vehicles due to the curtailment of other shelters pushing against the limits set by the incidence of employer/union-based pension plans, and the changing constraints on employee RPP and RRSP contributions.

While most RPP contributions will stay "locked-in" until retirement, people may withdraw RRSP funds at any point, and each year there is a significant flow of preretirement withdrawals. When attempting to get an idea of the extent of net asset accumulation in this form, it is important to take into account these withdrawals. Unpublished tabulations from the Department of Finance indicate that aggregate withdrawals as a percentage of contributions for taxpayers aged less than 60 years were 16.7, 21.4, and 19.2 percent in 1981, 1982, and 1984, respectively. The age profile shows a strong negative relation between withdrawals and age from age 25 to age 60. (Withdrawal rates rose until age 25 and again after age 60.) In the recession years, 1981 and 1982, withdrawals were 30 percent of contributions for those aged 25–34. However, in 1984, which was perhaps more "normal," withdrawals were just 21.6 percent in this age group, and the relationship between age and withdrawals was overall much flatter than in the recession years.

It would be interesting to look at more recent information on RRSP withdrawals for those of working age, especially in view of the curtailment of several alternative tax shelters since 1984. Nevertheless, one may provisionally conclude that withdrawals average about 15–20 percent of contributions for those of working age. This conclusion is used to help with some rough calculations (below) of the stock of RRSP wealth which people would build up at various ages if they continued to contribute at recently observed rates.

Table 2.6   RRSP Ownership by Age and Income, Families and Unattached
                   Individuals, 1984 SCF

	Incidence (%)	Mean Amount ($)	% of Assets	% of Financial Assets	Mean Net Worth ($)
Age					
<25	10.6	230	1.6	9.4	9,104
25–34	27.2	1,683	2.8	19.3	42,845
35–44	34.1	3,636	3.4	23.6	85,775
45–54	42.8	7,110	5.0	25.5	128,411
55–64	43.8	8,214	5.7	21.3	136,904
>65	15.6	2,562	2.7	7.6	93,468
Income (thousand $)					
<5	3.9	260	0.9	5.8	24,028
5–10	3.5	220	0.8	3.7	25,238
10–15	10.3	810	1.6	6.8	45,891
15–25	22.7	1,780	2.5	10.9	63,396
25–35	35.1	2,920	3.3	16.8	74,807
35–45	45.3	5,070	4.5	24.3	94,328
45–60	54.9	7,490	4.9	22.6	130,450
>60	70.9	18,730	5.8	23.0	293,468
Total	30.2	3,900	4.0	18.2	85,344

Source: Cols. 1, 3, and 5 are taken directly from Statistics Canada, *The Distribution of Wealth in Canada, 1984,* Publication no. 13-580 (Ottawa, 1986), 64–73, tables 24–27; cols. 2 and 4 were calculated by the authors from these tables.

Stocks

As discussed earlier, Statistics Canada has conducted wealth surveys at roughly seven-year intervals as part of its annual Survey of Consumer Finance (SCF). Amounts held in RRSPs, but not in RPPs, are surveyed. Unfortunately, the most recent survey was conducted in 1984, so that this data source is now somewhat dated. However, the results of the survey appear to check out fairly well with independent information. They are summarized here in table 2.6.

Table 2.6 shows the incidence of, and average amounts held in, RRSPs by age and income groups for families and unattached individuals in spring 1984. On average, overall, just $3,900 was held in this form, which is only 4.6 percent of a mean net worth of $85,344. For comparison, this amount is comparable to the value of cars and trucks (5.3 percent of net worth), but is just 12 percent of equity in owner-occupied houses. As a fraction of overall financial assets, RRSPs were 18 percent—up considerably from the 1977 SCF (see figs. 2.5 and 2.6.)

The amounts held in the form of RRSPs, according to the 1984 SCF, are fairly modest. It should be borne in mind, however, that RPPs are likely to be about twice as great as RRSPs in value. On this basis, the combined RRSP/

Table 2.7   **Simulated "Steady-State" Sheltered Saving Stocks (1989 $)**

| Age | 1981 | | | 1986 | | | 1989 | | |
	RPP	RRSP	Total	RPP	RRSP	Total	RPP	RRSP	Total
25	646	119	765	502	317	819	531	458	989
30	3,455	882	4,337	3,586	1,942	5,528	3,676	2,653	6,329
35	7,039	1,855	8,895	7,523	4,015	11,538	7,691	5,454	13,144
40	12,917	3,701	16,618	14,713	7,839	22,553	15,343	10,449	25,793
45	20,419	6,056	26,475	23,890	12,720	36,610	25,110	16,826	41,936
50	29,944	9,920	39,864	35,374	19,755	55,130	38,184	26,032	64,216
55	42,101	14,851	56,952	50,032	28,735	78,766	54,869	37,781	92,651
60	56,272	20,790	77,062	67,039	41,053	108,092	73,433	54,094	127,527
65	74,359	28,370	102,729	88,746	56,775	145,521	97,125	74,913	172,038

Source: Authors' own calculations. See text.

RPP wealth of the 1984 SCF sample would be about 15 percent of their net worth, which is considerably more impressive.

In terms of patterns across age and income groups, note first that the qualitative patterns picked up for *contributions* are echoed for stocks. The incidence of RRSP ownership rises with both age and income. The relative importance of RRSPs in the portfolio also tends to rise with both age and income.

Another way of getting an idea about stocks of sheltered retirement saving is to do a perpetual inventory calculation based on flows. In order to get an actual estimate of RRSP/RPP ownership in a particular year, one would want to have a complete time series of contributions by age. In fact, what we have is data for just three years: 1981, 1986, and 1989. What we have done, therefore, is to compute three alternative "steady-state" age profiles of RRSP/RPP stocks which would be obtained if the contribution patterns from the three different years had remained in place (in real terms) forever. A 5 percent real rate of return (conservative in light of real interest rates in the 1980s in Canada) and a 15 percent withdrawal rate at all ages have been assumed.[20] It is also assumed that employer and employee RPP contributions were equal.

The most striking thing about the steady-state calculations presented in table 2.7 is that the amounts built up in RRSPs and RPPs are much larger than one would expect on the basis of the survey evidence. In 1989 dollars, the RRSP balances at age 60 are $20,790, $41,053, and $54,094, using the 1981, 1986 and 1989 data, respectively. These figures, which are for individual taxpayers, compare with mean *family* holdings (converted to 1989 dollars) of just $10,121 in 1984 according to the SCF. Part of the explanation for the difference is that because RRSP contributions have been trending up over time, the *steady-state*

20. The results are relatively insensitive to the assumed withdrawal rate, as long as it is kept in the plausible range of 10–20 percent. Results are more sensitive to the interest rate. If the real rate of return was only 3 percent (more representative of the 1960s and early 1970s than the 5 percent rate used in the calculations), RRSP accumulation at age 60 would be about one-third smaller.

stocks implied by any year's contributions will naturally exceed current stocks. However, some part of the explanation may lie in survey underestimation of RRSP holdings.

2.4.4   Social Security[21]

The earnings-related component of social security is much less important in Canada than in the United States. The three principal federal programs are Old-Age Security (OAS; its budget for the 1989–90 fiscal year was $11.8 billion), the Guaranteed Income Supplement (GIS; $3.9 billion) and the Canada Pension Plan (CPP; 1990 expenditures were $9.5 billion).[22] In addition, several provinces provide means-tested payments to the elderly, and many of the provinces and their municipalities provide transfers in the form of subsidized services (medical care, homes for the aged, and so on).

Old-Age Security is payable to all who are age 65 or older and who meet certain residency requirements. As of January 1, 1991, the maximum pension was $354.92 per month, or $4,259 per annum. It has been indexed quarterly to the consumer price index (CPI) since April 1, 1973. Old-Age Security benefits are taxable under the Income Tax Act and are also subject to the social benefits repayment tax introduced in 1987, which taxes back OAS payments at a rate of 15 percent on an individual's net income in excess of a threshold which is partially indexed and stood at $51,765 in 1991.

Guaranteed Income Supplement is an income-tested supplement payable to OAS recipients. As of January 1, 1991, the maximum GIS was $421.79 per month for a single pensioner and $211.93 for each member of a married couple, both of whom had to be at least 65 years old. Thus OAS and GIS together guarantee elderly married couples an income of $15,111.60 per annum. However, the "tax-back rate" for GIS is 50 percent on income over and above GIS and OAS.[23]

Canada Pension Plan is a compulsory, contributory pension plan which pays benefits in a variety of circumstances and which requires those working to make certain contributions. Retirement pensions are based on each individual's earnings history. They are designed to replace 25 percent of earnings at age 65, up to the average industrial wage which stood at $30,500 in 1991.[24] Benefits are indexed to the CPI and are taxable. In 1991, employers and employees each contributed 2.3 percent of earnings between $3000 and $30,500 to cover the costs of the program. Since CPP's inception (in 1966) revenues have exceeded

21. This section draws heavily on various issues of the Canadian Tax Foundation's annual publication, The National Finances, as well as on Burbidge (1987).

22. Quebec operates its own public pension program, QPP.

23. The equivalent of OAS/GIS for persons aged 60–64 years is "spouse's allowance," which has a tax-back rate of 75 percent on the OAS component.

24. Contributors may choose to collect retirement benefits at any age between 60 and 70. The pension is reduced 0.5 percent per month before age 65, and increased 0.5 percent per month after. Thus someone retiring at age 60 collects 70 percent of the age-65 retirement pension (130 percent for someone aged 70).

John B. Burbidge and James B. Davies

Table 2.10   **Revenue Impacts of Tax Incentives for Saving, Canada: 1983**

Incentive	Amount (million $)	% of Federal Revenue
RRSPs/RPPs	4,900	18.3
Investment income deduction	835	3.1
Dividend tax credit	785	2.9
Life insurance	290	1.1
Pension income deduction	150	0.6
RHOSPs[a]	125	0.5
Oil, gas, and mining	45	0.2
Total	7,130	26.6

Col. 1, Department of Finance, *Account of the Cost of Selective Tax Measures* (Ottawa, —48, table 1; col. 2 equals col. 1 divided by total federal PIT refvenue in 1983, which 26,809 million.

[a] Registered Home Ownership Savings Plans.

10 do not provide a guide to the current revenue impacts of incentives. However, some fairly shrewd guesses can be made about the magni- current shelters. Those shown in table 2.10 that have since disap- vided benefits equal to 4.7 percent of federal revenue. The only new added is the $100,000 lifetime capital gains exemption. Even if d capital gains fully it would not reduce revenue by anything like accounted for by RRSPs/RPPs. An educated guess is that the reve- to this new shelter is likely to be less than 2 percent of total federal finally, RRSP/RPP contributions have increased sizably since out two-thirds by 1989, for example, whereas PIT revenue rose cent in real terms. But by 1995, RRSP contribution limits will doubled relative to 1989, so that in the new steady state that is hed, the RRSP/RPP shelter could well expand 40–50 percent relative size in 1983. This would imply total revenue losses percent of federal revenue. Adding up, when the new RRSP/ completely phased in, it appears that the total revenue impact ings incentives might be in the neighborhood of 30–35 percent ue, that is considerably higher than the 26.6 percent figure for 0.

mpacts

ntries, there has been much interest in the impact of taxati da. Renewed interest in this question was stimulated in oskin (1978), who found that, in contrast to earlier stud

enditure accounts estimated that the half-taxation of capital gains re If the revenue from capital gains taxation was in the same neighbor would add up to about 1.6 percent of federal revenue.

Table 2.8   **Components of Pretax Income for Urban, Married-Couple Families with Husband Retired: 1977, 1984, and 1989 SCFs (1990 $)**

	Income Year					
	1976		1983		1989	
	Weighted Means	Income Shares (%)	Weighted Means	Income Shares (%)	Weighted Means	Income Shares (%)
Earnings	5,000	20.9	4,692	16.5	6,532	17.7
Investment income	4,474	18.7	5,780	20.3	6,943	18.8
OAS and GIS	7,346	30.7	7,889	27.7	7,825	21.2
C/QPP	1,866	7.8	3,803	13.4	5,803	15.7
Pensions and annuities	4,358	18.2	4,507	15.8	8,013	21.7
Other income	902	3.7	1,770	6.3	1,781	4.9
Total income	23,946	100	28,441	100	36,897	100
No. of observations	364		534		1,468	
Average age	70.2		69.8		69.7	

Source: Authors' calculations using Statistics Canada's SCF public-use microdata tape.

expenditures and the surplus has been loaned to the provinces at below-market interest rates.[25] These surpluses are scheduled to fall so that CPP will become more like a pure pay-as-you-go program.

Table 2.8 uses the 1977, 1984, and 1989 SCFs to give some idea of the relative importance of different sources of income for elderly, urban, married-couple families in which the husband is "retired" and is at least 65 years old.[26] "Earnings" may arise from the activities of the wife in the labor market or from the self-employment income of the family (e.g., renting a room to a boarder). "Investment income" includes interest, dividends, and realized capital gains, but not the annuity income originating from having turned an RRSP into a retirement annuity. Unfortunately, SCF data do not permit one to isolate retirement income resulting from RRSPs; all such income is included with private pension income in "pensions and annuities." "Other income" includes the provincial supplements such as Ontario's Guaranteed Annual Income Supplement (currently $83 per month with a 50 percent tax-back rate).

Table 2.8 makes some important points: First, even though for all age groups together average real income was fairly constant from 1975 to 1990, mean income of *retired couples* increased by 50 percent. Second, the combination OAS/GIS has declined sharply in importance, while the share of C/QPP has doubled from 7.8 to 15.7 percent. Third, by 1989, "pensions and annuities"

25. The accumulated surplus stood at $39 billion in 1990.

26. The 1990 SCF has been released by Statistics Canada, but at the time this paper was being prepared, it had not been installed at our universities.

had become the most important component of retirement income. Fourth, the share of "investment income" was virtually unchanged at 18.8 percent between 1976 and 1989; that its share was a little higher in 1983 may reflect the high interest rates during the early 1980s.

What can we say about "replacement rates"? First, since the OAS/GIS safety net guarantees elderly, married couples an income over $15,000 per year, low-income workers likely experience an increase in after-tax income on retirement. Second, for middle-income workers earning less than the average industrial wage, the replacement rate built into CPP is 25 percent; this sets a lower bound because such workers would still receive at least OAS if not some GIS. Many defined-benefit private pension plans integrate CPP with the private pension and pay about 65 percent of final earnings, so for some workers, replacement rates on private and public pensions alone could exceed 70 percent. Finally, for higher-income workers, private arrangements dominate the public system; depending on RRSP wealth and for some private pensions, replacement rates could once again exceed 70 percent.

Various calculations of replacement rates have been made by students of pensions in Canada. The most comprehensive appears to have been by Wolfson (1979), who simulated the lifetime consequences of OAS, GIS, and C/QPP. In line with our above suggestion, Wolfson found that, looking at the impact of compulsory programs alone, "for the poorest 10 or 20% of the population, average post-retirement consumption levels could well exceed average pre-retirement consumption levels. For the upper 50 or 70% of the population, however, average post-retirement consumption levels could well be 25–50% below corresponding pre-retirement levels if no other provisions for retirement are made" (Wolfson 1979, 5–38).

To say more about actual replacement rates, it would be exceedingly helpful to have panel data that followed individuals through the retirement period. Unfortunately, such data are not publicly available for Canada.[27] Since earnings were so stable, at least over the 1980s, one may be able to build on table 2.8 by comparing the after-tax incomes of the families included in table 2.8 with the after-tax incomes of "similar" families where the head is aged 55–64. We use head's education as an extra control to achieve better comparability between the working and the retired samples.

We present the results of this exercise in table 2.9. As one might expect, before-tax and after-tax family income rise with the husband's education level. It is also not surprising that replacement rates are higher for after-tax income than for before-tax income. What is striking is how little replacement rates vary with education level. Using after-tax income, the replacement rate for

27. The Department of Finance has several longitudinal files of taxpayers which are used in-house. Those data could be used to study actual replacement rates, but we are not aware of any studies that have been done.

Table 2.9

Weighted Means and Replacement Rates of After-Tax (AT) Income for Urban, Married Selected Education Groups: 1989 SCF (19

Education Level of Husband	Working Aged 55–64		Retired Aged 65
	BT Income	AT Income	BT Income
Less than high school	62,211	49,689	31,513
High school	72,964	57,994	40,722
University degree	103,953	76,517	60,005
All groups	72,034	56,229	36,89
No. of observations	1,193		

Source: Authors' calculations using Statistics Canada's

those with less than a high school educa
university-degree group is 65 percent.

2.5 Evidence of Impacts

2.5.1 Revenue Impacts

The revenue impacts of governm
been most carefully studied by the
tax expenditure accounts in 1979,
1985 exercise are set out in table
impact of the seven measures list
actual federal revenues. Impacts
estimated but would have been
gate loss of revenue would b
income.

It is clear from table 2.10
the others. The revenue los
total from the seven measu
$1,000 investment income
credit (since, cut back co
ing under life insurance
$1,000 pension income
There has been so m

28. Currently, an update
yet available.

in table 2
for saving
tude of th
peared pro
shelter to
this shelter
the amount
nue loss du
revenue.[29]
1983—by a
only 46.6 pe
have almost
being approa
compared to
equal to 25–3
RPP system is
of personal sav
of federal reven
1983 in table 2.

2.5.2   Savings

As in other cou
on saving in Cana
United States by

29. The 1985 tax ex
revenue by $440 millio
as seems reasonable, it

there was a fairly large interest elasticity of aggregate saving. Boskin's best-known estimate of this number was 0.4. West (1987) replicated Boskin's study for Canada, but found that the interest rate effect on saving was negative and insignificant. He also replicated the approach of Summers (1982), based explicitly on the life-cycle model, and again found either zero or negative effects. Positive effects were only obtained when the nominal interest rate was used instead of the real rate. Beach, Boadway, and Bruce confirmed these results using alternative real interest rate variables (see Beach et al. 1988, 31–34). Beach et al. suggested that the divergence in U.S. and Canadian results could be explained by the upward trend in the generosity of Canadian tax incentives for saving in the 1960s and 1970s. Real interest rates declined in both the United States and Canada, but the impact one would otherwise expect on saving was reversed in Canada by the missing tax incentives variable, it was suggested.

There has been a great deal of discussion in the United States about whether IRAs stimulate saving or are simply inframarginal. Curiously, this issue has received much less attention in Canada, where RRSPs are relatively more important.

Since very few people are observed to save *only* in the form of an IRA or RRSP, simple economic analysis would suggest that most IRA/RRSP saving is inframarginal. From this viewpoint, IRAs/RRSPs just represent a rationed reduction in the price of retirement consumption. An increase in contribution limits may have only wealth effects, and no substitution effects.

There are important critics of this position. They point out, for example, that many people who contribute less than the IRA/RRSP limit also save in nonsheltered forms, suggesting that the two forms of saving are not perfect substitutes. Why aren't they perfectly substitutable? Clearly, the transactions costs of opening and closing IRAs/RRSPs may differ from those of other saving vehicles. Also, it has been argued, the high advertising of IRAs/RRSPs may help to make them a distinct commodity in many people's eyes. It is difficult to evaluate such arguments *a priori*. The question of whether IRAs/RRSPs stimulate fresh saving is really an empirical issue.

There are three pieces of evidence on the impact of RRSPs on saving in Canada: simulations by Michael Daly and colleagues, studies done using in-house Department of Finance data sets by David Wise, and the well-known Carroll and Summers (1987) study.

In the early 1980s, some Canadian researchers became interested in the properties of a tax system where both registered retirement savings vehicles and nonregistered but tax-exempt savings were present. Daly (1981) and Hood (1982) both showed that, under certainty and with perfect capital markets, in the absence of contribution limits such a system would allow ideal lifetime tax averaging, and would effectively convert the personal tax base from annual to lifetime income. Androkovich, Daly, and Naqib (1993) follow this up with a simulation of the effects of introducing unlimited RRSPs in a stylized representation of the Canadian tax system. They find that there is a very sizable effect on capital accumulation—in fact a greater effect than would be obtained via a progressive annual consumption tax.

While we believe that tax policy simulations are interesting, in the present context they seem to beg the question. (Simulated households behave according to the simple economics we outlined to start with. Real households apparently do not all do so.) Also, individual or household-specific effects, and variations in preferences, may be important. Thus serious empirical work, as well as simulation, is required.

In cooperation with Steven Venti and Anil Gupta, David Wise has conducted a series of studies for the Department of Finance since 1984. These have been motivated by a desire to predict the effects of the comprehensive RRSP/RPP reform which was originally projected in 1984 and has now been implemented (see the previous section). Attention in these studies has focused on the impact of higher contribution limits, and carry-forwards of unused contribution room, on taxpayers' likelihood of contributing and on their size of contribution. The effect on total saving has not been modeled explicitly.

The Venti and Wise approach is well known, and its features will not be detailed here (see Venti and Wise [1990], as well as the critical treatment in Gravelle [1991]). Rather we will confine ourselves to noting some of the quantitative results that Wise et al. have found for Canada. Wise (1984, 79) concluded that a 57 percent increase in limits would cause a 28 percent rise in contributions, neglecting the possible impact of increased contribution limits on the number of contributors.[30] Gupta, Venti, and Wise (1992, 32) estimate that the seven-year carry-forward provision of the new RRSP arrangements "will raise average contributions by 60 to 70 percent in the long run, with a peak increase of almost 100 percent occurring six or seven years after the introduction of the program."

Carroll and Summers (1987) compared savings rates in Canada and the United States from 1961 to 1985. The authors try to explain why the Canadian and U.S. savings rates, after being similar for many years, diverged in the mid-1970s. One of their independent variables is RRSP contributions. This variable was statistically significant in explaining part of the difference in savings rates between the two countries, although the variable was not significant in a stand-alone regression for the United States. It would be interesting to see the results of a repetition of the study after a few more years, given the current phasing-in of higher RRSP limits in Canada versus the post-1986 curtailment of IRAs in the United States.

---

30. Wise (1984) simulates the impact of alternative schemes for changing contribution limits. No convenient summary measure indicating the degree of sensitivity of contributions to changes in the limits is provided by these experiments, however. The numbers quoted here come from a simpler experiment: indexing contribution limits between 1979 and 1985 to offset the 57 percent increase in prices over this interval.

2.6 Conclusion

This paper has examined the evolution of tax incentives for saving in Canada, particularly tax-deferred retirement saving plans, over the period 1970–91. From 1970 until about 1981, these incentives increased both in number and, broadly speaking, in generosity. Subsequently, incentives were for the most part cut back. Finally, a new phase began in 1991 with the gradual introduction of considerably higher contribution limits and other liberal features in the RRSP/RPP system.

An interesting result of this paper is the identification of a strong gross correlation between tax incentives for saving and the personal saving rate. The latter peaked in 1982 and displayed a hump-shaped time profile over the 1970–90 period, matching the rise and fall of tax incentives very closely. In contrast, real interest rates, which one might have expected to lie behind the saving trends, behaved quite differently over the two decades. They fell until 1975 and then began an upward trend to 1990. A tentative conclusion is that the effects of tax incentives were much stronger than those of real interest rates over this period. Careful empirical work would be required to properly assess this conclusion.

References

Androkovich, Robert, Michael J. Daly, and Fadle Naqib. 1993. The impact of a hybrid personal tax system on capital accumulation and economic welfare. *European Economic Review.* In press.

Beach, Charles M., Robin W. Boadway, and Neil Bruce. 1988. *Taxation and savings in canada.* Ottawa: Economic Council of Canada.

Boskin, Michael J. 1978. Taxation, saving, and the rate of interest. *Journal of Political Economy* 2:S3–S27.

Burbidge, John. 1987. *Social security in canada: An economic appraisal.* Tax Paper no. 79. Toronto: Canadian Tax Foundation.

Canadian Tax Foundation. 1992. *The national finances, 1991.* Toronto: Canadian Tax Foundation.

Carroll, Chris, and Lawrence H. Summers. 1987. Why have private savings rates in the United States and Canada diverged? *Journal of Monetary Economics* 20:249–80.

Dagenais, Marcel G. 1992. Measuring personal savings, consumption, and disposable income in Canada. *Canadian Journal of Economics* 92:681–707.

Daly, Michael J. 1981. The role of registered retirement savings plans in a life cycle model. *Canadian Journal of Economics* 14:409–21.

Davies, James B. 1979. On the size distribution of wealth in Canada. *Review of Income and Wealth* 25:237–59.

———. 1993. The distribution of wealth in Canada. In *Research in economic inequality,* ed. E. Wolff. Greenwich, Conn.: JAI Press.

Gravelle, Jane G. 1991. Do individual retirement accounts increase savings? *Journal of Economic Perspectives* 5:133–48.

Gupta, Anil K., Steven F. Venti, and David A. Wise. 1992. Storing the option and saving for retirement in Canada. Mimeograph.

Hood, Ron. 1982. *A two asset model of personal taxation.* Ph.D. thesis, Department of Economics, University of Western Ontario.

Horner, Keith. 1987. Policy foundations of the new tax treatment of retirement savings. In *1986 Conference report,* Toronto: Canadian Tax Foundation. 17:1–17:18.

Statistics Canada. 1989. *A guide to the financial flow and national balance sheet accounts.* Publication no. 13–585E. Ottawa: Statistics Canada.

Summers, Lawrence H. 1982. Tax policy, the rate of return, and savings. NBER Working Paper no. 995. Cambridge, Mass.: National Bureau of Economic Research.

Venti, Steven F., and David A. Wise. 1990. Have IRAs increased U.S. savings? Evidence from consumer expenditure surveys. *Quarterly Journal of Economics* 105:661–98.

West, David A. 1987. Taxation and the interest elasticity of saving. M.A. essay, Queen's University.

Wise, David A. 1984. The Effects of policy changes on RRSP contributions. Tax Policy and Legislation Branch, Department of Finance, Government of Canada. Mimeograph.

Wolfson, Michael. 1979. The lifetime impact of the retirement income system, a quantitative analysis. In *The retirement income system in Canada: Problems and alternative policies for reform.* Vol. 2, Appendices. Ottawa: Task Force on Income Policy, Government of Canada.

3 Taxation and Personal Saving Incentives in the United Kingdom

James Banks and Richard Blundell

3.1 Introduction

In the United Kingdom in 1991 personal sector saving accounted for £42 billion of a total personal sector disposable income of £410 billion. To understand the relationship between taxation and savings it is critical to focus on behavior at the household level, where after-tax returns on particular assets can be precisely defined. It is also useful to separate two stages of decision making—how much to save and how to save it—although these will not usually be independent. In this paper we will look predominantly at the second of these decisions, although the evolution of the level of aggregate savings[1] will be considered when we look at the U.K. experience over the last 20 years in section 3.2 below.

Although many of the anomalies in the United Kingdom's tax treatment of assets and asset income have been ironed out during the past decade, it remains (in common with many other systems that have evolved over a considerable length of time) characterized by a ranking of pretax returns that differs markedly from that of posttax returns. Tax incentives have joined, and in some cases

James Banks is senior research officer at the Institute for Fiscal Studies, London. Richard Blundell is research director at the Institute for Fiscal Studies, London, and professor of economics at University College, London.

The authors are grateful for helpful discussions with many colleagues at the Institute for Fiscal Studies and with the participants of the NBER project on international comparisons of household saving. We would particularly like to acknowledge the comments of Andrew Dilnot, Anne Howarth, and Paul Johnson. Any errors or views expressed are entirely attributable to the authors. The support of the Economic and Social Research Council (ESRC) is gratefully acknowledged. The work is part of the program of the ESRC Research Centre for Fiscal Policy.

1. We will try to use "saving" to indicate flows and "savings" to indicate stocks throughout this paper to reduce ambiguity.

replaced, economic incentives in determining the allocation of saving. In addition, though, the government may want to use the tax system as an instrument to increase the level of aggregate savings or divert saving into a particular vehicle and will therefore introduce a nonneutral tax specifically for that purpose. In the United Kingdom this has usually resulted in new acronyms, with the advent of tax-exempt special savings accounts (TESSAs) or personal equity plans (PEPs), for example, both discussed below. The purpose of this paper is to examine the tax incentives in existence for the different forms of household saving in the United Kingdom and to consider the distribution of personal sector wealth across these assets.

An important distinction to make in this area is that between intermediated household saving and saving through direct investment. A complete treatment of the taxation of saving requires a complete treatment of the taxation of direct investment, in particular for the self-employed. By becoming self-employed or registering as a company, individuals can enjoy tax relief on saving in assets that become treated as investment for tax purposes. For obvious reasons we cannot, in this paper, comprehensively treat the taxation of saving through direct investment, and so we choose simply to ignore such forms of saving and consider only intermediated household saving. We do, however, consider housing and mortgages to be a form of household saving, as is conventional, even though these could be interpreted as saving through investment.

In the subsections below we summarize the existing tax regime and report the important changes instigated in the U.K. tax system in recent years. Section 3.2 looks at the household balance sheet for the U.K. personal sector and briefly considers how this has changed over time along with the distribution of wealth. Sections 3.3–3.6 consider the taxation of specific asset types in more detail and examine more closely the extent to which the personal sector has responded to special tax incentives. Section 3.7 concludes the paper.

3.1.1 The Taxation of Personal Saving in the United Kingdom

The two most important taxes that have implications for saving in the U.K. personal sector are income tax and capital gains tax (CGT), as opposed to National Insurance and VAT, which are equally important from a revenue point of view. In the 1990–91 tax year, 25.7 million people paid a total of £59.6 billion in income tax, and £1.4 billion in CGT revenue was raised from 165,000 individuals. In addition, however, about £1.3 billion was raised from inheritance tax (IHT), but throughout most of this paper we will be more concerned with income tax and CGT. This is in part because very few individuals actually pay IHT (of the order of one-tenth of the estates notified for probate—representing about 30,000 individuals each year), but also because many U.K. commentators (for example, Kay and King 1990; IFS Capital Taxes Group 1988) have shown that IHT is relatively easy to avoid. For completeness, however, we describe IHT briefly in section 3.3 below.

Income tax is payable by any tax unit on income (above their personal tax-free allowance) from many forms of savings and is charged at a basic rate of 25 percent and a higher rate of 40 percent. Currently the single person's allowance stands at £3,445, and the higher rate threshold is £23,700 of *taxable* income. (In his budget of April 1992, the chancellor introduced a reduced rate band of 20 percent to apply to the first £2,000 of taxable income. However, no data exist as yet for the impact of this reform on savings, and it is expected that only 4 million people will pay the reduced rate.[2] Consequently, for the purposes of this paper we will define the "current" tax system to be the pre–April 1992 tax system.)

Capital gains tax operates in a similar way although the distinction between capital gains and income as defined by the tax system is not always clear. Investors receive an exemption of £5,800 per annum, below which any gains are entirely tax-free, and above which any *real* gains are taxed at the investor's marginal rate of income tax.

In reality the tax advantage or disadvantage associated with a particular asset will depend upon a number of other elements. A common measure of tax privilege, the "effective tax rate" (ETR), is computed by taking the ratio of the tax payment to the real pretax return. The three elements in this calculation—tax payments, inflation, and pretax yields—can vary across individual, time, and asset accordingly. First, the pretax yield on intermediated saving will depend on the way that the financial intermediary's portfolio itself is taxed. More important, however, is that some savings tax payments are calculated on nominal returns, and consequently the tax penalty of such assets is made significantly more severe in times of high inflation. Finally, tax exemptions offer significantly higher advantage to high-rate taxpayers than basic-rate taxpayers, and despite the fact that only 1.6 million people paid the higher rate in 1989, the effective tax rates can often be significantly lower for such individuals and as such the total effects could be quite large.

A final issue that clouds the analysis of savings taxation is the well-known process of capitalization of tax privileges into asset prices or pretax yields. In the United Kingdom this effect has been strong in the market for owner-occupied housing, but a less well known example exists in the case of low-yield National Savings Certificates (see Saunders and Webb 1988). The effect of capitalization is to shift the benefit of the tax privilege from the investors who own the asset to the people who invested in the asset before it became privileged. The actual (risk-adjusted) returns realized by investors are significantly equalized by this process.

---

2. It is worth noting, however, that a significant portion of these 4 million reduced-rate taxpayers will be pensioners, and so much of the taxable income will be unearned and the reduced rate band could prove to be quite an important issue in the taxation of savings.

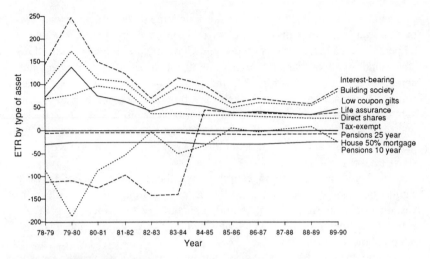

Fig. 3.1   Effective tax rates by asset type, 1978/79–1989/90 (basic rate taxpayers, actual inflation)
Source: Reproduced from IFS Capital Taxes Group (1989).

3.1.2   Major Changes in Tax Regimes

Although this paper seeks primarily to address the current U.K. tax system, any investigation of personal saving that has a time-series element would need to account for some important changes in the tax regime in recent years, in particular in the past decade. The majority of major changes and trends in the taxation of savings occurred in the 1980s, and their net result has been to equalize effective tax rates across assets over the time period concerned. This process is shown in figure 3.1, which is reproduced from the report of the Institute for Fiscal Studies Capital Taxes Working Party (IFS Capital Taxes Group 1989). The equalization has been aided by falling inflation, however, and figure 3.2 presents ETRs by asset calculated at constant inflation—showing distinctly less convergence over the 11 years. Remember that the ETR is the tax paid expressed as a proportion of the pretax return, and those calculated in the figures were calculated on the assumption of constant (real) pretax returns across assets—almost certainly unrealistic since properly functioning capital markets would act so as to equalize *after-tax* returns across assets. The figures do, however, show the direction and scale of the effects induced by fiscal reform in the past 10 years.

The Conservative government, since its election in 1979, has seen fit to reduce and to some extent simplify the direct tax system and has also reduced the rates of most direct taxes (albeit at the expense of the indirect tax burden). Most well known is Nigel Lawson's penchant for abolishing a tax in every budget during his tenure as chancellor of the exchequer in the mid-1980s. In

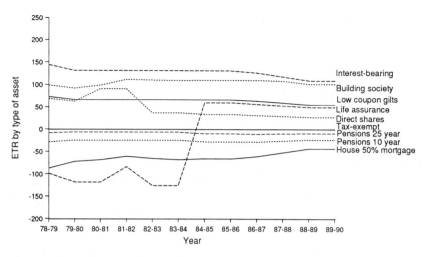

Fig. 3.2   Effective tax rates by asset type, 1978/79–1989/90 (basic rate taxpayers, constant [10.1%] inflation)
Source: Reproduced from IFS Capital Taxes Group (1989).

what follows we will try to describe the major regime changes in the last two decades along with the path of savings—both at the aggregate level and disaggregated by asset. Obviously we cannot describe every tax change, nor do data exist that are powerful enough to fully describe the path of household savings; however, in what follows we try to capture the important factors influencing the ETR profiles illustrated above.

Fewer and Lower Marginal Income Tax Rates

The rates and bands of income tax have important implications due to the tax relief at either the basic or marginal rates for deductible asset purchases and payments. As is well known, after a period of increasing direct taxes during the 1970s, there has been a wide-scale removal of direct tax bands and a reduction in direct tax rates over the last 13 years. This is illustrated in figure 3.3 and has had the effect of equalizing ETRs and therefore fiscal privilege across income ranges. It is worth remembering, however, that the number of higher-rate taxpayers has always been relatively small—as illustrated in the lower part of figure 3.3—rising recently to 6.5 percent of the total number of taxpayers. This has arisen as a result of the broad fixing of the higher rate threshold in real terms in a period of real earnings growth.

Capital Gains Tax

Two major changes in CGT rules have significantly changed the effective tax rates faced by households. First, indexation provisions were introduced into CGT in 1985, considerably reducing the penalties for holding assets in

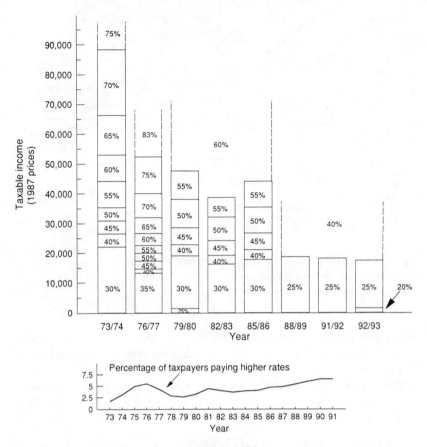

Fig. 3.3   Tax thresholds and tax rates since 1973

times of high inflation. Second, prior to the 1988 budget, CGT was charged at a flat rate of 30 percent thus giving higher-rate taxpayers particularly strong incentives to seek returns via capital gains. The switch to taxing capital gains at the investor's marginal rate of income tax reduced fiscal privilege but did not eliminate it due to the differing bases of the two taxes. Any tax penalties associated with CGT were also reduced by a gradual upward trend in the real value of the tax-free annual exemption until 1988 when the restructuring of CGT rates was combined with a reduction in the real value of the annual exemption.

Abolition of the Investment Income Surcharge and the Extension of the Composite Rate

Prior to 1984 the United Kingdom had an investment income surcharge (IIS) of an extra 15 percent above the investor's marginal income tax rate on investment income above a threshold. This resulted in a situation in 1976, say, in which income arising from investments was taxed at 98 percent for some individuals. The abolition of the IIS in 1984 and the subsequent reduction in the higher rate of income tax have reduced this to 40 percent, although this may have been less dramatic than it seems because many people believe that the 98 percent rate could only persist because it was easily avoided (e.g., by converting income into capital gains) and the excess burden reduced (Kay and King 1990).

The composite rate was introduced to ease the collection of a large number of relatively small tax payments from building society account income and is a weighted average of the marginal tax rates of zero- and basic-rate account holders that the building society pays on its total deposits. In 1984 this composite rate was extended to bank accounts, thus increasing the number of tax-penalized account holders. Taxation at the composite rate (usually about 21 percent when the basic rate was 25 percent) represented a significant tax penalty for zero-rated taxpayers, who could not reclaim the composite rate payment, and a slight subsidy for basic- and higher-rate taxpayers. Basic-rate tax units were not required to pay the extra (about) 4 percent tax, and higher-rate taxpayers were required to pay additional tax only on the interest grossed up as if the full basic rate had been paid.

Introduced only as an administrative aid and almost universally disapproved of, the composite rate was eventually abolished in the 1990 budget of the then-chancellor, John Major, to wide approval.

Replacement of Capital Transfer Tax

The budget of 1986 saw the replacement of the capital transfer tax with the inheritance tax. The capital transfer tax had attempted to tax transfers of wealth and gifts between the living but had gradually been eroded by base narrowing, high levels of avoidance, and rate reduction (Keen 1991) and was therefore a good candidate for the chancellor's ax. In its place a seven-banded inheritance tax was introduced, and in the following two budgets the number of bands was reduced (from seven to four to one) and the threshold increased to £110,000. The threshold has been increased annually to its current level of £140,000.

Erosion of the "Mortgage Interest Relief Deducted at Source" Ceiling

While there have been no structural changes in the taxation of mortgages, there has been a steady downward trend in the mortgage ceiling resulting in the upward trend in the ETR for housing observed in figure 3.2. The ceiling for "mortgage interest relief deducted at source" (MIRAS) has been fixed in nominal terms at £30,000 since 1983, and 1983–90 has been a period of rapid house price inflation; consequently the real value of the tax relief has fallen to the point at which almost no new mortgages are entirely covered by MIRAS anymore and the attractiveness of saving through owner-occupied housing has diminished. In addition, the abolition of tax relief for home improvement loans and the switch to MIRAS entitlements being calculated per property rather than per tax unit, both in the 1988 budget, have also contributed to this decline. More recently, an important MIRAS reform was the replacement of tax relief at the investor's marginal rate by tax relief at the basic rate in the 1991 budget, thus reducing the privilege that higher-rate taxpayers gain from saving through housing.

Abolition of Domestic Rates

The only value-based tax on housing—domestic rates—was abolished in 1990 in favor of the community charge (or poll tax). This, unlike most changes outlined above, served to disperse ETRs among asset types and income groups, as it made saving through owner-occupied housing more privileged as the value of the house increased. The public discontent with the poll tax is well known, and the replacement—the council tax—although related to the house price by a nine-banded system, will still not return the taxation of owner-occupied housing to its original status.

3.2 The Household Balance Sheet

It is useful, before we look at asset types in more detail, to consider the way in which personal sector wealth is distributed both across the population and across the different types of assets themselves. While the latter question can be assessed from aggregate data, most of the interesting aspects of the distribution of wealth require some recourse to a microeconomic data set. In the United Kingdom the first preference of most economists is the Family Expenditure Survey, but information on the value of wealth holdings is extremely sparse and unreliable. In general the quality of any one data set is poor, but a study by Saunders and Webb (1988) utilizes a private microeconomic survey of 30,000 households carried out in 1987, and we draw on their results in some of what follows.

3.2.1 The Distribution of Personal Sector Wealth

In table 3.1 we simply report the concentration of wealth in the United Kingdom in three recent years, and this shows, not surprisingly, the large amount of marketable wealth held by the top few percentiles of the population. One noticeable feature is that although the most wealthy 5 percent have retained their share of the total, there has been a slight increase in the share owned by the middle percentiles over the past 13 or so years. This trend is evident under both definitions of wealth (including and excluding pension rights), but the other predominant characteristic of table 3.1 is that the wealth distribution which does not include pension rights (col. [ii]) is significantly more unequal. This emphasizes the importance of state pension rights that accrue to every employed individual in the distribution of personal wealth and also highlights

Table 3.1   **Concentration of Wealth among the Adult Population**

	1976		1982		1989	
% of Wealth Owned by:	(i)	(ii)	(i)	(ii)	(i)	(ii)
Most wealthy 1%	13	21	11	18	11	18
Most wealthy 2%	18	27	15	24	16	25
Most wealthy 5%	26	38	24	36	26	38
Most wealthy 10%	36	50	34	49	38	53
Most wealthy 25%	57	71	56	72	62	75
Most wealthy 50%	80	92	79	91	83	94

Source: Inland Revenue (1990).
Note: For col. (i), wealth is as defined in U.K. *Inland Revenue Statistics* (ser. E), i.e., the current valuation of total marketable wealth including occupational and state pension rights. In col. (ii), wealth is as defined in U.K. *Inland Revenue Statistics* (ser. C), i.e., excluding all rights accruing to individuals under occupational and state pension schemes.

the need for a consistent and relevant definition of wealth itself.

Given this breakdown we might be interested to know the structure of portfolios within different wealth and income categories, and these breakdowns are presented below. It is important to bear in mind that factors influencing the differential choice of assets by differing population groups can often be related to the kinds of variation in ETR described above. For example, there is an association between risk and fiscal privilege because, for tax purposes, gains that arise from the change in value of a tradable asset are treated as capital gains and therefore are taxed more lightly than interest payments. Risk-averse investors will tend to choose less risky, usually nontradable, assets, which also tend to carry a greater tax penalty. In addition, tradable assets tend to have higher holding and transaction costs and require greater information (this is clearly the case for gilts and equity, but also for the Business Expansion Scheme—see below—which has been highly privileged in the past). These fixed costs tend to become more significant when small amounts are invested and can lead to concentration of certain types of financial assets by income or wealth population subgroups. It is probably not feasible for small investors to hold well-balanced portfolios, and they may well simply resort to low-risk, less-privileged forms of saving that cost less to administer and also are more liquid.

Tables 3.2 and 3.3 show exactly these symptoms. When the population is broken down by income or wealth range, there is a clear shift toward equity and away from bank and building society deposits for the richer investors.

Nonfinancial or less-liquid assets such as housing or life assurance have significantly lower information costs but are still tax-privileged and consequently have wider take-up, as can be seen from table 3.4. These assets provide a privileged tax status to a much wider group of the population and will therefore

Table 3.2   Holdings of Financial Assets by Investor's Wealth

| | Investor's Level of Wealth | | | | |
| | Top | | | Bottom | |
% of Savings Held in:	1%	2%–5%	6%–25%	26%–75%	25%
Bank and building society accounts	34.2	68.4	⁻76.9	83.8	83.5
Equity	42.0	21.1	13.9	6.4	7.5
Gilts and local authority bonds	16.6	1.2	0.3	0.0	0.0
Tax-free National Savings	3.6	2.7	2.4	1.0	0.8
Other National Savings and savings clubs	3.6	6.7	6.6	8.7	8.2

Source: Saunders and Webb (1988).

Table 3.3   Holdings of Financial Assets by Tax Rate

% of Savings Held in:	Zero Rate	Basic Rate	Higher Rate
Bank and building society accounts	71.0	68.8	51.8
Equity	7.7	20.4	34.3
Gilts and local authority bonds	3.5	3.4	4.5
Tax-free National Savings	1.8	2.1	5.9
Other National Savings and savings clubs	15.9	5.4	3.3

Source: Saunders and Webb (1988).

offset, to a certain extent, the wide disparity in tax status of the portfolios of different population subgroups that is implied by the take-up and ETRs on the liquid assets reported in tables 3.2 and 3.3 and figure 3.1.

Finally in this section we report the distribution of aggregate personal wealth over various asset types in 1989. It can be seen from table 3.5 that over 60 percent of U.K. wealth is held in the form of housing or pension rights and life assurance. Of the £579 billion of wealth held in pensions and insurance funds, £275 billion is held through life assurance companies, and £213 billion of this is life assurance itself (as opposed to pensions)—almost 10 percent of personal sector wealth (Association of British Insurers 1990). Saving through life assurance is addressed in more detail in section 3.5. However, the heavily penalized bank and building society deposits still account for one-eighth of net wealth, between them, and this proportion has remained constant over recent years reflecting, perhaps, the attractiveness of the reduced riskiness of such a portfolio.

3.2.2   Personal Saving over the Past 20 Years

There have been a large number of changes to the savings regime in the United Kingdom in the past few years, both in the structure of existing taxes and tax rates, and in the addition and removal of new taxes themselves. The path of personal saving has also been variable, with positive saving taking place in the 1970s, despite persisting negative real interest rates, and a recent and well-documented fall in the saving rate throughout the 1980s illustrated in figure 3.4.

Although a consistent series of wealth data is quite difficult to find, it is possible to construct such a series from 1975 from the personal sector balance sheets in the U.K. National Accounts (1987) and *Economic Trends* (August 1991). In figure 3.5 we present a time series of proportions of total net personal sector wealth for six selected asset types. The most striking feature is obviously the doubling of the proportion of wealth held in pensions and life assurance since 1979, and this has occurred with the progressively increasing attractiveness of contracted-out pension schemes and life assurance. In addition, however, there has been a gradual fall in the proportion of wealth held as shares, and this represents a switch from holding equity directly to holding it through some intermediary (e.g., the pension fund). Finally, bank and building society deposits have held their share at around 12 percent, even in the late 1970s when real interest rates were negative and such accounts were being massively penalized by being taxed on nominal gains.

Table 3.4   **Proportion of Investors Holding Less-Liquid Assets by Tax Rate**

Asset	Zero Rate	Basic Rate	Higher Rate
Savings-based life assurance policy	39.1	46.7	54.1
House owned outright	23.0	22.0	27.6
House with mortgage	8.7	42.7	60.6

Source: Saunders and Webb (1988).

Table 3.5   **Distribution of Personal Wealth by Asset Type, 1989**

Asset Type	Value (£ billion)	% of Total
Housing (net of mortgages)	842	36.8
Pension and insurance funds	579	25.4
Bank deposits	146	6.4
Building society accounts	141	6.2
U.K. securities and unit trust units	172	7.5
Consumer durables	160	7.0
National Savings	35	1.5
Gilts and other interest-bearing assets	23	1.0
Agricultural and commercial land and buildings	102	4.5
Notes and coins	13	0.6
Other	71	3.1
Total	2,284	100

Source: CSO (1991a).

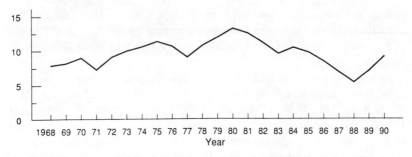

Fig. 3.4 Personal saving as a percentage of disposable income, 1968–90
Source: CSO (1992).

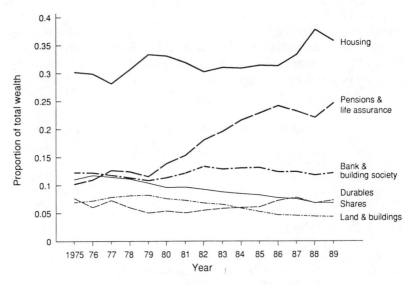

Fig. 3.5 Composition of Wealth, 1975–89

The most recent figures for flows of saving of different assets are for 1990, and these are presented in table 3.6. Unfortunately, the series for dwellings and durables ceased to exist after 1989, so we omit housing and mortgages and consumer durables in what follows.

3.3 The Taxation of Capital Income

As briefly mentioned in section 3.1, the main personal taxes that are relevant to this paper are income tax and CGT, and the taxation of most capital income is related in some way to these rates. This has not always been the case, as is clear from section 3.1.2 above. An individual pays income tax at either the

Table 3.6   **Personal Sector Asset Flows, 1990**

Asset Type	Financial Surplus or Deficit (£ million)
Pension and insurance funds	37,138
Bank deposits	16,143
Building society accounts	17,964
U.K. securities and unit trust units	−13,536
National Savings	783
Gilts and other interest-bearing assets	−1,209
Notes and coins	−134

Source: CSO (1991b).

basic rate of 25 percent or the higher rate of 40 percent on earned income above their personal allowance, but they also pay National Insurance (NI) contributions of 9 percent on earnings falling between prescribed limits. National Insurance is described in more detail in section 3.4, but the important fact for the taxation of capital income is that such income is not liable for NI. When we talk about the investor's marginal rate in what follows, we refer to the marginal rate of income tax, not the "true" marginal rate of income tax plus NI.[3]

Bearing in mind the caveat in the introduction concerning saving through direct investment, capital income can broadly be split into three categories— interest income, dividends, and capital gains. Income from capital (i.e., rent) is simply taxed as other income.

Interest income and dividends are usually taxed at the same rate—the investor's marginal tax rate—and the only difference between their tax treatment might be the timing of the tax payments in some cases. An imputation system exists for all dividend payments, so basic-rate tax is deducted at source, and higher-rate taxpayers are required to pay the extra 15 percent in tax every six months. Higher-rate taxpayers are required to complete a tax return annually (unlike basic-rate tax units, of which only a few are sent tax returns in any given year), so the interim tax payment is estimated. Most interest income also has income tax deducted at source, again at the basic rate. Such a system usually exists for bank and building society accounts for example, and again a higher-rate taxpayer will pay the tax difference later in the year. On the other hand, some interest income (e.g., that from National Savings) is net of tax, and tax payments are deferred. In both these cases, zero-rate taxpayers require some form of refund. For interest income they can simply provide a certificate of zero-tax status to qualify for removal of income tax deductions at source,

---

3. In fact, the threshold above which an individual ceases to pay NI lies below that at which they move on to the higher rate of income tax, resulting in the well-known fall in the true marginal direct tax rate—from 34 to 25 percent—as income rises over the NI ceiling (£20,280) but before it reaches the higher rate threshold (at least £27,145).

but for dividend income zero-rate taxpayers are required to claim a tax rebate at the end of the tax year.

Since the 1988 budget, indexed capital gains above the annual £6,000 exemption have also become taxable at the investor's marginal rate of income tax. In addition, any chattels that have a value of £6,000 or less on disposal are automatically exempt from CGT and do not count toward the individual's annual exemption, whereas chattels with a disposal value above this but a capital gain of less than the exemption earn marginal relief. The main exemption from CGT is that of gains realized on disposal of an individual's principal private residence, and this accounts for much of the tax-privileged status of housing, but certain other assets also have exemption from CGT. These include gains arising from occupational pensions, sales of motor vehicles, decorations for valor(!), certain gilt-edged stocks and qualifying corporate bonds or options for these stocks, life assurance policies, betting winnings, gains of approved pension schemes, gains accruing to authorized unit trusts, gains of unit trusts for exempt unit holders, contracts for deferred annuities, and gains within personal equity plans (see below). Retirement relief of £150,000 plus 50 percent of gains up to £600,000 (i.e., a maximum of £375,000) is available for individuals age 55 and over.

Finally, savings can ultimately become liable to inheritance tax under certain circumstances. Under the inheritance tax rules, the first £140,000 of any bequest on death or in the seven years preceding death is tax-free,[4] and above that bequests are taxable at 40 percent on the value over £140,000. This tax is payable immediately by the beneficiary. Inheritance tax exemptions apply to some bequests, including lifetime transfers between spouses (i.e., when the bequestor is still alive), gifts of up to £3,000 per year, gifts to political parties, and trusts for the mentally or physically disabled.

3.4   Retirement Saving and Pensions

Pension rights make up a significant proportion of personal wealth—about 15 percent in 1989—and saving in the form of pensions in particular is quite heavily tax-privileged. Pension regulations have also been an area of rapid change in the United Kingdom in recent years, with much work being done by economists in this area. In this section we look at the treatment of saving through the various types of pension schemes and the extent to which these schemes have been taken up, and then in section 3.5 we turn to the treatment of life assurance policies.

Any U.K. worker has a certain amount of pension rights arising from their NI contributions (NICs). National Insurance is paid by every employee on

4. Transfers within seven years of death are taxed on their value on the date of death but subject to a tapering scale going down to 20 percent of the full charge for transfers between six and seven years of death.

Table 3.7   **Composition of Retirement Income**

Source of Income	% of Gross Normal Weekly Income (retired households only)
Wages and salaries	11.8
Self-employment	0.5
Investments	16.5
Annuities and pensions	20.0
Social security benefits	41.5
Imputed income from owner-occupation	9.2
Other	0.5

Source: CSO (1990).

earnings falling between the lower earnings limit (LEL) and the upper earnings limit (UEL), and by employers on any earnings above the LEL. Once an individual's total NICs rise above a minimum level, he becomes entitled to the basic state pension. In addition, all individuals are, by default, contracted into the State Earnings-Related Pension Scheme (SERPS), which is calculated on the total amount of contributions paid. The individual can, however, choose to contract out of the SERPS into either an occupational pension scheme or a personal pension plan (PPP), and they are then entitled to the "contracted-out rebate" on some of their NICs, which is paid into the approved pension scheme by the government. Rules governing contracting out have been frequently changed in the last five or so years, and the contribution and tax structure of all three forms of pensions is described in more detail below. For the individual, the major savings choice is *whether*, and *how*, to contract out, and therefore we will concentrate mainly on personal and occupational pensions (in particular, personal pensions) in what follows, describing the SERPS only as the alternative against which to base the decision. Broadly, however, the U.K. pension tax system exempts pensions from tax (i) when contributions are made and (ii) when income is derived from investments but levies tax when benefits are withdrawn from the fund.

In 1989, one-fifth of the income of retired households in the U.K. Family Expenditure Survey (FES) was derived from annuities and private pensions, despite the fact that PPPs will have had negligible effects on retirement incomes so close to their inception in 1986. The complete breakdown of income of retired households in the 1990 FES is given in table 3.7. A comprehensive description of the FES as a data source can be found in Kemsley, Redpath, and Holmes (1980).

The replacement rate for retired households (and indeed for all households) falls continuously as a function of household preretirement income, as retirement and social security benefits are not means-tested (although there is a small means-tested SERPS entitlement).

3.4.1   SERPS and the Basic State Pension

National Insurance contributions are paid at a rate of 9 percent by every individual on earnings falling between £54 per week (the LEL) and £405 per week (the UEL) and at 2 percent on the first £54 per week (if earnings exceed the LEL).[5] Employers pay contributions in banded rates varying from 4.6 to 10.4 percent on all earnings over the LEL. The LEL is set annually by regulation and must, by statute, be approximately equal to the value of the basic state pension for a single person. In turn, the UEL must lie between six-and-a-half and seven-and-a-half times the LEL. Individuals who contract into the SERPS receive a pension based on a cumulated fraction of their average annual earnings falling between the LEL and the UEL. In calculating pensions entitlements, annual earnings are revalued in line with an index of earnings, but the earnings limits themselves are linked to the basic state pension, which is only revalued in line with prices. The price indexation of the UEL in particular seems likely to cause a compression of SERPS entitlements relative to those that would arise from a symmetric indexation of earnings and the earnings limits. National Insurance contributions are not income tax–deductible, nor, since the scheme is pay-as-you-go, is there any real fiscal privilege attached to the investment of accumulated contributions.

3.4.2   Occupational Pensions

Occupational pension schemes were originally the only alternative for an individual who wanted to contract out of the SERPS. They typically offer a "defined-benefit scheme," in which pension benefits are based on an earnings formula. In the 1986 Social Security Act, however, the government widened the range of schemes into which an individual could contract out. Occupational schemes must offer a guaranteed minimum pension based on average indexed earnings during years within the scheme, although they are typically more generous than this. A replacement rate (i.e., the pension payments themselves) of up to two-thirds of final salary is permitted, and one-and-a-half times final salary can be converted into a lump sum on retirement.

Employees and employers are entitled to the contracted-out rebate on their NICs. This currently stands at 5.8 percent of earnings between the LEL and the UEL—3.8 percent applicable to employers' contributions and 2 percent applicable to employees' NICs. Employers' contributions can be offset against corporation tax, and employees' contributions can be deducted from their taxable income. Any income or capital gains from occupational funds are exempt from tax, as is the converted lump sum, but pensions in payment are taxable at the normal rate of income tax.

---

5. The 2 percent introductory NI rate was introduced in the 1989 budget, replacing a 5 percent starting rate on all NICs if the level exceeded the LEL, which in turn replaced an even more extraordinary 9 percent starting rate in 1985.

3.4.3   Personal Pensions and "Money Purchase" Schemes

As mentioned above, the 1986 Social Security Act significantly widened the number of schemes into which an individual could contract out, most importantly allowing "defined-contribution schemes," in which the returns to investment essentially depend on the real rate of return of assets in the fund rather than on the real earnings growth which underpins the SERPS and all defined-benefit schemes. This led to the advent of personal pensions (individual defined-contribution) and also "money purchase" schemes (group defined-contribution). Such pensions can be bought in addition to investments in occupational pension schemes, and these are "free-standing additional voluntary contributions" (FSAVCs).

The benefits of contracting out into personal pensions are even greater than those of occupational pensions because the government simultaneously introduced an extra two-percentage-point rebate to encourage the take-up of personal pensions. This is valid until April 1993, and in addition, for people contracting out before April 1989, the incentive was paid for the previous two tax years as a lump sum into the scheme. These are added to the existing rebate, and the whole contracted-out rebate is then grossed up to account for the income tax relief, resulting in a total rate of contribution to the fund of 8.46 percent of eligible earnings. As with an occupational pension, individuals can then supplement this with contributions from their earnings up to the prescribed maximum, which ranges from 17.5 percent of earnings for a 35-year-old to 35 percent of earnings for someone over age 56, and these contributions are deductible against income tax. A tax-free lump sum can also be withdrawn from a defined-contribution scheme on retirement, and this can be a maximum of one-quarter of the value of the accumulated fund.

3.4.4   The Take-Up and Coverage of Personal Pensions

The incentives to take up personal pensions at the expense of NI revenues have been criticized for being too generous by many groups, including the National Audit Office, and initial take-up has exceeded expectations by a factor of eight—4.6 million individuals have taken them up since 1988, representing 20 percent of the working population. Coverage of defined-benefit schemes in comparison stands at about half the total employed, or 11 million people. Figure 3.6, taken from Disney and Whitehouse (1992), illustrates the striking rates of take-up for groups in the working population differing by age and sex. Indeed, Disney and Whitehouse cite this as evidence contradicting the claim that younger workers often exhibit myopia as to their retirement income 40 years in the future.

As would have happened with a switch from defined-benefit to defined-contribution schemes, though, this take-up of personal pensions has not been coincident with a large reduction in occupational schemes, the coverage of which has stood at around one-half the working population since the mid-

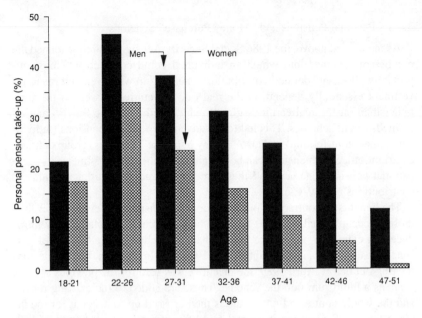

Fig. 3.6   The Take-Up of Personal Pensions by Age
Source: Reproduced from Disney and Whitehouse (1992).

1960s. Employees have either contracted out for the first time into personal pensions or have taken a personal pension in addition to a defined-benefit scheme.

Once again, contracted-out defined-contribution schemes are relatively new in the United Kingdom, and as yet, figures on the distribution of asset holdings within pension funds are difficult to calculate. For occupational pensions, however, some data exist, and these are presented for three recent years in table 3.8.

3.5   Saving through Life Assurance

Although there are rules governing the amount of insurance that life assurance policies must contain, in reality, by far the largest portion of the value of such contracts lies in the sum which is paid out at the end of the contract. Hills (1984) quotes a figure of 1 percent of the premiums paid as the actuarial value of the insurance element alone. For simplicity, in this section we follow the tradition of most analyses of life assurance in the United Kingdom and assume that the pure insurance element in such a scheme is nil.

In 1989 the value of life assurance holdings was £213.4 billion—about 10 percent of personal sector wealth holdings. Yet the tax privilege associated with this form of saving is not that large. Life assurance policies are often described as tax-free, but although on maturity the pay-out is usually free of

Table 3.8   **Distribution of Occupational Pension Fund Assets**

% of Fund Held in:	1981	1986	1991
U.K. equities	52	55	58
Overseas assets	13	21	28
U.K. fixed interest	23	15	4
U.K. index-linked gilts	1	2	2
Sterling cash	3	3	6
Property assets	8	4	2

Source: Pensions Pocket Book (1992).

tax, this is misleading as the insurance company itself is liable to tax on the returns that it earns on invested funds. The taxation of life assurance companies is, however, complex and also rather cumbersome. Profits have to be allocated between policyholders and shareholders, and companies pay tax at the basic rate on dividends, corporation tax on any interest income, and the basic-rate CGT on capital gains; these taxes combine, in theory, to a tax rate which a basic-rate taxpayer would face (although there are some rules on franked versus unfranked income that mean a life assurance portfolio is actually marginally less attractive than the same portfolio held independently).

Higher-rate taxpayers are required to pay an exit charge equal to the difference between the basic and the higher rates if they withdraw funds before the maturity date. This charge is only levied on the difference between withdrawals and total contributions (unadjusted for inflation) and also depends on the length of time the policy has still to run.

The complexity of issues in the taxation of financial intermediaries, however, means that it is difficult to say whether life assurance policies are on the whole privileged or penalized for the basic-rate taxpayer. This has not always been the case, as life assurance premiums have earned full tax relief in the past. In the budget of 1984, tax relief on life assurance premiums was ended for new contracts. Even nontaxpayers benefited from this relief as it was deductible at source from premiums, and the reform considerably reduced the privilege associated with life assurance. However, premiums on policies taken out before that date still receive tax relief at the investor's marginal rate.[6]

Given the discussion above, it would appear difficult to understand why life assurance is such an important element of personal saving in the United Kingdom. To some extent this can be explained by the large existing stock of policies taken out when privileges were still enormous due to the tax relief on premiums. The other important factor, however, has been the increased incidence of tying life assurance into mortgage borrowing by means of endowment

---

6. Despite the supposed secrecy of the U.K. budget process, it is well known that the two-week period prior to the announcement (and in particular the night before) saw a monumental escalation in the number of policies being taken out.

mortgages. The housing boom of the late 1980s created a massive increase in personal sector mortgage borrowing, of which most was financed through endowment mortgages (where the household repays only the interest on the loan and takes out a life assurance policy to repay the principal when the mortgage expires). Indeed, 64.9 percent of the premium value of new annual life policies taken out in 1991 was mortgage-related (calculated from Association of British Insurers [1992]).

3.6 Tax-exempt Accounts and Targeted Incentives

Over the last few years a number of initiatives have been implemented with the aim of increasing and directing personal saving. Major schemes usually occasioned acronyms—TESSAs, PEPs, and BES—and have enjoyed varying degrees of success as described below. Personal pension plans were another of these savings initiatives, but have been detailed separately in section 3.4 above.

3.6.1 Tax-exempt Special Savings Accounts

Tax-exempt special savings accounts (TESSAs) were introduced in the Finance Act of 1990 to encourage small savers. From January 1991, investors aged 18 or over were able to open one TESSA with an approved bank or building society. Any interest earned on a TESSA is entirely tax-free provided the savings are left in the account for five years, although it is possible to withdraw some of the interest as it arises (equal to the net-of-tax interest). Withdrawal of capital at an earlier date leads to complete loss of the tax advantage.

There is a limit of £3,000 for savings in TESSAs in the first year and £1,800 for each subsequent year, subject to an upper limit of £9,000 in total over the full five years. These savings can be made in single, regular, or irregular payments, and TESSAs are designed to be as flexible as possible. After five years any further interest on funds becomes liable for tax in the usual way, although the investor can simply open a new TESSA and transfer £3,000 into it in the first year.

Obviously TESSAs have not been in existence long enough for their impact to be analyzed comprehensively, but table 3.9 shows that they have already had a quite substantial impact. As more figures become available it will become clear whether these numbers represent an addition to aggregate saving or simply a diversion of existing (probably bank and building society) funds. At present it appears that there has been a simple transfer of existing building society funds into TESSAs, which would result in a big take-up initially, followed by a much reduced flow.

3.6.2 Personal Equity Plans

In his 1986 budget, the then-chancellor, Nigel Lawson, announced the introduction of personal equity plans (PEPs)—a new measure in the government's policy of encouraging wider share ownership. It is beyond the scope of this

Table 3.9   The Take-up of TESSAs

Quarter Ending:	Building Society Accounts		Bank Accounts		All Accounts	
	Number (thousands)	Amount (£ million)	Number (thousands)	Amount (£ million)	Number (thousands)	Amount (£ million)
March 1991	1,351	3,487	731	1,654	2,082	5,142
June 1991	1,613	4,222	858	2,025	2,471	6,247

Source: Inland Revenue (1991).

paper to debate the benefits or otherwise of wider share ownership per se, but the introduction of PEPs in 1986 was an important initiative designed to lure the first-time investor into saving in the form of U.K. equity. Investors in PEPs are exempt from income tax on dividends arising from shares held in a plan, and in addition there is no capital gains tax when shares are sold. This compares favorably with the normal tax treatment of equity or unit trusts. Indirect investment via a unit trust or an investment trust is permitted, and the administration of the plans is carried out by approved plan managers. In 1991 PEPs were extended to cover shares in companies in other EC member states. Individuals can put a lump sum into a plan or a regular amount, and PEPs may be "managed" or "own choice" (where the investor makes the portfolio decisions).

In January 1992, PEPs were split into two subplans—the "single-company PEP" and the "general PEP"—and investors are now allowed to subscribe to one of each of these in any one year. The limit for investing in a single-company PEP is £3,000 and for a general PEP is £6,000, so an investor taking full advantage of the two plans can invest £9,000. Initially, PEPs were set up on a calendar year basis and investments were required to be retained and dividends reinvested for one year to qualify for tax relief. Since April 1989, however, the maximum permitted investment has been calculated on a fiscal year basis, and the minimum holding period has been abolished.

It is clear that the government engaged in a substantial amount of tinkering with the PEP rules, and this represents a response to poor initial take-up, which can be seen in table 3.10. Lee and Saunders (1988) use the same survey as Saunders and Webb (1988) to show that less than 1 percent of their sample were PEP investors and that of these only a low proportion were first-time investors. They give a number of reasons for this initial failure of the scheme. The first factor is the disillusionment with the equity market in general following the crash of October 1987 and the outbreak of insider-dealing scandals. But even before then, investment in PEPs was still very limited compared with, say, unit trusts. In addition the tax advantages may not actually be that substantial to the small investor. Recall that the current CGT exemption is £5,800 of real gains per annum, anyway, so the PEP exemption is of absolutely no addi-

Table 3.10   The Take-up of PEPs

Period	Number of New Plans Taken Out (thousands)	Amount Invested (£ million)	Average Amount per Plan (£)
1987	270	480	1,800
1988	120	200	1,650
1989/90:1	580	1,600	2,750
1990/91	500	1,600	3,200

Source: Inland Revenue (1991).

tional value to most of the population. The income tax exemption is also clearly of more value to higher-rate than to basic-rate taxpayers, and from 1983 to 1988 the average dividend yield was typically around 4.5 percent compared with average capital gains of 17.5 percent, so the income tax incentive was less important anyway (Lee and Saunders 1988). Consequently, PEPs have received criticism for being incorrectly targeted and failing to appeal to the small, first-time investor.

Against these tax advantages, saving through PEPs also has three negative features. First, they have relatively high administration charges compared with other forms of investment, such as unit trusts, mainly due to government regulations on the administrative responsibilities of plan managers and the fact that stamp duty and dealing costs are borne by the investor. Second, initially there were substantial restrictions on the way that PEP investment was allocated, with only one-quarter allowed to be invested in unit trusts and most equity being restricted to shares in one to five companies. This was not sufficient for investors to achieve a diversified portfolio within the plan, and PEPs were relatively risky to the small investor. Finally, at their introduction, the one-year holding period meant that the PEP investor was effectively locked into the U.K. equity market with a relatively illiquid asset.

As shown in table 3.10, the relaxation of PEP rules in the light of this poor initial response appeared to have significant effects on the amount of saving through PEPs,[7] with the number and size of new plans increasing almost two-fold after 1988. The targeting of PEPs (through income tax and CGT exemptions) has remained problematic, with some of the drawbacks outlined above remaining relevant, and the overall effect seems to be one of deepening share ownership among current investors rather than widening the holdings of equity among noninvestors. Despite this, the government remains committed to PEPs and promises to expand the scheme in the future.

7. There is now a lower limit of £1,500 for PEPs that fail to meet a 50 percent EC equity criterion in addition to the split into single-company and general PEPs, the change in holding periods, etc.

3.6.3   The Business Expansion Scheme

The Business Expansion Scheme (BES; formerly the Business Start-Up Scheme) was designed to help small unquoted companies raise finance, but, viewed as a personal savings vehicle, also presented considerable tax advantages to the individual investor. The BES was introduced in 1983 and provides full tax relief at the investor's highest rate on new investments of up to £40,000 in qualifying U.K. trading companies, provided that the shares are held for a minimum of five years and that the shares were being newly issued (i.e., not traded). In 1988 the scheme was extended to cover investment in companies letting properties on assured tenancies. Individuals may invest in an approved investment fund or may use unapproved funds or syndicates provided that the individual becomes the actual owner of the shares. Dividends are taxed in the normal way but any capital gain will be free of CGT.

Indeed, the attractiveness of BES funds that is derived from their tax position completely dominates any incentives arising from the expansion of the business itself, encouraging investment in companies that do little more than hold assets for the five-year period. Consequently, the BES has fallen out of favor. It is already essentially a lame duck, and all the major political parties are committed to abolishing the scheme in the near future.

The take-up of BES shares since the scheme's inception in the early 1980s has not been spectacular despite the massive concessions available, with £211 million being raised between 916 participating companies in 1989–90. With the introduction of rental companies into the scheme the year before, however, the figure was temporarily higher—raising £420 million for 2,511 companies.

3.7   Conclusions

In this paper we have tried to sum up the main issues in the taxation of saving in the United Kingdom and to describe to some extent the form in which personal-sector wealth is held. The tax regime for savings is far from simple, even when one chooses to ignore the complexities of the distinction between saving and direct investment, but, even so, many anomalies of the past have been (or are in the process of being) ironed out.

Broadly speaking, the tax system gives high privileges to saving through housing and pensions, mild privileges to gilts, equity, National Savings, and some unit trusts, and penalizes bank and building society accounts (sight accounts). The size of tax privileges, however, depends on time-, asset-, and individual-specific factors. There also seems to be some systematic relationship between risk and fiscal privilege, and this has sometimes been interpreted as the tax system's encouraging risk-taking.

The government has introduced a number of initiatives to encourage saving in various forms but, with the exception of personal pension plans, these have appeared so far to simply deepen savings from existing savers rather than widen particular asset holdings among first-time or small investors. In contrast to savings plans such as the individual retirement account in the United States, these incentives have been asset-specific rather than simply encouraging any form of saving. The schemes are really too young for an evaluation of their success or failure, whether this be measured by a redirection of or an increase in personal saving. Initial evidence, however, seems to suggest that aggregate saving has not been strongly affected by special incentive schemes (with the possible exception of personal pensions).

Finally, in the past 20 years there have been substantial reforms to the taxation of savings and capital income and also marked trends in the personal sector's holdings of assets. Most noticeable of these is the enormous increase in the proportion of wealth held in pension funds, which has resulted in the two most privileged forms of household saving (pensions and housing) now accounting for over 50 percent of net personal sector wealth.

References

Association of British Insurers (ABI). 1990. *Insurance statistics.* London: ABI.
———. 1992. *Quarterly long-term business statistics: 1st quarter 1992 results.* London: ABI.
Central Statistical Office (CSO). 1990. *Family spending: A report on the 1990 family expenditure survey.* London: Her Majesty's Stationery Office.
———. 1991a. *Economic trends.* London: Her Majesty's Stationery Office.
———. 1991b. *U.K. National Accounts.* London: Her Majesty's Stationery Office.
———. 1992. Economic trends annual supplement. London: Her Majesty's Stationery Office.
Disney, R., and E. Whitehouse. 1992. *The personal pensions stampede.* IFS Report. London: Institute for Fiscal Studies.
Hills, J. 1984. *Savings and fiscal privilege.* IFS Report, ser. 9. London: Institute for Fiscal Studies.
Inland Revenue. 1990–91. *Inland Revenue Statistics.* London: Her Majesty's Stationery Office.
IFS Capital Taxes Group. 1988. *Death: The unfinished business.* IFS Commentary no. 10. London: Institute for Fiscal Studies.
———. 1989. *Neutrality in the taxation of savings: An extended role for PEPs.* IFS Commentary no. 17. London: Institute for Fiscal Studies.
Kay, J. A., and M. A. King. 1990. *The British tax system,* 5th ed. Oxford: Oxford University Press.
Keen, M. 1991. Tax reform. *Oxford Review of Economic Policy* 7(3): 50–67.
Kemsley, W., R. Redpath, and M. Holmes. 1980. *Family expenditure survey handbook.* London: Her Majesty's Stationery Office.
Lee, C., and M. Saunders. 1988. Personal equity plans: Success or failure? *Fiscal Studies* 9(4): 36–50.
Pensions Pocket Book. 1992. Henley-on-Thames: NTC Publications.
Saunders, M., and S. Webb. 1988. Fiscal privilege and financial assets: Some distributive effects. *Fiscal Studies* 9(4): 51–69.

4   Savings in Germany—Part 1: Incentives

Axel Börsch-Supan

4.1. Introduction: Overview of Household Savings

This paper is the first of two that report on household saving in Germany. This paper concentrates on incentives for saving; the second paper will provide an analysis of the composition of household savings and the factors that influence it.

Germans are said to value saving per se, by tradition. They were reluctant to follow American consumerism despite strong American influence on German postwar development. Although this attitude appears to be changing with each new generation, it does so surprisingly slowly. Table 4.1 presents comparable personal savings rates for Germany and the United States. It shows that, since 1960, savings rates have always been higher in Germany than in the United States but that this discrepancy is particularly large in recent years. Although savings rates in both countries have declined since 1975, the relative decline is much smaller in Germany than in the United States.

The different historical experiences of Germans and Americans may help to explain the higher aggregate savings rates that emerged in Germany as soon as a moderate standard of living was achieved in the 1960s. The elderly in the decade 1982–92 have all experienced World War II. This catastrophe, however, affected Americans and Germans very differently. During wartime and until the German currency reform in 1948, most Germans could not even satisfy such basic needs as food and clothing, an experience not shared by their American contemporaries. In addition, during the so-called economic miracle in the

Axel Börsch-Supan is professor of economics at the University of Mannheim, a research associate of the National Bureau of Economic Research, and a research fellow of the Centre for Economic Policy Research.

The author thanks Karl-Heinz Nöhrbaß, Wolfram Richter, and Volker Ulrich for most valuable comments. Matthias Meier and Bernhard Boockmann provided able research assistance.

Table 4.1   **Aggregate Savings Rates (personal savings as % of personal disposable income)**

Year	West Germany	United States
1960	8.6	5.7
1965	12.2	7.0
1970	13.8	8.0
1975	16.2	8.7
1980	14.2	7.9
1985	13.0	6.4
1990	14.8	5.1

Source: Monatsberichte der Deutschen Bundesbank (Frankfurt am Main: Deutsche Bundesbank, 1992); *Economic Report of the President,* Statistical Appendix (Washington, D.C.: Government Printing Office, 1992).

1950s in Germany, saving was heavily promoted in large-scale public campaigns.

Tables 4.2 and 4.3 report on how these large savings are invested. The tables are based on two very different surveys: table 4.2 is based on the German Income and Expenditure survey, which excludes the very rich[1]; table 4.3 is based on property tax returns, which need only be filed by the very wealthy, due to the large exclusions. On average, about 70 percent of net household wealth is held in real estate, as is evident from the last column in table 4.2. Another 10 percent is invested in company shares and the remaining 20 percent in financial assets. However, portfolio choice varies greatly with the total amount of wealth available. Company shares and bonds are preferred by the rich, while the less wealthy prefer general savings accounts. According to table 4.3, more than 70 percent of all company shares and almost 60 percent of all stocks and bonds are held by the wealthiest 1 percent of households in Germany. Real estate, however, is much more equally distributed.

The attitude that saving is good per se (and that personal loans are to be avoided) is reflected in the German tax treatment of savings and loans. Although all income is nominally taxed equally, the taxation of interest income and capital gains is only half-heartedly enforced. In addition, there are several schemes subsidizing savings in Germany, many of them heavily advertised. A description of these incentives is the main topic of this paper.

Section 4.2 will detail the taxation of capital income in Germany. Section 4.3 is devoted to a discussion of property taxes. Because this paper is concerned with tax incentives to household saving, we concentrate on personal taxation and largely ignore the taxation of corporations. Sections 4.4 and 4.5 describe the incentives for retirement and precautionary saving in relation to pension provisions and health and unemployment insurance. Section 4.6

1. Households with net incomes exceeding DM 250,000 per annum (U.S. $156,000).

Table 4.2   Distribution and Composition of Household Wealth (based on the 1973 Income and Expenditure Survey)

Total Net Household Wealth	Average Net Household Wealth (DM)									All Households
	0 and Less	1 to 4,999	5,000 to 9,999	10,000 to 19,999	20,000 to 34,999	35,000 to 99,999	100,000 to 499,999	500,000 to 999,999	1,000,000 and More	
Population share (%)	8	11	11	15	11	20	21	2	1	100
Company shares	1,165	68	146	246	731	4,266	19,660	66,594	507,397	11,606
Real estate	16,298	785	874	2,046	7,184	39,856	163,366	537,495	1,538,713	70,697
General savings	2,280	2,708	5,150	8,145	12,266	13,410	17,807	29,383	107,621	11,715
Bausparkassen	1,258	314	814	1,842	3,226	3,767	4,405	7,295	14,026	2,824
Bonds	298	104	286	804	2,028	3,030	5,075	13,739	406,926	6,451
Life insurance	550	361	587	1,527	2,509	3,706	8,621	28,072	132,907	5,107
Cash and checking accounts	884	639	1,333	2,401	3,959	4,875	8,158	20,181	104,095	5,214
Gross wealth	22,717	4,979	9,389	17,011	31,903	72,910	227,090	702,755	2,811,710	113,614
Home mortgages	21,773	1,006	1,026	1,852	4,502	9,465	16,210	35,013	104,903	9,787
Consumer loans	6,950	1,461	1,016	888	1,052	1,549	2,094	4,565	40,295	2,321
Net wealth	−6,006	2,508	7,347	14,272	26,349	61,896	208,786	663,175	2,666,285	101,505

Source: Mierheim and Wicke (1978).

Note: Excludes households with annual incomes above DM 250,000 ($156,000 U.S.).

Table 4.3   Distribution and Composition of Household Wealth among the Very
                   Rich (based on 1980 property tax returns)

Average Household Wealth of Top x % (thousand DM)
and
% of Total Wealth Held by Top x %

x	Agricultural Property	Real Estate	Company Shares	Stocks and Bonds	Other	Gross Wealth	Debt	Net Wealth
0.5	12	1,240	1,522	441	537	3,754	379	3,374
	3.6	13.2	61.8	50.7	6.1	17.2	12.0	8.1
1.0	9	894	877	251	355	2,389	243	2,146
	5.2	19.1	71.3	57.9	8.1	21.9	15.5	23.0
1.5	7	721	624	179	278	1,811	184	1,627
	6.4	23.1	76.2	61.8	9.5	24.9	17.6	26.1

Source: Baron (1988, 188).
Note: Excludes households with wealth below property tax exclusion. Property tax considered is
the Vermögensteuer in section 4.3.1.

examines special incentive programs for saving in Germany, in particular the
Vermögensbildungsgesetz, a wealth accumulation program for the lower middle class that has existed since 1961. Section 4.7 concludes and delivers a summary of the programs and their associated expenditures from 1975 to 1990.
We will refer to this summary (table 4.11) throughout the paper.

4.2. Taxation of Capital Income

The basic principle of German personal income taxation is that all income
of German residents—wherever and however earned—is taxed equally. Therefore, the original intention of the German legislature was to provide no special
provisions for capital income taxation and to avoid any distortions related to
differential taxation. All asset income is supposed to be taxed as ordinary income. This includes capital gains: Germany does not have a capital gains tax
like the one in the United States, and there is no distinction in statutory tax
rates among different income sources like the different Massachusetts state
income tax rates. Moreover, Germany has only a federal income tax, with no
state or local income taxes that can create additional regional distortions.[2]

Reality, however, deviates from this principle. Effective tax rates differ between various income sources, not because of differential statutory tax rates
but because of differential valuation methods, differential exclusion rules, and
differential enforcement of taxation.[3]

2. However, property taxes are regional or local, see sections 4.3.1 and 4.3.2.
3. Summaries of the German tax system can be found in Petersen (1988) and Stiglitz and Schönfelder (1989).

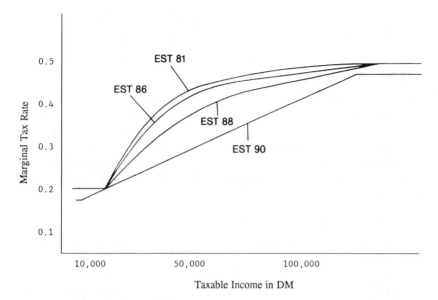

Fig. 4.1   Marginal personal income tax rates before and after German tax reform
Source: Einkommensteuergesetz (various issues).
Note: EST 81 refers to the *Einkommensteuergesetz* (1981), i.e., the German personal income tax code in 1981. The notation is analogous in 1986, 1988, and 1990, when the three steps of the tax reform took place.

The German federal income tax code has a single tax schedule defined piecewise by polynomials. The polynomials are stated in the law as mathematical formulae. Germans do not use the notion of "tax brackets," although three pieces of the schedule can be distinguished: two proportional zones and a progressive zone. Until 1989, the basic structure consisted of a constant marginal tax rate of 22 percent for low incomes, then a degree-four polynomial for middle incomes, and finally a top marginal tax rate of 56 percent for high incomes. All three pieces were smoothly tied together. The 1990 tax reform reduced the marginal tax rates and flattened the so-called middle-class belly by replacing it with a quadratic polynomial, resulting in a flat increase of the marginal tax rate from 19 percent to the top rate of 53 percent. Figure 4.1 displays the marginal tax rates of the German federal income tax schedule before and after the 1990 tax reform.

Marriages are subsidized by a splitting rule that is applied to the tax schedule outlined above: a married couple filing jointly pays twice the tax on half of their joint income. Due to the progressivity of the German income tax schedule, this results in substantial tax savings relative to two single earners if the individuals have different incomes.[4]

As mentioned, this tax schedule is to be applied to the sum of income from all sources. Mainly for technical reasons, German tax law distinguishes among

---

4. The maximum subsidy—to a married couple filing jointly with a single income subject to the top marginal tax rate—is DM 22,842 (U.S. $14,300) per annum.

seven income categories: (1) agricultural income, (2) income from business, (3) labor income from self-employment, (4) labor income from employment, (5) income from capital, (6) rental income, (7) other income, in particular speculative capital gains and pensions returns. Not included among these income sources and therefore not subject to federal income tax is income in the form of gifts, inheritances, and prizes such as those from lotteries. There is, however, a special tax for gifts and inheritances, which we will discuss in section 4.2.4.

Only taxes on labor income from employment and taxes on profit shares are withheld at source. All other income has to be declared in the yearly income tax statement. Compared to the United States, less income is withheld at source. The most important difference here is the tax treatment of interest income.

4.2.1   Interest Income

Of interest income, the first DM 600 (DM 1,200 for married couples filing jointly; about U.S. $375, U.S. $750 for married couples) is formally tax-exempt.[5] This exclusion was originally intended to avoid the taxation of interest from insignificant savings but is now explicitly considered a subsidy to savings. Interest income in excess of the exclusion is taxable income. Table 4.11 presents the estimated tax losses as a result of this exclusion, from 1975 to 1990.

However, the main feature of interest income taxation in Germany is its lax enforcement. Interest income from passbook savings or similar liquid capital and bonds is currently not subject to automatic withholding but is self-reported on the tax return. Direct notification of the internal revenue service by the bank (as routinely done in the United States on Form 1099) would be considered a violation of German privacy laws. Bankers' discretion in Germany is almost as sacred as in Switzerland. Hence, interest income remains widely undeclared, and the public does not really share the notion that this constitutes tax evasion.

Two mechanisms enforce some degree of interest income taxation. First, there is a provision which states that, when land and houses are purchased, the sources of payment must be specified. If these sources include financial assets or inheritances, the revenue service routinely cross-checks whether the appropriate income and estate taxes have been paid. There are, of course, obvious ways to avoid revealing the primary sources of payment. Second, the German internal revenue service freezes all assets of a deceased person. The estate is redistributed to the heirs only after a careful check that all taxes have been paid by the decedent. If this is not the case, the heirs have to pay the tax liability before the estate can be released.

Five years ago the government tried to introduce automatic withholding of

---

5. This amount is called the *Sparer-Freibetrag*. It is to increase 10-fold, when automatic withholding is reintroduced (see below).

interest income taxes (*Quellensteuer*) at a rate of 10 percent. This rule was heavily opposed and induced substantial flows of capital from German banks to banks in neighboring countries such as Luxembourg. It ultimately led to the demission of the secretary of finance and a repeal of the withholding rule only half a year later (Nöhrbaß and Raab 1990).

However, in 1991 the German supreme court issued a decision that the government must take action to enforce equal taxation of all income sources. In response to this, the government has stepped up its public relations effort to stimulate compliance with the tax code but has been reluctant to change the privacy laws that might enable enforcement. Moreover, it will revive withholding taxes on interest at source, now at a rate of 30 percent, beginning in 1993. However, this only appears to be a dramatic change. In fact, the government will increase the interest income exclusion tenfold to DM 6,000 (DM 12,000 for married couples filing jointly; about U.S. $3,750, U.S. $7,500 for married couples). Hence, the reform will continue to shield most interest income from taxation, with the exception of income of the very rich. Because the tax liability will be transferred as a lump sum from each bank with no possibility for the internal revenue service to trace each individual taxpayer, the very rich can still cheat on the difference between the withholding tax of 30 percent and the, presumably higher, marginal tax rate applicable to them.

Somewhat of a counterpart to the lax taxation of interest income is the non-deductibility of interest expenditures for any kind of consumer loan. In particular, German consumers cannot deduct mortgage interest on land and housing purchases, an important deductible item in the United States.[6] Interest payments are deductible only if they can be considered business expenses. The most important example here is mortgage interest related to a dwelling that is rented to somebody else.

The symmetry between lax taxation of interest received and no deduction for interest paid is not a statutory one. In fact, while interest income ought to be taxed by law, the law also explicitly forbids the deduction of consumption and mortgage interest payments.

4.2.2   Dividends and Corporate Income Taxes

Income from dividends and other kinds of profit shares is, in general, subject to automatic withholding at a rate of 25 percent, which is then credited against the actual income tax burden. There is no exclusion for dividend income, unlike interest income. Thus, a rule is applied to dividend income that was politically infeasible for interest income.

In addition, dividends are subject to corporate income tax (*Körperschaftsteuer*) at a flat rate of 36 percent. However, this tax too is credited against

---

6. Temporary and restricted exceptions were in place in 1986–89 and 1992–1994. The current exception allows for the deductability of mortgage interest up to DM 12,000 (U.S. $7,500) per annum for three consecutive years after buying a newly built house.

personal income taxes. Hence, Germany has no double taxation of dividend income as in the United States.

Because it can be deducted from personal income tax, the German corporate income tax is in essence not a separate tax. Effectively, corporate profits—unless they are retained earnings—are taxed at the applicable marginal income tax rates of the corporation's owners, in proportion to their ownership shares.

Retained earnings are treated very differently. They are taxed at a flat 50 percent at the company level and cannot be credited against the personal income taxes of the shareholders.

4.2.3   Capital Gains

The taxation of capital gains in Germany deviates from the Anglo-Saxon principle of a specific, often complicated capital gains tax. In fact, capital taxation of households in Germany is very simple.[7]

Capital gains are subject to personal taxation only when they are obtained by what the law considers speculation. Speculation is defined as selling a financial asset (e.g., bonds) within six months of the purchase date, or selling land or land leases within two years of the purchase date. In these cases, capital gains are computed as the nominal difference between actual sales price and actual purchase price, reduced by associated transaction outlays. This amount is then taxed as ordinary income. If capital is held longer than six months (or two years, in the case of land) capital gains are not taxed.

In addition, the first DM 1,000 (about U.S. $625) of capital gains are tax-exempt in all cases. Capital gains of one asset and capital losses of another asset within a given calender year can be consolidated.

Income achieved by investing in a pension scheme is also only partially taxed. German tax law distinguishes between the insurance part of pension income and the internal return of a pension scheme. The share of the second part is tabulated by age at retirement. These tables are computed as imputed interest earned on fictitious pension wealth based on an annuity rule that underestimates the actuarial fair accrual and ignores the intergenerational redistribution between contributions and pensions. For a worker retiring at age 65, the assumed internal return of his pension investment amounts to 24 percent of annual pension income. This part is taxable as ordinary income. Because of the actuarially unfair computation and the omission of transfer gains, pension income is effectively taxed at a substantially lower rate than ordinary income.

4.2.4   Gift and Estate Tax

Capital transfers in the form of gifts and inheritances are not subject to German federal income tax but to a specific gift and inheritance tax (*Schenkung-* and *Erbschafsteuer*). Bequests and inter vivos gifts are taxed at the same statutory rate. This should in theory eliminate distortions between inter vivos gifts

---

7. Tax treatment of capital gains at the company level is different.

and bequests. In fact, however, taxation is a disincentive to leave bequests because it is much easier to evade taxation by transferring wealth while still alive, while German law requires the freezing of all assets as soon as a person dies.

Tax rates and initial exclusions depend on one's relation to the donor (see table 4.4).[8] Spouses and children are allowed very large exclusions (DM 250,000 and DM 90,000, respectively; about U.S. $150,000 and U.S. $56,000, respectively) and subject to low tax rates (3–35 percent: e.g., 4 percent for DM 100,000 and 10 percent for DM 1,000,000), while nonrelatives face a low exclusion (DM 5,000) and high tax rates (20–70 percent: e.g., 24 percent for DM 100,000 and 48 percent for DM 1,000,000). Because real estate is valued at assessed values, which are very low, substantial estates remain tax-free.

4.3   Property and Transaction Taxes

Property taxes play a minor role in the German tax system except for the very wealthy. In contrast to those in the United States, they have little effect on middle-class taxpayers on the one hand and are only a minor source of revenue for local governments on the other.

The German system has two kinds of property taxes: a general property tax on all asset types (*Vermögensteuer*), which is uniform across Germany—though technically a state tax—and a local property tax on land, which differs among communities (*Grundsteuer A und B*).

4.3.1   State Property Taxes

State property taxes are due on net wealth, that is, the sum of all assets minus debt. The tax base is total net wealth at the beginning of each calender year, reduced by an exclusion of, normally, DM 70,000 per household member (about U.S. $44,000). A proportional tax rate of 0.5 percent is applied to the tax base. In addition, corporations pay another 0.6 percent state property tax, nonrefundable to owners.

Computation of total wealth is regulated by a special evaluation law (*Bewertungsgesetz*). This law defines the value of financial assets as basically their current market value and the value of real property as basically their assessed value. The law also specifies assessment rules. These rules result effectively in assessed values for land and housing that are on average about one-seventh of actual sales values (Schöffel 1986). However, this ratio varies both between and within communities. Assessed values are updated every six years for land and housing, and every three years for business property. The updating procedure is commonly not a property-specific but a universal adaptation of prop-

---

8. This is quite different from the United Kingdom, the United States, and Japan. See Richter (1987).

Table 4.4   **Gift and Inheritance Tax Rates (%)**

Taxable Wealth (thousand DM)	Relationship Category			
	I	II	III	IV
0–50	3	6	11	20
50–75	3.5	7	12.5	22
75–100	4	8	14	24
100–125	4.5	9	15.5	26
125–150	5	10	17	28
150–200	5.5	11	18.5	30
200–250	6	12	20	32
250–300	6.5	13	21.5	34
300–400	7	14	23	36
400–500	7.5	15	24.5	38
500–600	8	16	26	40
600–700	8.5	17	27.5	42
700–800	9	18	29	44
800–900	9.5	19	30.5	46
900–1,000	10	20	32	48
1,000–2,000	11	22	34	50
2,000–3,000	12	24	36	52
3,000–4,000	13	26	38	54
4,000–6,000	14	28	40	56
6,000–8,000	16	30	43	58
8,000–10,000	18	33	46	60
10,000–25,000	21	36	50	62
25,000–50,000	25	40	55	64
50,000–100,000	30	45	60	67
More than 100,000	35	50	65	70

Source: Author's calculations based on *Erbschaft-* and *Schenkungsteuergesetz.*

Note: The relationship categories and, in parentheses, their corresponding tax-free exclusions are as follows: I—spouses and children (spouses: DM 250,000, children: DM 90,000 plus supplements for minors), II—grandchildren (DM 50,000), III—parents and siblings (DM 10,000), IV—everybody else (DM 3,000).

erty values to general increases in land and housing prices. The last major individual reassessment was in 1964.

The combination of large exclusions and small assessment ratios render the state property taxes fairly irrelevant for all but the very wealthy. For a three-person household with no other wealth, for example, the sales value of a house must be larger than DM 1.5 million (about U.S. $900,000) to be subject to the state property tax. Moreover, a small amount of financial debt is sufficient to offset great real estate wealth, resulting in zero taxable net wealth.[9]

9. The amount of financial debt necessary to wipe out property taxes is the assessment ratio times real estate wealth.

4.3.2   Local Property Taxes

Local property taxes are due on land only. While assessed values are the same as for state property taxes, tax rates are set by communities. Variation across communities, however, is relatively small, particularly in comparison to the variation among communities in the United States. Effective tax rates vary by land usage. Land for housing is effectively taxed at rates between 0.15 and 0.2 percent of market value, rates much lower than in the United States.

Because of the small tax burden, the problem of differential effective taxation due to different assessment ratios and the resulting call for reassessment are not political issues in Germany.

4.3.3   Transaction Taxes

Transaction taxes were levied when stocks, companies, and land were sold. With the exception of that on land transactions, these taxes have been abolished. The former transaction tax on the sale of stocks (*Börsenumsatzsteuer*) was 1 per mill of the sales value for the seller as well as for the buyer. It was abolished effective January 1, 1991. The former transaction tax on the sale of companies (*Gesellschaftsteuer*) was 1 percent of the sales value for the seller. This tax was abolished effective January 1, 1992. Finally, the transaction tax on the sale of land (*Grunderwerbsteuer*) is 2 percent of the assessed value. This tax is still being levied on the buyers of land.

4.4   Pension Plans and Retirement Saving

Germany has a pay-as-you-go public pension system, which supplies, in effect, a minimum level of retirement income to almost every worker. Coverage is very broad. Only the self-employed (8.9 percent of the labor force in 1988) and workers with very small incomes (5.6 percent) are not required to participate, although they may do so (Casmir 1989).

However, the basic principle of the German retirement system is not the provision of a last-resort retirement income but the appropriate replacement of individual lifetime income. The German public retirement system is more insurance than a social safety net or transfer program, which is reflected in the name *Gesetzliche Rentenversicherung* (mandatory retirement insurance) as opposed to "Social Security" in the United States. Private pensions, either on an individual or a firm-based level, are therefore much rarer than in countries with a less pronounced link between individual labor and retirement income.

4.4.1   The German Public Pension System

Until 1992, public pension benefits were computed by a formula in which, in principle, number of years of service, current wage level, and relative former income position of the individual worker entered multiplicatively. This resulted in three features: pension benefits were only slightly affected by retirement

Table 4.5   Net Replacement Ratios of Social Security Old-Age Pensions[a]

Relative Income (% of APW wages)[b]	United States	Germany
50	61	67
75	55	66
100	53	71
150	45	77
200	41	75
300	30	53

Source: Casmir (1989, 508, 512).
[a]Net replacement ratios for a worker with 40 years of service. Married-couple supplement not included.
[b]Wages of an "average production worker" according to the OECD.

age, pensioners benefited from labor productivity increases achieved by the younger generation, and, even more important for savings, pension income for the middle class was roughly proportional to labor income and thus conserved relative income positions even after retirement. Because the lifetime income base had a lower and an upper limit, this proportionality holds only roughly.

The system was reformed in 1992, but essentially retains these features, except that the relation between pension benefits and retirement age is more actuarially fair. In addition, the link between pension benefits and current wages was changed from a before-tax to an after-tax basis.[10]

The philosophical difference between this and other pension systems, most notably the U.S. Social Security system—the German system is not designed to prevent poverty but to provide approximately the same living standard before and after retirement—results in substantially higher replacement rates than, for example, the U.S. Social Security system, particularly for higher income levels. As a matter of fact, the rationale for not having a 100 percent replacement ratio in Germany is not the added utility of leisure but the cessation of work-related expenses after retirement.

Table 4.5 presents net replacement ratios by income class, that is, after-tax retirement incomes as percentages of the preceding after-tax labor incomes. On average, German social security income is about 33 percent higher than American, resulting in an average net replacement ratio of more than 70 percent.

Payments to the retirement insurance program are directly subtracted from wages, similar to Social Security contributions in the United States. The current contribution rate is 17.7 percent on the first DM 6,800 of gross monthly earnings, shared equally between employer and employee (about U.S. $51,000

10. More precisely, "before" and "after" mean before and after personal income taxes and social security contributions.

per annum), a low point between the 18.7 percent rate in 1980 and the expected increase to 20.1 percent in 2000, and even higher thereafter. Even so, the German contribution rate is perceptibly higher than the contribution rate in the United States, due partly to the higher replacement ratio and partly to the different age structure of the German population.

German public retirement insurance is augmented by mandatory accident insurance, an institution close to a combination of disability insurance and workers' compensation in the United States. Every employee, except for civil servants, is enrolled in this branch of the German social insurance system. Accident insurance covers on-the-job accidents and provides compensation, full or partial pensions in case of accident-related early retirement, and pensions for widows and widowers in case of accident-related death. Contributions are paid exclusively by employers.

4.4.2   Employer-provided Pension Plans

Employer-provided private pensions play only a minor role in Germany. They provide approximately 3 percent of the retirement income of the German elderly. In 1984, 82 percent of all elderly in West Germany received *only* social security income. Another 8.5 percent had additional private pension income (mainly annuities from life insurance), and only 7.6 percent had both social security and firm pension income (Börsch-Supan 1992a). This is in stark contrast to the United States, where employer-provided pensions provide a significant fraction of retirement income (about 15 percent of American retirement income). About half of Americans age 60 and older are covered by pension plans. For 13 percent of these, pensions contribute more than 20 percent of their retirement incomes; for 2 percent, pensions make up more than half (Hurd 1989, table II 6).

Contributions are treated as taxable income for the employee, but there are tax incentives for employer-provided pension plans on the employers' side, because pension funds can escape corporate income taxation in certain circumstances when they are used as reserves. This is relevant mainly for large companies.

4.5   Health Insurance, Unemployment Insurance, and Precautionary Saving

Germany has a considerably tighter social safety net than the United States. Health insurance is mandatory, and unemployment compensation can last up to two years.[11] One is tempted to conclude that Germans need precautionary savings less than Americans.

---

11. Extensive descriptions of the German social policy system are contained in Frerich (1987) and Lampert (1985).

4.5.1   Health Insurance

In Germany, virtually every worker is enrolled in the health insurance system, which covers all health expenditures, the only exception being long-term institutionalized care not related to acute illness. Coverage includes hospital costs, costs of doctor visits, and medication and medical aids. It covers expenditures not only for catastrophic illnesses but also for many bagatelles (over-the-counter medicines), and until recently even cold remedies.[12] Therefore, German coverage is far more comprehensive than that of the U.S. Medicaid and Medicare systems.

Germany has a dual health insurance system, partly private, partly social. The social health insurance system is not like the British National Health Service. Rather, it consists of several heavily regulated insurance companies—some public, some private—that engage in limited competition. Enrollment in the social health insurance system is mandatory for employees with monthly incomes below about DM 5,000 (about U.S. $37,500 per annum). Wealthier households and self-employed workers are free to choose which insurance to enroll in or to self-insure. However, once private insurance has been chosen, there is no way back into the social system. Competition in the private sector is also limited because government regulations enforce rather high service standards and require the redistribution of surpluses to customers. Although social health insurance serves as last-resort insurance because it is required to accept every customer initially, there is little adverse selection. The main reason is, of course, the mandatory participation of all households except upper-middle-class and wealthy households. Moreover, standards in the social insurance system are high, and the system is not considered inferior, unlike, for example, the British system.

Monthly contributions to social health insurance are subtracted from wages, like contributions to retirement insurance. Payments are shared equally between employer and employee and amount to 12.5 percent of the first DM 5,000 (U.S. $3,125) of monthly gross income.

The only significant gap in the safety net for health expenditures is costs of long-term institutionalized care not related to acute illness. The government has promised to establish long-term care insurance that would fill this gap by 1994. After much discussion about a fully funded system, which would be a novelty in the German social insurance system, the present coalition government has decided on a pay-as-you-go system, much like the social health insurance system. It features an initial contribution rate of about 2 percent of gross income, shared equally between employer and employee, and would cover most costs of long-term institutionalized care.[13]

4.5.2   Unemployment Insurance

The third component in the German social insurance system is unemployment insurance. All employees must be enrolled; only the self-employed and civil servants do not participate. Monthly contributions to unemployment insurance are subtracted from wages, like contributions to health and retirement insurance. Payments are shared equally between employer and employee and amount to 6.3 percent of monthly gross income.

In case of unemployment, there are two kinds of payment. During an initial period, in general lasting one year, the unemployed worker receives unemployment compensation (*Arbeitslosengeld*). The replacement rate is 68 percent of net wages for workers with children, 63 percent of net wages for workers without children.

After this period, if the worker is still unemployed, he or she is eligible to receive unemployment relief for one more year (*Arbeitslosenhilfe*). This relief is much like welfare because it requires the exhaustion of the personal wealth of the worker and his immediate family.[14] The replacement rate for unemployment relief is 58 percent of net wages for workers with children and 56 percent of net wages for workers without children.

Eligibility rules and the duration of the first period actually depend on years of service as well as on age (see table 4.6). In order to receive unemployment compensation at all, the worker has to demonstrate a minimum duration of service of one year. In this case, unemployment compensation is paid for half a year. Each additional four months of service add another two months of unemployment compensation, so that a minimum of two years of service is required to be eligible for one full year of unemployment compensation. For workers age 42 and older, this scheme is continued. At a maximum, workers age 54 and older with at least five years and four months of service are eligible to receive two years and eight months of unemployment compensation. In each case, another year of unemployment relief can be added if the worker is eligible. Thus, compared to unemployment insurance in the United States, German benefits last substantially longer and feature a higher replacement rate.

4.6   Special Incentive Programs

The German government has several programs that subsidize savings. These programs had their heyday in the seventies and early eighties but have recently been reduced. A general program designed to foster wealth accumulation among lower income groups (*Vermögensbildungsgesetz*) is a means for wealth redistribution. Several other programs are incentive programs for specific kinds of savings, most prominently savings in building societies (*Bausparkassen*) and life insurance policies.

---

14. This requirement includes parents and own children. Housing wealth is not counted.

Table 4.6   Duration of Initial Period of Unemployment Compensation
(weekdays)

Employment Duration		Age				
Total Number of Days Worked	Years since First Workday	0–41	42–43	44–48	49–53	54+
360	3	156	156	156	156	156
480	7	208	208	208	208	208
600	7	260	260	260	260	260
720	7	312	312	312	312	312
840	7		364	364	364	364
950	7		416	416	416	416
1,080	7		468	468	468	468
1,200	7			520	520	520
1,320	7			572	572	572
1,440	7				624	624
1,560	7				676	676
1,680	7					728
1,800	7					780
1,920	7					832

Source: Bundesminister für Arbeit und Sozialordnung (1990).

4.6.1 Vermögensbildungsgesetz

The *Vermögensbildungsgesetz* (wealth accumulation program) was put in place in a rudimentary form in 1961 and substantially extended in 1970. It very much exemplifies the German idea of a social market economy. Its stated intentions were to at least partially equalize the wealth distribution in order to stabilize trust in a market economy, cushion the conflict between labor and capital, and induce savings to provide sufficient capital for economic growth.

The basic mechanism of the program is as follows: Employees authorize the deduction of a certain amount from their pay, which is direct-deposited into long-term funds. Originally, the contributions were paid by the employer only. Currently, no distinction is made between employer and employee contribution. The employer may not impose the selection of a particular fund. The funds must remain on deposit for at least six years. If the employee's income is below a certain limit, the government supplements the contributions at a fixed percentage until an upper limit is reached.

Currently, funds eligible for a subsidy include shares in the employee's own or any other company and savings accounts at building societies.[15] Until recently, regular long-term savings accounts at banks and contributions to life insurance qualified, as well. Currently, contributions of up to DM 936 (roughly U.S. $600) for individuals and twice that amount for married couples are subsi-

15. These are the provisions of the *Fünftes Vermögensbildungsgesetz, Fassung* 1990.

Table 4.7   **Premia in the Wealth Accumulation Program**

		Subsidy (%)					
	Limit of Contribution	General Savings		*Bausparkassen*		Productive Capital	
Year	(DM)	(a)	(b)	(a)	(b)	(a)	(b)
1975–82	624	30	40	30	40	30	40
1983–89	936	16	26	23	33	23	33
1990–92	936	0	0	10	10	20	20

Source: Author's calculations based on *Vermögenbildungsgesetz.*
Note: (a) households without children; (b) households with 3 children.

dized. Company shares are currently subsidized by a 20 percent premium, while the subsidization rate is 10 percent for savings accounts at building societies. The current income limit for participation in this program is DM 54,000 per year for married-couple households (about U.S. $33,750), a lower-middle-class income in Germany, and half that amount for single-member households. In the seventies, these premia were as high as 40 percent, and the income limit for eligibility was sufficiently high to cover incomes far into the middle class. An overview is provided in table 4.7.

In addition to the above program, employees can receive shares of their employers' companies as tax-exempt income, if they do not sell these shares for six years and if the market value does not exceed DM 500 per annum (about U.S. $312). There are no income limits to this tax subsidy.[16] Estimated government expenditures on these programs are tabulated in table 4.8.

4.6.2 *Bausparkassen*

Savings to accumulate the down payment for housing purchases are subsidized by a special incentive program (*Wohnungsbauprämiengesetz*). The system centers on the German building societies (*Bausparkassen*). Each building society is a completely closed and self-financing savings and loan institution in which all funds for housing mortgages are taken from savings in the building society, and only former savers in the society are eligible for home mortgages. This pay-as-you-go system is almost completely detached from the general capital market. The combined savings and loan contracts in building societies have the following form: Building society and saver agree on a specified contract sum. The saver accumulates 40 or 50 percent of the contract sum. If this amount has been accumulated, the contract is called "mature" and the saver is eligible for a mortgage of the remainder amount, 60 or 50 percent of the contract sum, respectively. Neither the time for the accumulation of the savings nor the time of the payout of the loan are part of the contract. Average accumu-

---

16. These are the provisions of §19a of the *Einkommensteuergesetz.*

Table 4.8   Government Expenditures in Savings Subsidies, 1975–90 (million DM)

Year	General Interest Income Exclusion (1)	Tax Deduction Bausparkasse (2)	Premium for Bausparkasse (3)	Premium for General Savings (4)	Wealth Accumulation Program (5)	Company Participation Program (6)	Total Savings Subsidies Nominal (7)	Total Savings Subsidies Real (8)
1975	300	765	3,169	1,633	3,230	0	9,097	14,326
1976	300	800	2,241	2,508	3,415	0	9,264	13,973
1977	315	780	1,852	4,367	3,500	0	10,814	15,741
1978	330	750	1,870	2,390	3,450	0	8,790	12,468
1979	350	720	1,926	1,351	3,000	100	7,447	10,132
1980	365	690	1,974	1,270	2,900	100	7,299	9,430
1981	380	500	1,967	1,408	2,835	70	7,160	8,710
1982	390	570	1,941	1,692	2,130	70	6,793	7,853
1983	400	840	1,076	2,332	1,780	40	6,468	7,235
1984	410	820	938	1,492	1,850	50	5,560	6,070
1985	425	790	878	1,023	1,790	120	5,026	5,375
1986	440	640	885	845	1,800	130	4,740	5,075
1987	455	720	862	532	1,935	200	4,704	5,026
1988	470	630	842	5	2,040	210	4,197	4,427
1989	1,300	600	980	0	2,050	225	5,155	5,293
1990	1,200	320	590	0	1,000	225	3,335	3,335

Source: Bundesminister der Finanzen (ed.), Subventionsberichte des Deutschen Bundestages (Annual Report of the German Parliament on Subsidies Granted) (Bonn: Heger, 1978–90).

Note: The associated parts of the German tax code are: (1) §20.4 Einkommensteuergesetz (EStG), (2) §10.1 EStG, (3) Wohnungsbauprämiengesetz (WoPG) including state contributions, (4) Sparprämiengesetz (SparPG), (5) §§13, 15 5th Vermögensbildungsgesetz (5.VermBG) and the corresponding earlier versions, (6) §19a EstG and §8 Kapitalerhöhungsgesetz (KapErhG). Col. (7) is the sum of cols. (1) through (6). Col. (8) is col. (7) divided by the consumer price index, 1990=100.

lation time is about six to seven years, and the waiting time between the accumulation of savings and the payout of the total contract sum (loan and savings) can be between one and two years. The waiting time is the crucial mechanism used to balance the pay-as-you-go system. The interest paid on savings is very low (currently 3 percent, whereas market interest is about 7.5 percent) but so is the mortgage interest (currently 5 percent, whereas market rate is about 10 percent).

There are basically three incentives for participation in the system. First, the nominal interest differential between loan and savings interest is lower than in the market. However, this "incentive" is deceiving because it ignores the time structure of the payments. Second, the contract forces households to save, and they appear to like this. Although this is not an argument that appeals to economists, it appears again and again in surveys that ask people why they participate. Finally, the government subsidizes this kind of savings, and the subsidy was both deep and widespread until recently. Table 4.9 provides participation rates by sociodemographic group.

The law specifies two kinds of subsidies which are exclusive of each other but are on top of subsidies granted by the wealth accumulation program described above. The mechanism of the first kind of subsidy is the same as for the wealth accumulation program: a percentage premium with a cap for households below an income limit. The second mechanism is independent of an income limit and allows contributions to building societies to be deducted from federal income tax. Contributions are implicitly capped by the provision that the deduction not exceed the permissible sum of deductions for what the law calls "precautionary expenses" (*Vorsorgeaufwendungen*). These include contributions to the social insurance system (health, unemployment, and retirement insurance) and contributions to private health and life insurance.

Like the wealth accumulation program, this program was rather generous in the seventies and early eighties but recently has been severely cut. Table 4.8 summarizes the impact of these changes on estimated government expenditures. Currently, the premium of the first mechanism is 10 percent of contributions up to DM 1,600 (about U.S. $1,000), and the income limits are DM 54,000 per year for married-couple households and DM 27,000 for single-member households, exactly as for the wealth accumulation program. The subsidization rate was in excess of 40 percent in the mid-seventies. Subsidies have since dramatically decreased, see table 4.10.

The viability of the second mechanism has been severely hampered by a deduction limit for precautionary expenses that has not been changed in spite of substantially increased contributions, particularly to health insurance payments. In many cases, health insurance payments alone have crowded out the possibility of deducting contributions to building societies. Moreover, after the 1990 tax reform, only 50 percent of contributions to building societies can be deducted. Table 4.8 shows the impact on tax expenditures.

A similar incentive program existed for general long-term savings, the *Spar-*

Table 4.9   **Participation in the *Bausparkassen* Program, Contributions, and Percentage of Financial Wealth in *Bausparkassen* Accounts.**

Demographic Categories	Participation (%)		Contributions (DM per year)		Wealth Share (%)	
	1978	1983	1978	1983	1978	1983
All households	43.9	49.4	2,356	2,270	17.9	16.6
Age:						
18–34	61.3	60.2	3,039	2,457	23.8	23.2
35–44	59.6	65.6	2,787	2,672	17.0	15.7
45–54	47.2	58.0	2,233	2,566	14.5	13.5
55–64	33.9	38.2	1,964	1,973	15.4	13.3
65–99	16.8	18.1	1,735	1,495	17.3	15.8
Married	47.6	55.4	2,495	2,488	17.5	15.7
Single	17.1	21.9	1,353	1,270	25.1	27.3
No children	30.0	33.4	2,026	1,877	20.2	19.5
One child	52.3	56.7	2,699	2,413	18.3	16.5
Two children	61.9	69.3	2,744	2,801	16.5	15.0
Three or more children	61.3	71.7	2,531	2,803	14.1	12.8
Renter	33.8	35.6	2,418	2,065	26.9	25.8
Homeowner	56.0	63.5	2,279	2,478	11.3	11.3
Single income	38.6	43.5	2,061	1,989	17.6	16.8
Double income	61.0	67.0	3,307	3,110	18.5	16.1
Income (DM):						
<1,000	6.2	8.5	755	727	40.0	45.6
1,000–1,999	16.8	15.3	1,366	941	25.5	32.9
2,000–2,999	39.8	31.8	1,890	1,371	20.0	21.8
3,000–3,999	55.3	51.3	2,587	1,964	17.5	17.3
4,000–4,999	64.2	63.8	2,999	2,450	15.5	15.3
5,000–10,000	68.8	71.2	4,835	3,763	13.0	13.3
>10,000	63.3	56.5	10,117	7,764	12.0	9.0
Self-employed	57.7	60.9	3,212	2,808	12.9	8.5
Civil servant	66.5	70.6	3,207	3,139	21.2	19.4
White-collar	54.6	58.5	2,712	2,627	18.0	16.6
Blue-collar	49.4	58.2	2,134	2,006	16.6	15.4
Unemployed	19.7	22.1	1,687	1,487	18.7	17.8

Source: Einkommens- und Verbrauchsstichprobe 1978 and 1983, quoted from Börsch-Supan and Stahl (1991)

Note: "Participation" is the percentage of households with *Bausparkassen* contracts in the corresponding household group. "Contribution" is the average annual contribution of households in the program. "Wealth share" is the average percentage of financial net wealth held in *Bausparkassen* contracts among participating households. "Income" is nominal monthly net household income.

Table 4.10   **Subsidies in the *Bausparkassen* Program**

Year	First Mechanism: Premium (%)	Second Mechanism: Tax Deduction (%)
1975	23 + 2 for each child	100
1976–81	18 + 2 for each child	100
1982–89	14 + 2 for each child	100
1990	10	50

Source: Author's calculations based on Wohnungsbauprämiengesetz.

prämiengesetz. However, it was removed in 1990. Together, the special incentive programs and the general wealth accumulation program have historically provided a substantial subsidy to saving. Table 4.11 presents some illustrative examples for the 1988–89 fiscal years, before the 1990 tax reform severely reduced the subsidies.

4.6.3   Life Insurance

Savings in the form of contributions to life insurance funds are subsidized because they can be deducted from federal income taxes. However, the same implicit cap exists as in the second mechanism used to subsidize contributions to building societies: the deduction must not exceed the permissible total of all precautionary expenses. The internal returns from investing in a life insurance system escape taxation, much like the returns from a pension scheme. This is very much like the tax treatment of life insurance contributions in the United States.

4.7   Conclusions

Capital markets per se do not differ greatly between the United States and Germany. In the two countries, financial markets are only mildly regulated, and portfolio options are quite comparable. The only difference may be that the wealthy in the United States face more portfolio options due to a somewhat more dynamic market for financial instruments than their German counterparts. Policy-induced differences in savings options between Germany and the United States include mainly different dedicated savings programs. In the United States, IRAs and Keoghs are subsidized savings dedicated to retirement income. In Germany, bequeathable savings dedicated to housing investments and company shares have been substantially subsidized and still play a major role in private wealth accumulation.

If we sum up the incentives for savings in Germany and the extent of German social safety provisions, we receive a mixed message about the impact of public policy on savings. On one hand, tax treatment of savings is more favorable in Germany than in the United States, which should, ceteris paribus, induce relatively higher savings rates in Germany. On the other hand, two of

Table 4.11   Examples for Total Savings Subsidy

Household Type	Bausparkassen Savings			General Savings			Total Subsidized Savings DM	Total Subsidy	
	Maximum Contribution	Premium %	DM	Maximum Contribution	Premium %	DM		DM	%
			1988						
Single, no children	800	14	112	624	23	144	1,424	256	17.9
Married, no children, one earner	1,600	14	224	624	23	144	2,224	368	16.5
Married, no children, two earners	1,600	14	224	1,248	23	287	2,848	511	17.9
Married, two children, one earner	1,600	18	288	624	23	144	2,224	432	19.4
Married, two children, two earner	1,600	18	288	1,248	23	287	2,848	575	20.2
Married, three children, one earner	1,600	20	320	624	33	412	2,224	526	23.6
Married, three children two earners	1,600	20	320	1,248	33	412	2,848	732	25.7
			1992						
Married, one earner	1,600	10	160	936	10	94	2,536	254	10.0
Married, two earners	1,600	10	160	1,872	10	187	3,472	347	10.0

Source: Author's calculations based on *Wohnungsbauprämiengesetz, Sparprämiengesetz,* and *Vermögensbildungsgesetz.*

the main economic rationales for saving—assuring a comfortable retirement income and precaution against high health-care expenses—are less important in Germany than they are in the United States because the safety net is tighter in Germany. This should, ceteris paribus, reduce savings among households below retirement age.[17] Among the older elderly, however, the tighter safety net in Germany might actually increase net savings since the generous retirement income might not only prevent the German elderly from depleting their assets but even provide income levels sufficiently large to induce savings in old age (Börsch-Supan 1992b).

In order to gauge the impact of the incentive programs on one side and of the tight safety net on the other, we need to know the elasticity of savings with respect to after-tax returns, as well as the substitution elasticities among different kinds of savings, including especially the substitution between private

17. That is, provided the young generation believes in the stability of the current pension system in spite of the dramatic aging of the German population.

and public savings. Börsch-Supan and Stahl (1991) provide evidence that the special incentive program favoring saving in building societies had a positive net impact on total savings, i.e., new savings in building societies more than compensated for substitution out of general savings. Similarly, tabulations of household wealth in comparable data sets indicate that private household wealth is about 20 percent lower in Germany than in the United States. However, imputed social security wealth is about 33 percent higher in Germany (Börsch-Supan 1991a). Again, although there is some substitution, the total wealth effect is positive.

Finally, it is important to note that savings incentives in Germany have dramatically changed since the mid-eighties. While the favorable incentive programs are still in place and capital income frequently escapes taxation, many of the subsidies have been severely reduced, in particular since the 1990 tax reform. See table 4.8, which summarizes this. It is too early to observe changes in savings behavior. And, in fact, the aggregate savings rate went up from 1985 to 1989 in spite of a reduction in tax incentives.

References

Baron, Dietmar. 1988. *Die personelle Vermögensverteilung in der Bundesrepublik Deutschland und ihre Bestimmungsgründe.* Frankfurt am Main: Lang.

Beck, C. H. 1991. *Steuergesetze. Vols. 1 and 2.* München: Beck.

Börsch-Supan, Axel. 1992a. Population aging, social security design, and early retirement. *Journal of Institutional and Theoretical Economics (Zeitschrift für die gesamte Staatswissenschaft)* 148:533–57.

———. 1992b. Saving and consumption patterns among the elderly: The German case. *Journal of Population Economics* 5:289–303.

Börsch-Supan, Axel, and Konrad Stahl. 1991. Do dedicated savings programs increase aggregate savings and housing demand? *Journal of Public Economics* 44: 265–97.

Bundesminister für Arbeit und Sozialordnung. 1990. *Die Rentenreform 1992.* Bonn: Bundespresseamt.

Casmir, Bernd. 1989. *Staatliche Rentenversicherungssysteme im internationalen Vergleich.* Frankfurt: Lang.

Frerich, Johannes. 1987. *Sozialpolitik.* München: Oldenbourg.

Hurd, Michael D. 1989. Issues and results from research on the elderly: Economic status, retirement, and savings. *Journal of Economic Literature* 28: 565–637.

Lampert, Heinz. 1985. *Lehrbuch der Sozialpolitik,* Berlin, Heidelberg, and New York: Springer.

Mierheim, Heinz, and Lutz Wicke. 1978. *Die personelle Vermögensverteilung in der Bundesrepublik Deutschland.* Tübingen: Mohr.

Nöhrbaß, Karl-Heinz, and Martin Raab. 1990. Quellensteuer und Kapitalmarkt. *Finanzarchiv* 48:179–93.

Petersen, Hans-Georg. 1988. *Finanzwissenschaft II: Spezielle Steuerlehre.* Stuttgart, Berlin, and Köln: Kohlhammer.

Richter, Wolfram. 1987. Taxation as insurance and the case of rate differentiation according to consanguinity under inheritance taxation. *Journal of Public Economics* 33:363–76.

Schöffel, Heinrich. 1986. Kaufpreisuntersuchung des Statistischen Bundesamtes. Wiesbaden: Statistisches Bundesamt.

Stiglitz, Josef E., and Bruno Schönfelder. 1989. *Finanzwissenschaft.* München and Wien: Oldenbourg.

5   Government Incentives and Household Saving in Italy

Tullio Jappelli and Marco Pagano

The Italian saving rate has exhibited large variability since World War II, with a trend decline in the past two decades, following very high levels in the fifties and sixties. Since tax incentives and social security arrangements are potentially important determinants of private and national saving, it is natural to consider whether changes in the tax code and in the social security system have contributed to the changes in the Italian saving rate. For instance, is the decline due to reforms in the taxation of capital income or to the transition from funded social security to a pay-as-you-go system? Alternatively, would the private saving rate have declined even further were it not for the tax incentives introduced in the eighties?

The empirical literature on the Italian saving rate is of very limited help in answering these questions. This paper describes the tax and social security developments that are relevant to household saving choices, to provide a framework for future research on the effects of government incentives to save in Italy.[1]

Tullio Jappelli is associate professor of economics at the Istituto Universitario Navale, Napoli. Marco Pagano is associate professor of economics at Università Bocconi, Milano. Both are research fellows of the Center for Economic Policy Research.

The authors thank Antonio Cristoforo for helpful comments.

1. After the completion of this paper in August 1992, a number of reforms have reshaped several aspects of the Italian tax and social security systems. A real estate tax (*Imposta Comunale sugli Immobili* [ICI]) has been introduced for the first time and its proceeds devolved to local government. The tax on capital gains has been suspended. The social security system has become less generous. Over the next decade the minimum retirement age will be gradually raised from 60 to 65 years for men and from 55 to 60 for women; the minimum period of contribution will increase from fifteen to twenty years; the period of the working life on the basis of which pension benefits are computed (so far the last five years) will be gradually extended to the last ten years for the current employees and to the entire working life for employees hired after 1992; the degree of pension indexation has been reduced and contributions raised. Finally, private pension funds have been regulated, and employers' contributions to pension funds will gradually replace severance pay.

In section 5.1 we document the shifts in household portfolios in the past two decades. This is followed by a brief history and description of the present rules governing the tax treatment of capital income, the taxation of wealth, capital transfers, and capital gains, the integration of dividend taxation with the corporate income tax, and the tax treatment of interest on household debt (section 5.2). In section 5.3 we focus on the institutional arrangements that affect incentives to save for retirement, i.e., social security (section 5.3.1), private pension funds (section 5.3.2), and severance pay (section 5.3.3). In section 5.4 we describe the public incentives to hold life insurance policies that have been recently introduced into the Italian tax code and compute the excess return of a typical life insurance policy relative to the rate of interest on public debt.

5.1   The Household Balance Sheet

Throughout the postwar period the Italian national saving rate has been consistently above the OECD average. Italy's net national saving rate was 3.4 percentage points above the Group of Seven average in the sixties, 2 points in the seventies, and 1 point in the eighties (Dean et al. 1990). In all three periods, Italy ranked second only to Japan.

Another distinction of the Italian saving rate has been its variability, which has far exceeded that of most other industrialized countries. The net national saving rate rose from 7 percent in 1952 to 22 percent in 1961. The sixties registered high and relatively stable saving rates, ranging between 18 and 22 percent. The past two decades then witnessed a trend decline in saving, down to 9 percent of net national income in 1990 (see Guiso, Jappelli, and Terlizzese 1994).

In the past two decades, the composition of household net worth has changed considerably, as well. Table 5.1 shows that the share of housing and of nonresidential real estate declined by 12.2 percent over the 1975–89 period; conversely, the stock of durable goods and of net financial assets rose by 3.9 and 8.3 percent, respectively.

Table 5.2 indicates that, within the class of financial assets, households accomplished a massive portfolio shift from debt claims on banks and private companies to public sector debt. The sum of currency and deposits shrank from 62.1 percent of total household assets in 1975 to less than 40 percent in 1989. Private bonds declined even more steeply, from 8.2 to 3.1 percent. The mirror image of this decline in bank deposits and private bonds was the 10-fold increase of the share of government debt in household portfolios, from 3.2 percent in 1975 to 32.1 percent in 1989. Capital controls, in place until 1989, prevented Italian households from diversifying their portfolios away from public debt: this is witnessed by the minuscule share of foreign assets, which never exceeded 1.5 percent of total financial assets.

Other significant features of table 5.2 are Italian households' relatively small holdings of equities and their low borrowing, compared with most other

Table 5.1   **Composition of Household Net Worth, 1975–89**

	1975	1980	1985	1989
	Level (thousand billion current lire)			
Housing	322.1	913.9	1,807.5	2,365.3
Nonresidential real				
estate	29.0	74.5	87.1	111.7
Durables	43.1	143.6	335.6	520.1
Net financial assets	88.3	230.4	588.3	1,088.0
Net worth	482.4	1,362.4	2,818.5	4,085.1
Income	112.1	297.0	629.9	889.8
	As a % of Net Worth			
Housing	66.8	67.1	64.1	57.9
Nonresidential real				
estate	6.0	5.5	3.1	2.7
Durables	8.9	10.5	11.9	12.8
Net financial assets	18.3	16.9	20.9	26.6
Net worth	100.0	100.0	100.0	100.0
Wealth–income ratio	4.3	4.6	4.5	4.5

Source: Pagliano and Rossi (1992, tables 20 and 21).

OECD countries. The small share of equities reflects the thinness of the Italian stock market, even after the introduction of investment funds in 1984 and the stock market boom of 1985–86; the low level of household debt is due mainly to regulation, high enforcement costs, and the lack of substantial incentives to borrow (Jappelli and Pagano 1989, 1994). The high nominal interest rates of the seventies and early eighties placed an additional burden on debtors (due to the lack of indexed mortgage instruments) so that the share of household liabilities declined until the mid-eighties, not regaining the 1975 level until 1989.

Table 5.2 shows that most financial assets held by Italian households have short maturities (the average maturity of public debt was 3.5 years at the end of 1987). The only long-term saving instruments are those explicitly earmarked for retirement needs, i.e., life insurance, pension funds, and severance pay. Insurance policies and severance pay accounted for almost 20 percent of total financial assets in 1975, but declined to 11.3 percent in 1985 and to about 10 percent in 1989. But the data displayed in table 5.2 are a misleading indicator of the assets held to finance retirement consumption, because (i) the value of pension funds is omitted, (ii) the official figures for severance pay do not take into account that severance pay is partially indexed to the consumer price index, and (iii) the figure for insurance measures assets held by insurance companies against all insurance policies, not just life insurance, which is the only policy that can provide retirement income.

The estimates in table 5.3 overcome these measurement problems. The adjusted figures show that in Italy pension funds and life insurance policies form a tiny fraction of financial assets, in sharp contrast with most other industrial-

Table 5.2   Composition of Household Financial Assets, 1975–89 (%)

	1975	1980	1985	1989
Assets				
Currency and deposits	62.1	60.2	45.8	39.3
Currency	6.8	5.4	3.8	3.3
Bank deposits	44.5	45.2	34.1	26.7
Postal deposits	8.2	8.0	5.6	6.4
Deposits at SCI[a]	2.6	1.6	2.3	2.9
Government bonds	3.2	13.2	26.8	32.1
BOT[b]	0.1	8.6	12.7	14.5
CCT[b]	—	2.3	12.0	10.7
Other government bonds[b]	3.1	2.3	2.1	6.9
Private bonds[c]	8.2	2.7	2.7	3.1
Investment funds[d]	—	—	2.2	3.1
Equities	5.3	7.0	9.5	9.9
Foreign assets	1.4	1.0	1.0	1.5
Insurance	6.6	5.7	4.9 ⎫	
Severance pay	13.2	9.8	6.7 ⎬	10.9[e]
Other assets	0.1	0.5	0.2 ⎭	
Total financial assets	100.0	100.0	100.0	100.0
Liabilities				
Bank loans	39.9	56.4	58.4	53.9
SCI loans	56.5	37.8	34.7	31.9
Other liabilities[f]	3.7	5.9	6.8	14.2
Total liabilities	100.0	100.0	100.0	100.0
Liabilities/assets (%)	8.3	7.0	5.8	7.4

Sources: For 1975–85, Bank of Italy, "The Wealth of Italian Households, *Economic Bulletin* (English edition), no. 3 (1986); for 1989, Bank of Italy, *Annual Report,* Statistical Appendix (Roma, 1990), table aD29.

[a]Special credit institutions (SCI).

[b]BOT are treasury bills up to one-year maturity. CCT are floating-rate treasury credit certificates, 2 to 4 years in maturity indexed to BOTs; these certificates were introduced in 1977. Other government bonds include BTP (long-term government bonds), bonds issued by the PO Deposits and Loans Fund, bonds issued by local governments and by public sector enterprises.

[c]Bonds issued by private enterprises and by special credit institutions.

[d]Investment funds were authorized in 1984.

[e]For 1989 separate figures for insurance, severance pay, and other assets are not available.

[f]In 1989 this item also includes consumer credit extended by finance companies (see D'Alessio 1990).

ized countries. Only accrued severance pay entitlement accounts for more than a negligible share of household financial wealth, between 8 and 9 percent. The fact that private pension arrangements and life insurance wealth have such little attraction for Italian savers cannot be explained by lack of tax incentives: the tax treatment of both types of assets, and in particular of private pension funds, is quite favorable, as is documented in sections 5.3 and 5.4.

Table 5.4 completes the picture by providing information on the distribution

Table 5.3   **Pension Funds, Life Insurance, and Severance Pay**

Year	Pension Funds (1)	Life Insurance (2)	Severance Pay (3)	Financial Assets (4)
	Trillion Lire (end-of-period estimates)			
1980	—	—	40.6	—
1981	—	—	47.9	—
1982	—	—	55.9	—
1983	20	—	63.8	—
1984	—	9.6	73.2	—
1985	22.5	11.9	83.5	948
1986	—	15.0	95.3	—
1987	—	19.5	105.2	—
1988	40	24.7	115.1	1,467
	As a % of Household Financial Assets			
1985	2.4	1.3	8.8	100.0
1988	2.7	1.7	7.8	100.0

Notes: Col. (1)—no official statistics exist for pension funds. Sources are for 1983, Commissione tecnica per la spesa pubblica; for 1985, Banca d'Italia-IMI-INA (1986) estimate pension funds to be between 15 and 30 trillion lire; for 1988, Piatti (1990) estimates it to range from 35 to 45 trillion lire. In the table we report the midrange value for these two years.

Col. (2)—assets held by domestic and foreign insurance companies as a counterpart to life insurance policies sold to residents. Source is *Annuario ANIA* (Roma, 1990), table 13.

Col. (3)—the official estimates of severance pay do not take into account the indexation of severance pay. The figures in this table adjust for indexation and are drawn from Piatti (1990, table 5).

Col. (4)—these figures are obtained by replacing the official estimate of the value of severance pay with its adjusted estimate, and by adding the value of pension funds.

of wealth. We report data, by decile, on net worth, net real assets, financial assets, and bank deposits drawn from the 1989 Survey of Household Income and Wealth. The median net worth is about 103 million lire, while the median holding of financial assets and deposits are 10 and 9 million lire, respectively. The latter two values—approximately $8,000 in 1989—are considerably higher than in the United States, where Deaton (1992) reports that the median level of household liquid assets in the early eighties was less than $1,000. The difference between these numbers may reflect differences in the composition of household assets as well as in households' propensity to save.

In the next sections, we shall first provide an overall view of the tax treatment of capital income in Italy and then describe the specific provisions affecting retirement saving, i.e., the rules of the social security system and the tax provisions concerning private pension plans, severance pay, and life insurance.

5.2 Taxation of Capital Income

In Italy interest income is taxed at a flat rate or is tax-exempt, depending on the type of asset, and capital gains were effectively tax-exempt until 1990. The

Table 5.4   Distribution of Household Wealth and Financial Assets in 1989

	Net Worth		Real Assets		Financial Assets		Deposits	
Decile	V	S	V	S	V	S	V	S
Lowest	3,519	0.0	0.0	0.0	0.0	0.0	0.0	0.0
Second	13,361	0.5	1,760	0.1	2,500	0.4	2,000	0.6
Third	40,000	1.7	14,665	0.4	5,000	1.3	4,000	1.9
Fourth	70,500	3.7	56,000	3.2	7,873	2.2	6,000	3.0
Fifth	102,751	5.9	84,000	5.8	10,000	3.7	9,000	4.4
Sixth	128,652	7.8	106,000	7.9	15,000	4.7	11,000	6.0
Seventh	162,000	9.6	135,810	9.9	21,000	6.7	16,000	8.3
Eighth	219,000	12.6	183,255	12.9	33,333	9.8	21,429	11.4
Ninth	331,000	17.9	288,000	18.4	61,250	16.9	38,067	17.0
Highest	—	40.5	—	41.8	—	54.7	—	47.5
Mean	149,711		122,364		27,348		16,624	
Coefficient of variation	1.46		1.50		2.75		2.00	
Gini coefficient	0.58		0.61		0.69		0.63	

Source: The numbers are based on the sample of 8,274 households of the 1989 Survey of Household Income and Wealth. We thank Luigi Cannari for providing us with the data. The median income in the survey is 29,057 thousand lire.

Note: V = value of the assets held by the poorest household in the decile. S = share of the assets held by the households belonging to the decile (sum to 100 except for rounding errors).

rate at which interest income is taxed is well below the average marginal tax rate on income from labor, and Italy features a much lower overall tax rate on income from capital than the United Kingdom, the United States, West Germany, and Sweden (Giannini 1989).

The foundations of the current tax system were laid by the 1974 tax reform act, which introduced two separate taxes on personal income: a progressive income tax levied at the national level (*Imposta sul Reddito delle Persone Fisiche* [IRPEF]), whose base is formed by income from labor and income from capital excluding interest income (i.e., dividends, profits, and rents); and a proportional tax on all kinds of income from capital except interest income, presently levied at a flat rate of 16.2 percent (*Imposta Locale sui Redditi* [ILOR]), whose revenue is collected by the central government and originally devolved on local governments, as well as a proportional tax on corporate income (*Imposta sul Reddito delle Persone Giuridiche* [IRPEG]) presently levied at a flat rate of 36 percent.

In table 5.5 we report the composition of tax revenues of the general government by main categories. In 1991 more than 50 percent of total revenues were raised in the form of direct taxes. The IRPEF alone represented one-third of total revenues, while IRPEG and ILOR accounted for roughly 5 percent of revenue. As shown in table 5.5, while taxes on capital income represent a sub-

Table 5.5   **Sources of Government Revenue[a] (as a % of total revenues)**

	1980	1985	1991
Direct taxes	48.9	55.9	53.5
IRPEF	30.6	34.7	32.4
IRPEG	3.3	5.2	4.6
ILOR	5.5	5.9	5.5
Taxes on interest income	8.0	7.8	8.5
Deposits	—	7.0	4.0
Government bonds[b]	—	—	3.2
Others	—	0.8	1.3
Withholding tax on dividends	—	0.5	0.6
Estate, inheritance, and gift taxes	0.3	0.2	0.2
Others	1.2	1.6	1.7
Indirect taxes	51.1	44.1	46.5
Total	100.0	100.0	100.0

Source: Bank of Italy, *Annual Report,* Statistical Appendix (Roma, various years), table aC6.
[a]The figures exclude revenues of local governments and other government agencies. They also exclude direct taxes collected in Sicily.
[b]Tax-exempt before 1986.

stantial source of revenue, the withholding tax on dividends and the tax on estates, inheritances, and gifts have always represented a minuscule share of revenue. The composition of interest taxes has changed considerably, the main reason being that taxation of interest on government bonds was introduced in 1986.

Table 5.6 displays the current tax brackets and those in place before the tax reform of 1989. It shows that the degree of progressivity of IRPEF has diminished and the number of tax brackets reduced in the past two decades by a series of reforms (in 1983, 1986, and 1989). In fact, the number of brackets dropped from 32 in 1976 to 7 in 1989, while the top marginal tax rate was lowered from 72 to 50 percent.

An important innovation of the 1989 reform was indexing tax brackets for inflation. This partially eliminated the fiscal drag built into the previous rate schedules, which had caused a substantial increase in the tax burden during the seventies and eighties: the ratio of IRPEF receipts to GDP had risen from 3.8 percent in 1975 to 7.6 percent in 1985, and its ratio to total tax revenues rose from 17 to 35 percent.

Dividends, income from unincorporated business, rents, imputed income from home ownership, severance pay, income paid by life insurance policies, and pensions are subject to IRPEF and, with the exception of pensions, to ILOR. All other income from capital (mainly interest payments) is excluded from the tax base of IRPEF: a flat-rate withholding tax is in fact levied on all nominal interest income.

The extent to which recipients of capital income succeed in evading taxes is

Table 5.6   **Marginal Tax Rates on Labor Income (%)**

1976–82		1983–85		1986–88		1989–90[a]		1991[a]	
Bracket[b]	Rate	Bracket[b]	Rate	Bracket[b]	Rate	Bracket[b]	Rate	Bracket[b]	Rate
≤3	10	≤11	18	≤6	12	≤6.4	10	≤6.8	10
3–4	13	11–24	27	6–11	22	6.4–12.7	22	6.8–13.5	22
4–5	16	24–30	35	11–28	27	12.7–31.8	26	13.5–33.7	26
5–6	19	30–38	37	28–50	34	31.8–63.7	33	33.7–67.6	33
6–7.5	22	38–60	41	50–100	41	63.7–159.1	40	67.6–168.8	40
7.5–9	25	60–120	47	100–150	48	159.1–318.3	45	168.8–337.7	45
9–11	27	120–250	56	150–300	53	>318.3	50	>337.7	50
11–13	29	250–500	62	300–600	58				
13–15	31	>500	65	>600	62				
15–17	32								
17–19	33								
19–22	34								
22–25	35								
25–30	36								
30–35	38								
35–40	40								
40–50	42								
50–60	44								
60–80	46								
80–100	48								
100–125	50								
125–150	52								
150–175	54								
175–200	56								
200–250	58								
250–300	60								
300–350	62								
350–400	64								
400–450	66								
450–500	68								
500–550	70								
>550	72								

[a]In March 1989 tax brackets were indexed to the cost of living starting in 1990.
[b]Brackets are determined by annual income in millions of lire.

hard to gauge. Although there is a common perception that Italy has a significant hidden or underground economy, no estimates exist for the share of capital income that escapes taxation because it is not reported to the tax authorities.[2]

2. Various methods for estimating the size of the hidden economy have been proposed (Marrelli 1989). Visco (1983) evaluates the difference between earned income reported on tax returns and wage income from the national accounts at about 10 percent for employees and 35–40 percent for the self-employed. Estimates based on the difference between the labor force participation rate in Italy and in other Western countries range from 10 to 25 percent (Marrelli 1989).

5.2.1   The Taxation of Dividends and Corporate Taxation

Until 1974 individuals could choose between two regimes of dividend taxation: (i) let dividends be part of the income tax base and then be taxed at the personal income tax rate (which ranged from 10 to 82 percent), or (ii) pay a flat 30 percent tax rate—*cedolare secca* (final schedule withholding tax). In either case, there was no tax credit for corporate taxes. The 1974 reform eliminated the second regime: since then dividends must be included in the income tax base. At the same time, the previous system of corporate taxation was replaced by the two proportional income taxes mentioned above: a company tax levied at the national level (IRPEG) and the so-called local tax (ILOR). The tax rate for ILOR was the same as for individuals.

The tax bases for the two taxes were virtually the same, and initially ILOR was not deductible from the tax base of IRPEG. The IRPEG tax rate was 25 percent, while for ILOR, initially, each local authority was given the right to set its own tax rate, ranging between 9.4 and 14.7 percent. However, after 1977 ILOR was levied at a uniform tax rate of 15 percent and the proceeds transferred to the central government. The resulting corporate income tax was 40 percent.

In 1978 two major changes occurred. First, an imputation system was introduced for dividends and phased in over a two-year period. Full credit for IRPEG was allowed against the liability deriving from the personal income tax (IRPEF), although no credit was allowed for ILOR. Second, ILOR became deductible from IRPEG at the corporate income tax level. As a result, the corporate income tax rate fell to 36.25 percent.

From 1983 to 1992, IRPEG and ILOR were raised to 36 and 16.2 percent, respectively, so that the overall corporate tax rate rose to 46.36 percent. The IRPEG (but not the ILOR) has remained fully deductible from the personal income tax on dividends since 1983.

The average marginal tax rate on dividend recipients was estimated to be 43.6 percent in 1980 and 49.1 percent in 1985 (Alworth and Castellucci 1993).[3] Both estimates are based on tax return information on the distribution of dividend income and are obtained by multiplying the value of reported dividend income by the marginal tax rate which applies to each tax bracket. The corresponding value for 1990 was estimated to be 46.1 percent, assuming that the distribution of share ownership remained the same as in 1981, but allowing for the drift in tax brackets associated with inflation.

5.2.2   Interest Income

The tax rates on nominal interest income differ according to the type of investor, the type of financial instrument, and its issuer, and they have varied

---

3. A similar figure is reported by Giannini (1989), who estimates the 1980 average marginal tax rate on dividends to be 43.5 percent.

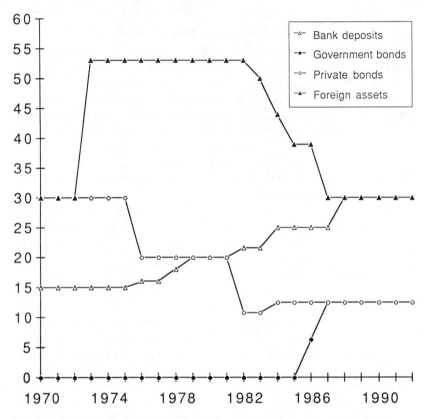

Fig. 5.1   Tax rates on interest income, by main asset categories: 1970–92

considerably over time. Figure 5.1 displays tax rates on interest income for four main asset categories; the appendix traces the past and current values of all tax rates on interest from financial assets. At present, all deposits and postal saving accounts are taxed at 30 percent, while public and private debt instruments are taxed at 12.5 percent (except for CDs with less than 18 months of maturity, which are taxed at 25 percent). Foreign assets have always been taxed at higher rates than domestic securities, reflecting restrictions on capital mobility. These restrictions have been partly removed in recent years, and the tax rate on foreign assets has accordingly declined to the current 30 percent level, down from 50 percent in 1984.

For comparison with the discussion in the previous paragraph, note that the marginal tax rate on interest income was estimated to be 19.7 percent in 1980, 22.5 percent in 1985, and 16.7 in 1990 (Alworth and Castellucci 1993), about half of that on dividends.[4]

4. These values were computed by weighting the tax rate that applies to each debt instrument by the respective ownership shares and allowing for indirect lending through the banking system via purchase of securities issued by companies and special credit institutions.

5.2.3 Taxation of Wealth and Capital Transfers

In Italy there are no taxes on personal financial wealth. The only wealth tax, other than on estates, inheritances, and gifts, which will be discussed below, is a capital gains tax on nominal price increases of real estate. The tax, introduced in 1974 and considerably revised in 1980, is paid only when property is transferred—whether through a sale, a bequest, or a gift—and is called INVIM (*Imposta sull'Incremento del Valore degli Immobili*). In contrast with ILOR, a local tax only in name, INVIM is truly a local tax, providing about 15 percent of municipal tax revenues.

The tax base of INVIM is the difference between the current price and the price recorded at the time of the previous ownership transfer. Until recently this value was assessed by the tax authorities. However, since this method of assessment often led to lengthy disputes that had to be settled by special tax courts, in July 1986 a new rule was introduced: the price declared by the parties cannot questioned by tax authorities if it equals or exceeds the value that is imputed to real estate of that class. This imputed value equals the corresponding statutory rent, or *rendita catastale,* multiplied by 100 (if the initial value refers to the period before 1963, the *rendita catastale* is multiplied by 35).

As shown in the top panel of table 5.7, the tax is progressive: rates vary from 5 to 30 percent, and the tax base depends on the initial value of the property and the number of years that it was held. Suppose that a house bought for 10 million lire in 1980 is resold in 1990 for 220 million lire. The total tax base is the price increment of 210 million lire. In the second panel of table 5.7 we compute the tax liability (units are million lire). The figures in the second column sum to 210 million lire, i.e., to the price increment. The overall tax liability—the sum of the figures in the third column—is 36 million lire, corresponding to an average tax rate of 17.1 percent and a marginal tax rate of 30 percent.

The average and marginal tax rates are so high because in this example the price increase is very high (2,200 percent) and the holding period is relatively short (10 years). In fact the tax is structured so that the marginal tax rate is an increasing function of the property's price increment and a decreasing function of the holding period. The bottom panel of table 5.7 shows that the marginal tax rate can be as low as 5 percent for a house with a relatively small price increase and a relatively long holding period, and as high as 30 percent for large price increases and short holding periods. For instance, if the price increase is 100 percent and the holding period is longer than 5 years, the marginal tax rate is 5 percent, but the same price increment is subject to a marginal tax rate of 15 percent if the house is held for only one year.

Inheritances and gifts are the only other cases in which taxes are levied on wealth, rather than on income. In contrast to all other OECD countries, which have either an estate tax—where the tax base and tax rate depend on the amount transferred by the decedent—or an inheritance tax—where the tax base and tax rate depend on the amount received by the beneficiary—Italy has both, inheritance taxes being levied only on legacies outside the immediate

Table 5.7   INVIM

Taxation of Capital Gains on Real Assets (INVIM)

Tax Rate	Portion of the Price Increment Taxed
5	20% of the initial value × number of years asset was held
10	30% of the initial value × number of years asset was held
15	50% of the initial value × number of years asset was held
20	50% of the initial value × number of years asset was held
25	50% of the initial value × number of years asset was held
30	any residual part of the price increment

An Example of INVIM[a]

Tax Rate	% × Initial Value × No. of Years	Tax Liability (million lire)
5	20% × 10 × 10 = 20	5% × 20 = 1
10	30% × 10 × 10 = 30	10% × 20 = 2
15	50% × 10 × 10 = 50	15% × 50 = 7.5
20	50% × 10 × 10 = 50	20% × 50 = 10
25	50% × 10 × 10 = 50	25% × 50 = 12.5
30	the residual 10 million lire	30% × 10 = 3

Marginal Tax Rates of INVIM

Holding Period (years)	% Increase in the Price of Real Estate					
	20	30	100	200	350	500
1	0.05	0.10	0.15	0.25	0.30	0.30
2	0.05	0.10	0.10	0.15	0.25	0.30
5	0.05	0.05	0.05	0.10	0.15	0.15
8	0.05	0.05	0.05	0.10	0.10	0.15
10	0.05	0.05	0.05	0.05	0.10	0.10
15	0.05	0.05	0.05	0.05	0.10	0.10
20	0.05	0.05	0.05	0.05	0.05	0.10

[a]In this example, the property is assumed to be worth 10 million lire in 1980 and sold for 220 million lire in 1990.

family. These taxes were first introduced in 1972, replacing earlier legislation. Tax brackets and tax rates for both types of taxes have been changed frequently in the past 20 years, but the general principles on which their provisions are based have remained the same.

Table 5.8 describes the current system of inheritance and estate taxes. Gifts are taxed in a similar way. The general principle is that of progressive taxation; as with IRPEF, the top marginal tax rates were considerably reduced in the seventies and eighties. Spouses and direct descendants are subject only to the estate tax. Relatives and other recipients are also subject to the inheritance tax, with tax rates that vary among classes of beneficiaries. Life insurance policies, social security benefits, and public debt are tax-exempt.

Table 5.8   **Marginal Tax Rates on Estates, Inheritances, and Gifts: 1992**

Tax Bracket (million lire)	Marginal Estate Tax (%)	Marginal Inheritance Tax (in addition to estate taxes; %)		
		Brothers, Sisters, Nephews, and Nieces	Other Relatives	Other Beneficiaries
<10	—	—	—	—
10–100	—	—	3	6
100–250	—	3	5	8
250–350	3	6	9	12
350–500	7	10	13	18
500–800	10	15	19	23
800–1,500	15	20	24	28
1,500–3,000	22	24	26	31
>3,000	27	25	27	33

Note: The spouse and direct descendants of the transferor are exempt from inheritance tax. In January 1992, the threshold for estate tax was 250 million lire. The threshold for inheritance tax varies and is graduated on the three classes of beneficiaries: 100 million lire for brothers, sisters, nephews, and nieces, 10 million lire for other relatives and for other beneficiaries. The tax regime for gifts is the same as that for bequests.

As was shown in table 5.5, inheritance, estate, and gift taxes have always been a minor source of government revenue (0.2 percent of total tax revenues). In particular, the revenue from gift taxes is extremely low (0.01 percent of total revenues), reflecting in part the difficulty of aggregating gift taxes and estate taxes (OECD 1988), and in part the ease with which taxes on gifts are evaded.

5.2.4   Capital Gains on Equities

Until 1990, as a practical matter, capital gains on equities were tax-exempt, although in principle they were subject to general income tax if the relevant transactions were undertaken with "speculative intent." However, as the definition of speculative intent was not objective and the burden of proof lay with the tax revenue service, no tax on capital gains on equities was effectively levied.[5]

After a rather confused transition between September 1990 and March 1991, a system was introduced according to which investors can choose one of two tax regimes. Under one regime, capital gains are taxed at a flat 25 percent, and losses can be deducted from taxable income for the subsequent five years. Alternatively, investors can pay a proportion of the resale value of their shares, irrespective of the realized capital gain; this proportion is set each quarter by

5. There were exceptional cases, however, where speculative intent was presumed by the tax code. The exceptions were the sale of shares held for less than five years in the following cases: until 1984, the sale of unlisted shares of real estate companies; between 1984 and 1990, the sale of more than 2 percent of the value of listed companies, more than 10 percent (5 percent after 1987) of unlisted companies, and more than 25 percent (15 percent after 1987) of unincorporated companies.

the Board of the Stock Exchange Brokers, and in no case can it be less than 0.3 percent or higher than 1.05 percent. The second regime can be chosen only for transactions involving relatively small volumes of shares: less than 2 percent of the share value of listed companies (less than 5 percent of the equity value of unlisted companies and less than 15 percent of unincorporated companies). Each year taxpayers must opt for one of the two rules and may not alter their choices for the whole year.

If shares are held by an investment fund, the tax regime is totally different: the income distributed to unit holders is tax-exempt, but the net worth of the investment fund is subject to a tax of 0.25 percent.

5.2.5   Tax Treatment of Household Liabilities

As was shown in table 5.2, one of the striking facts about the Italian economy is the extraordinarily low level of household borrowing. There are a number of reasons for this. The regulation of the banking industry and the costs of judicial enforcement of loan contracts have limited the availability of credit to households (Guiso et al. 1994; Jappelli and Pagano 1994). Another reason for the limited stock of household debt is the lack of substantial tax incentives, either for personal credit or home mortgage credit.

In some countries, such as Sweden and the United States until the tax reform of 1986, interest payments on consumer credit are tax-deductible. No such privileged treatment for consumer credit and personal loans is given to Italian households. In 1980–85 the ratio of consumer credit to personal consumption expenditures in Sweden was on average 17 times higher than in Italy, and in the United States it was 10 times higher (Jappelli and Pagano 1989). It is hard not to relate these huge differences in the personal credit market, at least partly, to the disparate tax treatment.

The other area in which households often benefit from tax deductions is mortgage loans for home purchase. In Italy, however, direct government intervention in housing finance is limited, and tax incentives have been reduced over time. Until 1976 all interest payments were tax-deductible; in 1976 a yearly ceiling of 3 million lire was set (raised to 4 million in 1980). But the deductibility of interest payments was abolished in 1990, for all but first-home buyers. In most European countries, and in the United States, deductions are more generous (EC Mortgage Federation 1990).

Other incentives to housing finance had been provided by a law enacted in 1984 and abrogated in January of 1991, offering loans at subsidized interest rates: the rate was inversely related to household income and ranged from 5.5 to 13 percent. The law set stringent eligibility requirements: the head of the household had to be under 45 years old, employed continuously for at least two years, and not already a homeowner. The maturity of the subsidized loan was 20 years, and the loan could finance up to 75 percent of the value of the house. However, the mortgage could not exceed 60 million lire, about twice the average household income, and the house could not be resold before the mortgage was repaid.

5.2.6 Summary

The overall picture of the taxation of capital income is one of relatively favorable treatment of interest income, compared to labor income and dividends, and of strict provisions on the deductibility of interest on household liabilities. Compared with the tax regime of the early seventies, tax rates on most forms of capital income have been raised considerably, while the deductibility of mortgage interest has been restricted. Government bonds, exempt until 1986, are now taxed; the tax rates on deposits have doubled, and since 1990 capital gains have been taxed more severely. The only assets for which the tax burden has eased are some private bonds and foreign assets, which traditionally have been a small share of households' portfolios, as was shown in table 5.2. Moreover, as was shown in figure 5.1, rates on government bonds and private bonds have converged to 12.5 percent and those on foreign assets and bank deposits to 30 percent, indicating an effort to reduce the substantial tax distortions that affected the portfolio choices of Italian households in the seventies.

5.3 Pension Plans and Retirement Saving

Social security provisions, pension arrangements, and the rules determining severance pay (*indennità di fine rapporto*) are generally held to be key determinants of the national saving rate.[6] However, very few studies have investigated how Italian national saving has responded to changes in the social security system, and none has analyzed the impact on saving of the tax treatment of private pensions and of the rules concerning severance pay.

As shown in table 5.9, social security benefits represent a large share (55 percent) of the income of households with retired heads. On average, an additional 25 percent of income is provided by labor earnings, and 10 percent by imputed income from housing. Interest income accounts for only 10 percent of the income of retirees, in the form of either financial wealth (4.0 percent) or other capital income (5.5 percent). These figures already show that voluntary accumulation schemes such as pension funds represent a fairly small source of income for the elderly. As will be seen below, the main reasons are that in Italy social security provides relatively generous benefits and that severance pay has a far more important role than in other industrialized countries.

5.3.1 Social Security

Until 1952 the Italian social security system was fully funded. Starting in that year, the government set minimum pensions, gradually extended compul-

---

6. Replacing a funded social security system with a pay-as-you-go system reduces national saving (Feldstein 1974) unless people fully discount the implied burden of future social security contributions (Barro 1974). Public policy also affects national saving through tax incentives to private pension funds and to deferred workers' compensation (severance pay). These incentives increase the present discounted value of retirement income; whether they induce young people to

Table 5.9 **Income Sources of Households with Retired Head (thousand 1987 lire)**

Age Group	% of Households	Social Security	Labor Income	Income from Financial Wealth	Other Income from Capital	Imputed Income from Housing	Total
≤40	1.1	5,629	13,243	246	197	2,637	23,941
		(25.6)	(60.3)	(1.1)	(0.9)	(12.1)	(100.0)
41–50	2.3	7,698	12,715	624	622	1,843	23,502
		(32.8)	(54.1)	(2.7)	(2.6)	(7.8)	(100.0)
51–55	4.5	9,653	11,441	1,308	881	2,082	25,365
		(38.1)	(45.1)	(5.2)	(3.5)	(8.2)	(100.0)
56–60	11.9	11,104	8,669	1,019	674	2,310	23,776
		(46.7)	(36.5)	(4.3)	(2.8)	(9.7)	(100.0)
61–65	19.3	12,034	5,089	998	1,021	2,310	21,452
		(56.1)	(23.7)	(4.6)	(4.7)	(10.8)	(100.0)
66–70	22.4	12,358	5,750	848	1,478	2,177	22,611
		(54.7)	(25.4)	(3.8)	(6.5)	(9.6)	(100.0)
71–75	16.6	10,818	3,104	820	1,314	2,006	18,062
		(59.9)	(17.2)	(4.5)	(7.3)	(11.1)	(100.0)
>75	22.0	10,030	1,829	444	1,000	1,497	14,800
		(67.8)	(12.4)	(3.0)	(6.8)	(10.1)	(100.0)
All retirees	100.0	11,088	5,172	814	1,102	1,992	20,168
		(55.0)	(25.6)	(4.0)	(5.5)	(9.9)	(100.0)

Source: Cannari and Franco (1990, table 7).
Note: The numbers in parentheses are percentages of total income in each age group.

sory contributions to farmers and the self-employed, and supplemented the system with unfunded social security benefits. However, one key principle of funded systems was retained: pension benefits were still proportional to contributions. Thus, between 1952 and 1968, the social security system was partly unfunded.

The link between contributions and benefits was severed in 1969, with three major innovations. First, benefits were made proportional to the number of years of contributions and to average earnings over the three years preceding retirement. Second, the system became entirely pay-as-you-go: anyone more than 65 years old was entitled to a "social pension," irrespective of contributions during working life. Third, the maximum pension rose to 80 percent of the last salary, and benefits were indexed to the cost of living.

The seventies witnessed a series of reforms relaxing the eligibility criteria. This led to rapid growth in social security benefits, from 7.5 percent of GDP in 1970 to 10.2 percent in 1980 and 13.9 percent in 1990. In 1975 the indexation system was changed: minimum pensions were indexed to the earnings of employed workers, leading to automatic increases in the real value of benefits. As the increase in contributions did not keep pace, the result was a growing social security deficit (Rossi and Visco 1994).

Currently, the eligibility requirements for pension benefits are: making contributions for 35 years or making contributions for a minimum of 15 years and being over age 55 for women and age 60 for men. For all private sector employees, yearly benefits are determined by $0.02nS$, where n is the number of years of contributions (maximum 40) S is average yearly salary over the 5 years before retirement, adjusted for the increase in the cost of living, and 0.02 represents the yearly accrual rate.[7] In 1988, there was a maximum pension of 33.5 million lire after 40 years of contributions, corresponding to a yearly salary of 41.9 million lire. In 1989 the maximum pension was increased by 1.5 percent for earnings between 41.9 and 55.6 million lire, 1.25 percent between 55.7 and 69.5 million, and 1 percent above 64.5 million lire. In 1990 the social pension, or old-age benefit to poor people over 50 years of age without contributions, was 6 million lire.

The degree of indexation of retirement benefits is inversely related to their amount. Pensions up to twice the minimum are fully indexed to the cost of living. Indexation falls to 90 percent for pensions between 2 and 3 times the minimum, and to 75 percent for pensions over 3 times the minimum. Social security contributions equal 25.15 percent of gross salary, 7.15 percent being contributed by the employee and 18 percent by the employer. Benefits are taxed at the general progressive income tax rate.

---

save less or more for retirement is not clear, because this depends on the relative strength of income and substitution effects.

7. For public employees, S is equal to the last yearly salary.

This brief account highlights the particularly high benefits and broad eligibility criteria of the Italian social security system. In most other OECD countries, social security benefits are lower, either because they are unrelated to earnings history, or because only a fraction of the benefits is so related, as in the United Kingdom. And where benefits are proportional to past salaries, eligibility requirements and pension award formulas are less generous than in Italy: (i) minimum retirement age is higher, (ii) pension benefits are not computed on the basis of the last five years' earnings but on the basis of the last 10 (France) or the entire career (Germany and Belgium), (iii) the accrual rate ranges from 1.33 percent in Belgium to 1.9 percent in Austria, compared to 2 percent in Italy, (iv) the maximum pension as a fraction of salary is lower everywhere, except Germany, (v) benefits are indexed to the prices, rather than to salaries as in Italy, and (vi) the rules concerning double pensions and benefits paid to survivors are stricter than in Italy.

As a result of these differences, in 1985 the ratio of social security benefits to the yearly salary of men with 40 years of contributions was 80 percent in Italy, compared to 60 percent in Germany, 55 percent in Belgium, 50 percent in France, and 25 percent in the United Kingdom (CREL 1990, 62).

The increasing generosity of Italian eligibility rules and award formulas is indicated by the rise in the ratio of the average retirement pension to the average salary from 26 percent in 1960 to 44 percent in 1987. According to macroeconomic evidence reported by Rossi and Visco (1994), the increased benefits paid by the social security system have been perceived by Italian households as an increase in social security wealth and have been a key determinant of the reduction in the private saving rate.

However, this very increase in benefits and the rapid aging of the Italian population may foster the perception that the current system cannot be sustained indefinitely. If so, perceived social security wealth is lower than the present discounted value of the net benefits implied by the rules of the current regime (Castellino 1986). Evidence of this is provided by Brugiavini (1987), who computes a measure of social security wealth using the 1984 Survey of Household Income and Wealth and finds that pension wealth is only a very imperfect substitute for private net worth. She suggests that increased pension benefit coverage may have had only a small impact on saving because people anticipate an increase in future contributions or a decrease in pension benefits.

In fact, the unsustainability of current social security arrangements is recognized by a number of studies. Franco et al. (1994) apply the method of generational accounting proposed by Auerbach, Gokhale, and Kotlikoff (1991) to the Italian case. This method measures how much present generations are expected to pay on net to the government over their remaining lifetimes. The social security system is found to be a critical factor in the huge generational imbalance of Italian fiscal policy, an imbalance that is unsustainable under the current fiscal regime. The National Institute for Social Security (INPS 1991) projects that the equilibrium social security tax rate (the ratio of total pension benefits to total income subject to pension contribution) will rise from 39.5 percent in 1990 to 45 percent in 2010. Similarly, the State Accounting Office (Ragioneria Generale dello Stato 1991) estimates this rate at 48 percent in 2010 and 57 percent in 2025.

These alarming figures indicate the urgency of reform: current proposals contemplate raising the retirement age by five years for both men and women, reducing benefits (especially maximum pensions), and increasing contributions.

5.3.2   Private Pension Funds

In contrast with the universal coverage of the social security system, private pension funds in Italy have always been minuscule, despite extremely favorable tax treatment. People are not allowed to join a pension fund as individuals. Participation in a private pension fund is possible only by explicit contractual arrangement between a group of workers or a union and a firm or group of firms. All the major Italian pension funds are defined-contribution rather than defined-benefit plans.

Guerra (1991) reports that in 1990 there were about 300 private pension funds, mainly serving employees of insurance companies and banks. In recent years pension funds have been set up also by some large corporations, such as IBM, ENI, Olivetti, Montedison, and FIAT. As was shown in table 5.3, the total outstanding value of pension funds was 40 trillion lire in 1988, or 4.5 percent of GDP. These funds serve about 400,000 workers, only 2 percent of the employed workers, by far the smallest proportion in any major OECD country (CREL 1990).

Workers' and employers' contributions to private pensions are fully tax-deductible, regardless of amount. Taxes are levied when the pension is cashed, either as an annuity or as a lump sum payment. In the former case, only 60 percent of the pension is considered part of the recipient's taxable income for income tax purposes. In the latter case, the lump sum payment is subject to separate taxation, like severance pay (see below). Since 1988 the tax base has been the difference between the lump sum payment and the sum of the worker's contributions, up to contributions of 4 percent of yearly earnings.

Pension funds are allowed to set their own rules on investment policy, the age at which benefits are payable, and treatment of withdrawal, death of the employee, layoff, and resignation. In most cases the portfolio of pension funds is formed by securities and real estate. Early withdrawal is generally possible, though sometimes is penalized. A study by Piatti (1990) indicates that Italian pension funds suffer from several limitations as savings instruments: (i) disparities among statutory regulations, (ii) nontransparency of investment policies, partly due to their defined-contribution nature, (iii) variable tax treatment of their capital income, depending on their legal nature and on their investment policy.

5.3.3   Severance Pay

Severance pay is a far larger component of household lifetime income in Italy than in most other countries. The size of the fund that firms accumulate to face their severance pay liabilities can be inferred from national account flow data on allocations and withdrawals. Castellino (1973) estimated the value of this fund at the end of 1972 in the range of 6.5 to 9.5 trillion lire, i.e., between 8.1 and 11.9 percent of GDP. As was shown in table 5.3, in 1988 it amounted to 115 trillion lire, 10.5 percent of GDP.

Initially, severance pay was intended to insure the employee against the risk of dismissal, but it gradually evolved into a form of deferred compensation, irrespective of the cause of termination of employment: the employee is entitled to it whether he retires, is laid off, or quits.

By law, the employer must pay a fraction of the wage bill into a fund, from which employees cannot draw until the termination of their employment (with exceptions noted below). Since 1982, severance pay has been computed as 7.4 percent of gross yearly salary for each year worked.[8] Severance pay is indexed and increases each year by $0.015 + 0.75\,\pi$, where π is the rate of change of the consumer price index. This implies that the worker's real return on the fund is negative for inflation rates above 6 percent, which has been the case in Italy since the law has been in force, except for 1986–88. Until 1982 the severance pay of each worker was effectively indexed to the rate of change of his nominal wage, so as to guarantee a positive real return.

Severance pay is rather illiquid and can be regarded as an example of forced saving in favor of firms. Workers can use part of their severance pay only for exceptional medical expenses or for the purchase of a first dwelling (i.e., the first house ever bought in the city of residence). Withdrawal is allowed only once during the employment contract, and only for a small fraction of each company's work force at any given time.

Severance pay enjoys a double tax advantage. First, there is a deduction from the tax base, which is determined by $P - nA$, where P is severance pay, n is the number of years of employment, and A is a constant allowance (equal to 500,000 lire in 1988). Second, the tax rate is substantially lower than the corresponding personal income tax rate would be: namely, it is the average tax rate corresponding to an income of $12P/n$. For workers with sufficiently high seniority, this is lower than their general income tax rate.

5.4   Life Insurance

Italian households hold very little wealth in the form of life insurance policies: until 1985 life insurance premiums hovered around 0.3 percent of GDP, a proportion which doubled in the late eighties, following a partial deregulation

8. Before 1982 this percentage was different for different sectors and occupations.

of the insurance market and the introduction of tax incentives. Nevertheless, at the end of 1987, Italy ranked twenty-third in the market for life insurance among OECD countries. Of the two forms of contracts—annuities and life insurance—the former is virtually nonexistent.

The number of pure annuity contracts ranged between 6,000 and 10,000 in the eighties (0.1 percent of the population over age 65), one-twentieth of the figure in the United States, where 2 percent of the elderly hold annuities (Friedman and Warshawsky 1990). Fornero (1986) suggests that the rarity of pure annuities is explained by the absence of tax incentives. Life insurance contracts are more popular. In 1988 they numbered 800,000. The corresponding reserves of the insurance companies were 24.7 trillion lire in 1988, 1.7 percent of GDP (see table 5.3).

Despite the partial liberalization of 1986, regulation in the life insurance industry remains pervasive. Guiso et al. (1994) report that three main factors still severely limit competition. First, new entrants must be licensed by the Ministry of Industry. Until 1986 authorization was on a totally discretionary basis, and in practice no new life insurance company was licensed between World War II and 1985. In 1986 licensing was made nondiscretionary: it is sufficient for applicants to satisfy a number of requisites, such as specified financial ratios.

Second, life insurance companies are required to turn over to INA, a public company, 30 percent of their premium income for the first five years, 20 percent for the following five years, and 10 percent thereafter,[9] obviously a powerful deterrent to potential entrants.

Third, minimum premiums for life insurance are set each year by the Ministry of Industry. The actual premiums are the sum of three components: a fair premium, a spread to compensate the insurance company, and a commission to agents. The first two are set by the central authority and the third by the insurance agents themselves. If a company sold insurance at a price below that set by the regulating agency, its license could be revoked. In 1990 the excess of actual premiums over fair premiums for standard life insurance policies ranged from 18 to 20 percent.

The returns on life insurance contracts were consistently negative until the mid-eighties. Contracts provided no protection at all against inflation until 1973. Starting in 1974 the yield on life insurance was adjusted at a fixed rate (3.5–4 percent). With inflation at 20 percent, returns were abysmally negative throughout the seventies and early eighties. From 1974 to 1983 very few individuals signed new life insurance contracts, and those bound by old ones suffered great losses: in the early eighties the life insurance market was near collapse. The response of insurance companies was to offer indexed contracts,

---

9. Before 1985, the rule was even more severe. Insurers were required to turn over to INA 40 percent of their premiums for the first 10 years of operation, 30 percent for the following 10 years, 20 percent for the next 20 years, and 10 percent thereafter.

with yields partially indexed to nominal interest rates: 80 percent of the premium has the same return as the portfolio of the insurance company. After 1984, the real rate of return on life insurance contracts became positive, comparable to that on Italian public debt.

Since 1986 the tax code has allowed a deduction from the policyholder's general income tax base of premium payments (P) up to 2.5 million lire per year. To be eligible for this deduction, the insurance contract must last a minimum of five years and the individual must not borrow for the first five years of the contract. Insurance premiums are taxed at the time they are paid at the flat rate of 2.5 percent, and a proportional commission is charged on the premium. As a result, the net amount invested each year equals $P/(1 + f)$, where f is the sum of the tax rate on premiums and the commission rate charged by the insurance company.

If the taxpayer takes the option of being paid a lump sum at the expiration of the policy rather than an annuity, he pays taxes at the rate of 12.5 percent on the difference between this payment and the sum of premiums paid.[10] If one instead opts for an annuity, 60 percent of it is considered taxable income. In case of early withdrawal, the individual is entitled to the reimbursement of nominal contributions.

Because of the different tax treatment between annuities and lump sum payments, almost invariably life insurance contracts terminate with the client choosing to collect the capital, rather than convert it into a stream of yearly income payments. Thus the lump sum option is the only one we consider below.

In order to compare the return on tax-favored life insurance contracts with that provided by an alternative financial asset, we compute the return of a typical life insurance policy with the following features: (i) the premium is a constant nominal amount P, equal to (or less than) 2.5 million lire so that it is fully tax-deductible from IRPEF, and is paid for a number of years $T \geq 5$, and (ii) the net amount invested per year, $P/(1 + f)$, is rewarded at a rate that equals the after-tax rate of interest r paid by an alternative financial asset of the same maturity (e.g., government bonds).

Denoting by τ_c the tax rate on the difference between the lump sum payment and the cumulated premiums TP, and by τ_p the marginal personal income tax rate, the value of the policy in year T is given by:

$$
(1) \quad
\begin{aligned}
\frac{P}{1+f}\frac{1+r}{r}\left[(1+r)^T - 1\right] - \tau_c&\left\{\frac{P}{1+f}\frac{1+r}{r}\left[(1+r)^T - 1\right] - TP\right\} \\
+ \tau_p P \frac{1+r}{r}\left[(1+r)^T - 1\right] &= \\
P\frac{1+r}{r}\left[(1+r)^T - 1\right]\left(\frac{1-\tau_c}{1+f} + \tau_p\right) &+ \tau_c TP.
\end{aligned}
$$

---

10. The current tax treatment of insurance contracts is in some respects more favorable in the other major European countries. In the United Kingdom, Germany, and France both premiums

The expression above is the sum of three terms: the value of the lump sum collected in year T, the tax liability on the difference between the lump sum and the sum of premiums TP, and the tax saving due to the deductibility of premiums. Given that the present value of the cash invested in the policy is:

$$(2) \qquad P\frac{1+r}{r}\left[(1+r)^T - 1\right]\left(\frac{1}{1+r}\right)^T,$$

the "excess return" of the policy over the interest rate r is:

$$(3) \qquad \left(\frac{\text{future value of the policy}}{\text{present value of cash invested}}\right)^{1/T} - (1+r)$$

$$= \left\{\left[\left(\frac{1-\tau_c}{1+f} + \tau_p\right) + \frac{\tau_c T}{[(1+r)/r][(1+r)^T - 1]}\right]^{1/T} - 1\right\}(1+r).$$

Figure 5.2 shows the excess return of the policy under the assumption that the annual premium equals 2.5 million lire, that the insurance's commission is 7.75 percent of the premium—so that $f = 10.25$ percent—and that the after-tax rate of interest is 10.57 percent.[11] The excess return varies according to the taxpayer's marginal personal income tax rate and the duration of the policy. The figure shows that the excess return of the policy over the market interest rate is higher, the higher the marginal income tax rate and the shorter the duration of the policy. For very low income individuals the return is negative, because the commission and the tax on premiums actually outweigh the tax incentive. For a taxpayer whose marginal income tax rate is 33 percent, the standard five-year policy produces an excess return of 4.4 percent, while for individuals in the highest tax bracket the return above the market rate can be as high as 7.4 percent.

5.5 Conclusions

The Italian saving rate is high by international standards. This is often attributed to Italy's relatively high productivity growth and relatively severe liquidity constraints. A second feature of national saving in Italy is its variability. After increasing sharply in the fifties and sixties, the Italian national and private saving rates have declined markedly for two decades. Most explanations of this decline have focused on the slowdown in population and productivity growth after 1975, the role of increased government debt and of public transfers to households, and the transition from a funded to a pay-as-you-go social security system.

---

and capital are tax-exempt—capital only if the contract exceeds a minimum duration (10 years in the United Kingdom, 12 in Germany, and 6 in France).

11. The 7.75 percent value is the "typical" commission, while the 10.25 interest rate is that reported for 1991 by ISVAP, the government regulatory agency of insurance companies.

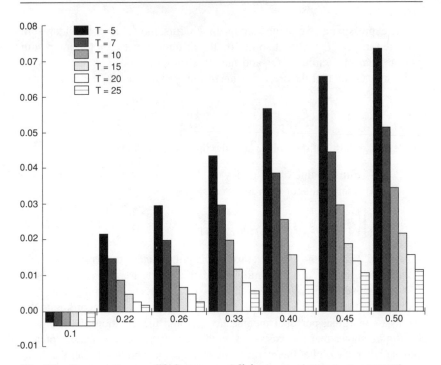

Fig. 5.2   Excess return on life insurance policies over return on government bonds, plotted by income tax rates and duration of insurance policy (T)

So far, no study has investigated whether changes in the tax code have contributed to changes in the household saving rate. Our analytical description of the Italian tax system suggests that the relatively high level of Italian saving may also be due to the favorable tax treatment of capital income and to the lack of incentives to borrow.

However, changes in the Italian tax code are unlikely to offer a satisfactory explanation for the decline in the Italian saving rate, since the tax reforms of the past two decades have been piecemeal and contradictory in this respect: the tax burden on capital income has increased, but new incentives for life insurance were enacted in the mid-eighties, and the deductibility of interest payments on mortgage loans was considerably restricted. One would expect these changes to have opposite effects on saving, and without more detailed empirical analysis one cannot assess their net impact. What does emerge, however, is that the new tax incentives have not prompted any substantial shift toward the favored assets. Few Italians have taken out life insurance policies, and very few have joined private pension funds. This is indirect evidence that the introduction of the new incentives has had a correspondingly minor impact on household saving.

It is easier to assess the impact of the dramatic changes in the Italian social security system, which has rapidly evolved from the funded to the pay-as-you-go model. Unless one subscribes to the dynastic view of Barro (1974), one would expect this to have contributed to the decline in the national saving rate in the seventies and eighties. Whether the generous social security benefits will continue to lower saving in the future is an open question, depending in part on the perceived sustainability of the current system and on expectations about the proposed reform plans.

Appendix
Summary of Taxes on Capital Income and Wealth and of Saving Incentives

1.   Taxation of Capital Income

Dividends and profits: top marginal tax rate 72 (1975–82), 65 (1983–85), 62 (1986–88), 50 percent (since 1989).

Interest income: flat rate

Bank and postal deposits: 15 (1970–75), 16 (1976), 18 (1978), 20 (1978–82), 21.6 (1982–83), 25 (1984–87), 30 percent (since 1988).

Postal savings: exempt until September 1986, 6.25 (1986), 12.5 percent (since 1987).

Certificates of deposit:

Less than 18 months: as bank deposits until 1988, 25 percent afterwards.

More than 18 months: 10 (1970–82), 10.8 (1982–83), 12.5 percent (since 1984).

Government bills and bonds and bonds issued by government agencies: exempt until September 1986, 6.25 (1986), 12.5 percent (since 1987).

Private bonds issued by:

Special Credit Institutions: 10 (1970–82), 10.8 (1982–83), 12.5 percent (since 1984).

ENI, IRI, and financial enterprises: 20 (1974–82), 10.8 (1982–83), 12.5 percent (since 1984).

Nonfinancial enterprises: 30 (1974–75), 20 (1976–82), 10.8 (1982–83), 12.5 percent (since 1984).

Convertible bonds: 15 (1974–75), 10 (1976–82), 10.8 (1982–83), 12.5 percent (since 1984).

Foreign assets: 30 (1970–72), 53 (1973–83), 50 (1984), 44 (1985), 39 (1986), 30 percent (since 1987).

Investment funds: income is tax-exempt; capital tax rate 0.25 percent (0.10 if at least 55 percent of the fund is invested in equities).

2. Households' Liabilities

Home mortgages
Full deductibility of interest payments until 1976; from 1976, interest payments deductible up to 3 million lire (4 million after 1980); except for first-home buyers, deductibility was abolished in 1990.
Consumer credit
No tax deductibility of interest payments.

3. Taxation of wealth and capital gains

Net wealth tax: no wealth tax exists.
Taxes at death and on gifts: both estate and inheritance tax exist (see text).
Capital gains: virtually tax-exempt until 1990. From 1990 choice of two regimes: flat rate of 25 percent or flat rate on the value of the shares between 0.3 and 1.05 percent.

4. Pension and Life Insurance Provisions

Social security
Employer pension contributions: no tax on contributions, taxed when paid as income.
Private pension funds
Employer pension contributions: no tax on contributions.
Benefits: if paid as annuity, 60 percent is taxed at the general income tax rate; if paid as lump sum, difference between capital and contributions is taxed at 12.5 percent (if contributions are less than 4 percent of yearly gross wage).
Severance pay
Deduction from the tax base and tax rate below the corresponding income tax rate (in both cases the tax benefit increases with the number of years of employment).

5. Life Insurance

Eligibility: universal.
Tax deductible contribution: 2.5 million lire/year.
Benefits: if paid as annuity 60 percent is taxed at the general income tax rate; if paid as lump sum, difference between capital and the sum of premiums is taxed at 12.5 percent.
Withdrawal provisions: if withdrawn before 5 years, reimbursement of nominal premiums only.

Sources: Alworth and Castellucci (1993); Giraldi, Hamaui and Rossi (1991); OECD (1988); see text.

References

Alworth, Julian S., and Laura Castellucci. 1993. The taxation of income from capital in Italy (1980–90). In *Taxation and the cost of capital*, ed. Dale Jorgenson. Washington, D.C.: Brookings Institution.

Auerbach, Alan J., Jagadeesh Gokhale, and Laurence J. Kotlikoff. 1991. Generational accounts: A meaningful alternative to deficit accounting. In *Tax policy and the economy*, vol. 5, ed. David Bradford. Cambridge: MIT Press.

Banca d'Italia, IMI, INA. 1986. Crisi finanziaria del sistema pensionistico pubblico e alcune linee di intervento per un riassetto della previdenza pensionistica. Roma: Bank of Italy. Mimeograph.

Barro, Robert. 1974. Are government bonds net wealth? *Journal of Political Economy* 81:1095–117.

Brugiavini, Agar. 1987. Empirical evidence on wealth accumulation and the effects of pension wealth: An application to Italian cross-section data. Financial Markets Group, Discussion Paper no. 20. London: London School of Economics.

Cannari, Luigi, and Daniele Franco. 1990. Sistema pensionistico e distribuzione dei redditi. Temi di Discussione, no. 137. Roma: Bank of Italy.

Castellino, Onorato. 1973. Alcune valutazioni in tema di indennità di anzianità. *Moneta e Credito* 26 (September).

———. 1986. Il futuro del sistema pensionistico italiano. *Rivista di Politica Economica* 76:1163–85.

Centro di Ricerche Economia e Lavoro (CREL). 1990. La previdenza integrativa in Italia: analisi, tendenze e prospettive. Roma: CREL. Mimeograph.

Dean, A., M. Durand, J. Fallon, and P. Hoeller. 1990. Saving trends and behavior in OECD countries. *OECD Economic Studies*, no. 14 (Spring): 7–58.

Deaton, Angus. 1992. *Understanding consumption*. New York: Oxford University Press.

D'Alessio, Giovanni. 1990. Le indagini campionarie sulle società di leasing, di factoring e di credito al consumo. *Supplemento al Bollettino Statistico*, no. 1 (January).

EC Mortgage Federation. 1990. *Mortgage credit in the European Community*. Brussels: Artigraph SA.

Feldstein, Martin. 1974. Social security, induced retirement, and aggregate capital accumulation. *Journal of Political Economy* 82:905–26.

Fornero, Elsa. 1986. Teoria del ciclo vitale del risparmio e assicurazioni di rendita vitalizia: un'applicazione al caso italiano. *Giornale degli Economisti e Annali di Economia* 45: 341–61.

Franco, Daniele, Jagadeesh Gokhale, Luigi Guiso, Laurence J. Kotlikoff, and Nicola Sartor. 1994. Generational accounting. The case of Italy. In *Saving and the accumulation of wealth: Essays on household and government behavior*, ed. Albert Ando, Luigi Guiso, and Ignazio Visco. Cambridge: Cambridge University Press.

Friedman, Benjamin M., and Mark J. Warshawsky. 1990. The costs of annuities: Implications for saving behavior and bequests. *Quarterly Journal of Economics* 105:135–54.

Giannini, Silvia. 1989. *Imposte e finanziamento delle imprese*. Bologna: Il Mulino.

Giraldi, Claudio, Roni Hamaui, and Nicola Rossi. 1991. Vincoli istituzionali e differenziali di rendimento delle attività finanziarie. Discussion Paper no. 91–9. Milano: Banca Commerciale Italiana.

Guerra, Cecilia. 1991. *Imposte e mercati finanziari*. Bologna: Il Mulino.

Guiso, Luigi, Tullio Jappelli, and Daniele Terlizzese. 1994. Why is Italy's saving rate so high? In *Saving and the accumulation of wealth: Essays on Italian household and government behavior,* ed. Albert Ando, Luigi Guiso, and Ignazio Visco. Cambridge: Cambridge University Press.

Instituto Nazionale per la Previdenza Sociale (INPS). 1991. Il nuovo modello previsionale INPS per le pensioni—Caratteristiche generali e risultati di sintesi della proiezione al 2010 del Fondo Pensioni Lavoratori Dipendenti. Roma: INPS. Mimeograph.

Jappelli, Tullio, and Marco Pagano. 1989. Consumption and capital market imperfections: An international comparison. *American Economic Review* 79:1088–105.

———. 1994. Saving, growth and liquidity constraints. *Quarterly Journal of Economics.* In press.

Marrelli, Massimo. 1989. The economic analysis of tax evasion: Empirical aspects. In *Surveys in the economics of uncertainty,* ed. John Hey and Peter Lambert. Oxford: Basil Blackwell.

Organisation for Economic Cooperation and Development (OECD). 1988. *Taxation of net wealth, capital transfers and capital gains of individuals.* Paris: OECD.

Pagliano, Patrizia, and Nicola Rossi. 1992. Il risparmio nazionale, privato e pubblico: una ricostruzione dal 1951 al 1990. Temi di Discussione, no. 169. Roma: Bank of Italy.

Piatti, Laura. 1990. Gli impieghi previdenziali del risparmio in Italia. In *Formazione e impiego della ricchezza delle famiglie,* ed. Elsa Fornero and Onorato Castellino. Torino: Collana Giorgio Rota.

Ragioneria Generale dello Stato. 1991. Fondo Pensioni Lavoratori Dipendenti. Una proiezione al 2025. Roma: Istituto Poligrafico dello Stato.

Rossi, Nicola, and Ignazio Visco. 1994. Private saving and government deficit. In *Saving and the accumulation of wealth: Essays on Italian household and government behavior,* ed. Albert Ando, Luigi Guiso, and Ignazio Visco. Cambridge: Cambridge University Press.

Visco, Vincenzo. 1983. L'evasione dell'imposta sul reddito delle persone fisiche in Italia. In *La crisi dell'imposizione progressiva sul reddito,* ed. Emilio Gerelli and Rolando Valiani. Milano: Franco Angeli.

6   Public Policies and Household Saving in Japan

Takatoshi Ito and Yukinobu Kitamura

6.1 Introduction

Many papers have been written on the issue of "high" Japanese household savings relative to other OECD countries, though some controversy remains about exactly how high savings are (the statistical measurement problem) and why they are so high.

Hayashi (1986) wrote a seminal paper correcting some statistical differences between Japanese and U.S. government statistics. Hayashi, Ando, and Ferris (1988) further studied Japanese household savings using the National Survey of Family Income and Expenditure (NSFIE). Horioka (1990) wrote a survey on the issue from the viewpoint of different motives for saving, in which he considered more than 30 factors to explain Japanese saving behavior. Ito (1992, chap. 9) and Hayashi (1992) provided overviews of the issues.

Among various aspects of Japanese saving, considerable attention has been paid to saving by the Japanese elderly. From various surveys, it appears that they do not spend down their savings. They even appear to continue accumulating wealth, particularly housing wealth, throughout their retirement years. There are three issues involved. First, this "observation" may reflect a statistical problem. Many surveys are conducted on the basis of household heads, but many (poor) elderly are merged into the households of offspring. Thus, what we see in the elderly are biased samples. Second, the elderly may indeed save at a high rate to accumulate funds bequests or for sudden illness, of which

Takatoshi Ito is professor of economics at Hitotsubashi University, a visiting professor at Harvard University, and a research associate of the National Bureau of Economic Research. Yukinobu Kitamura is an economist at the Institute for Monetary and Economic Studies of the Bank of Japan and a research associate of Hitotsubashi University.

The authors are very grateful to Michiko Matsumoto and Miho Yamaguchi of the Bank of Japan for data collection and manuscript editing. They also thank Richard Beason of the University of Alberta and Martin Feldstein of Harvard University for helpful comments.

some are destined to become "accidental bequests." Third, most of the savings of retired people are in the form of housing, and have thus accumulated unrealized capital gains. It may be difficult to spend down home equity, since the capital market does not seem to offer perfect annuity contracts. In this paper, tax incentives, related to the elderly's portfolio choices, will be discussed in detail.

We will place special emphasis on an examination of the relationship between tax incentives and saving. In the 1980s, both Japan and the United States enacted tax reforms, though with opposite intents. A quite notable change in Japanese capital taxation was the elimination of *maruyu* accounts (except for the handicapped, the elderly, and other special groups) in April 1988. Interest income is now taxed at 20 percent. A degree of tax credit for mortgage (housing loan) interest payments has been enlarged in Japan, so that borrowing for housing is encouraged. In the United States, however, the tax deductibility of loan and mortgage payments has been severely limited by tax reforms in the 1980s. Interest payments on home mortgages, which used to be fully deductible (when itemized), are now deductible only when applied to a principal residence or a second house. Interest payments for consumer loans, which used to be fully deductible (when itemized), are now only partially deductible.

Apart from tax incentives, since the early Meiji era the Japanese government has engaged in a variety of activities designed to promote saving. The postal saving system, established in 1875, was one of the most important instruments used to cultivate the public's appreciation of savings. Since the Second World War, the Japanese government has continued to engage in saving-promotion activities, in part through the Saving Promotion Department of the Bank of Japan (established in 1946), the Central Council for Saving Promotion (established in 1952), and the Saving Promotion Center of the Ministry of Finance (established in 1957). More recently, however, these committees have shifted the emphasis from saving to sound household management, including the avoidance of personal bankruptcy. The impact of saving-promotion activities on household saving is difficult to measure, but it appears that such activities have been much more pervasive in Japan than in other countries.

This paper is organized as follows. Section 6.2 presents an overview of Japanese household saving, with discussions of frequently used data sets and statistical measurement problems. Section 6.3 presents a comprehensive survey of tax incentives for household saving. In particular, incentives before and after the tax reform of April 1988 are compared. Section 6.4 is devoted to a survey of household portfolio selection over time. In section 6.5, we discuss tax incentives affecting the behavior of the elderly, including incentives for bequests. Section 6.6 concludes the paper with a summary.

6.2 Overview of Household Saving

The Japanese household sector provides funds in the form of savings for investment in the corporate sector, the government sector, and foreign countries

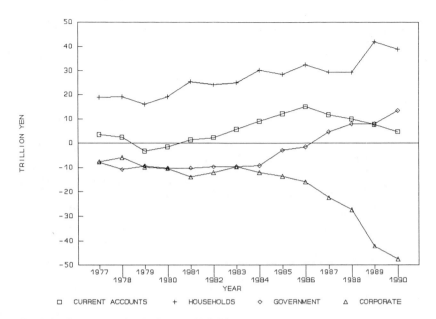

Fig. 6.1   Sectoral saving balance, 1977–90
Source: Economic Planning Agency, *Annual Report on National Accounts* (Tokyo, 1992).
Note: The sectoral balance is calculated as a saving surplus (i.e., saving minus investment) in the household, government, and corporate sectors. The current accounts absorb the domestic saving surplus.

(see fig. 6.1). Although the saving-investment identity does not imply any causal relationship, the following observations can be made: (1) high savings generally reduce the capital cost of investment, because they tend to make funds available to financial intermediaries at a lower interest rate; (2) high savings are likely to be accompanied by high investment; (3) high savings imply a tendency to run trade surpluses rather than deficits; and (4) high savings can finance government deficits without causing a high interest rate or borrowing from abroad.

This picture might lead one to criticize Japan's high savings as a cause of trade imbalance. The causal connection from excessive savings to trade imbalance, however, seems to be rather remote and seems to rely on various assumptions. In this paper, rather than debate whether savings cause trade imbalances, we will focus on household saving behavior itself—namely, on what factors determine household savings and how government policy influences the household saving decision.

In fact, the household sector faces three kinds of constraints. First, the macroeconomic environment determines income, inflation rate, current account balance, interest rate, and the like. Second, structural factors such as aging and financial market liberalization make the household sector adjust its behavioral pattern. Third, public policy, especially taxation, imposes a constraint on the household sector's budget. The household saving decision is formed by these

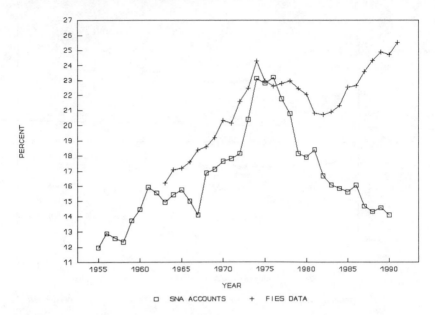

Fig. 6.2   Household saving rates in Japan (National Accounts and microdata), 1955–90
Sources: SNA accounts from Economic Planning Agency, *Annual Report on National Accounts* (Tokyo, various issues); FIES data from the FIES for various years.

environments, and no factor seems to play a dominant role. Bearing this in mind, researchers have to be careful to select a data set which matches their research agenda. A good example is in figure 6.2, which shows two series of the household saving rate in Japan. It is clear that the two series went in opposite directions in the 1980s. One could argue that the Japanese household saving rate was increasing over the 1980s if one uses the FIES data, but one would argue the opposite if one uses the *National Accounts* data. The divergence of the two data series has given rise to a recent research topic.[1]

It is well known that statistical adjustment for consumer durables makes the U.S.-Japan household saving rate gap much lower (see Hayashi 1986). If, however, savings are defined as the change in a stock of wealth, as argued by Bradford (1991), the U.S.-Japan household saving rate gap may have widened in the 1980s. In sum, the definition of savings and the statistical adjustment of it are crucial for policy analysis.

Table 6.1 presents a picture of the average household balance sheet. In general, Japanese households keep a high proportion of savings in time deposits,

---

1. The two statistics cover different samples—the FIES does not include one-person households and self-employed workers. The treatment of liabilities (mainly housing loans) is also different. However, a satisfactory explanation for such a large divergence is yet to be made.

Table 6.1   Composition of Household Net Worth (10,000 yen)

	1979		1984		1989	
	Mean	Median	Mean	Median	Mean	Median
Financial Assets	496	306	676	414	1,066	611
Demand deposit	57	30	53	25	72	33
Time deposit	237	120	328	172	455	224
Life insurance	86	54	128	80	242	150
Securities	99	0	140	0	257	0
Nonfinancial institutions	18	0	27	0	39	0
Liabilities	170	4	268	15	375	20
Housing loans (mortgages)	144	0	232	0	308	0
Others	26	0	36	0	66	0
Housing Assets	862	638	1,616	1,235	2,890	1,407

Source: NSFIE for 1979, 1984, and 1989.
Note: The data covers all households in Japan.

although the proportions of life insurance and securities have risen over the years. The same, but less obvious, trends can be observed in median households. The biggest difference between mean and median households lies in securities (mainly stocks). This implies that securities are distributed heavily among wealthy households. As to the balance between savings and liabilities, the mean household is more heavily in debt than the median household. In the case of the mean household, housing loans (mortgages) account for over 80 percent of total liabilities. In terms of numbers, those who have liabilities account for 54.2 percent of all households, and those with mortgages were 34.8 percent of the total in 1989.

Table 6.2 indicates the concentration of wealth among Japanese households. The general picture remains more or less the same, although the distribution worsens between 1984 and 1989. The reason for this is undoubtedly the boom in the stock and land markets in the late 1980s. Including real estate and durables in total wealth improves the distribution, as shown in column (ii) for 1989. This is probably because homeownership is widespread across households. The effect of the Nakasone-Takeshita tax reform (1988/89) can not be fully identified in the 1989 survey because it had been implemented too recently.

The following is a brief outline of data sources on household savings in Japan. To begin with macroeconomic data, aggregate time-series data is usually obtained from the *Annual Report on National Accounts*, which contains data on disposable income, so that the household saving rate can be calculated (and indeed it is given in the report). The *Flow of Funds Accounts* (Bank of Japan) give comprehensive data on financial flows among the different sectors and on financial stocks in each sector. Information on the composition of household portfolios is valuable.

For microeconomic data, the following four surveys from the Japanese gov-

Table 6.2   Concentration of Wealth

			1989	
Percentage of Wealth Owned by:	1979	1984	(i)	(ii)
Most wealthy 5 %	19	15	18	13
Most wealthy 10%	37	29	36	27
Most wealthy 25%	52	63	66	51
Most wealthy 50%	84	85	86	74

Source: NSFIE for 1979, 1984, and 1989.
Note: Figures for 1979, 1984, and 1989 (i) are financial wealth only. Figures for 1989 (ii) are total wealth, including real estate and durables.

ernment are the major ones. First, the Family Income and Expenditure Survey (FIES) aims at providing data on incomes and expenditures for all the nonagricultural households of two or more members and other related information. The FIES covers all consumer households in Japan except for those engaged in agriculture, forestry, or fishing, and except for one-person households. About 8,000 households are randomly selected for the survey out of about 26 million qualified households.

The Family Saving Survey (FSS; Statistics Bureau, Management and Coordination Agency) gives information on financial savings and liabilities of households, and their changes from the preceding year. The FSS tabulates the details of savings and liabilities with respect to various household characteristics, such as age cohort, income, number of household members, and geographic area. Stocks are evaluated at market value, and life insurance savings at the accumulated value of premium payments. The survey samples about 6,300 households, which have been sampled recently in the FIES. Since the sample households are a subsample of the FIES, single-member households and households in the business of agriculture, forestry, or fishing are excluded. A problem with this survey is that information on disposable income is not included so that the saving rate, in a conventional sense, cannot be calculated.

The National Survey of Family Income and Expenditure (NSFIE; Statistics Bureau, Management and Coordination Agency) is the most comprehensive survey of consumer behavior. It covers single-member households, agriculture, forestry, and fishery households, as well as other types of households, and its sample size is as large as 59,000. Households are categorized by age and occupation of household head and by type of household (a couple only, a couple and a child, a parent and a child, etc.). With respect to consumer durables, the survey asks the date of purchase of the goods and whether they were bought as a replacement or as an addition. With the 1989 survey, information on real estate (land and house) ownership was added.

The Comprehensive Survey of Living Conditions of the People on Health and Welfare (Ministry of Health and Welfare), begun in 1986, integrates four different surveys which had been conducted separately. One large survey, covering about 240,000 households, is scheduled to be conducted every three years. Smaller-scale surveys are conducted during the other two years. The large survey asks questions in three categories: households composition, health conditions, and income and savings. Income and savings (financial assets and housing conditions) questions are cross-tabulated along different household types, such as households with an elderly member (65 years or older). Information on housing is not included in this survey.

For a reference on the Japanese tax system written in English, the Tax Bureau, a branch of the Ministry of Finance, publishes an annual report on the Japanese tax system (*An Outline of Japanese Taxes*) and on the data (the *National Tax Office Yearbook*). Ishi (1989) is an authoritative survey of the Japanese tax system, and OECD (1991b) provides detailed information on personal and corporate tax systems in OECD-member countries.

6.3   Tax Incentives for Household Asset Accumulations

In Japan, tax incentives for household savings have gone through dramatic changes since the mid-1980s. Until April 1988, financial savings in the form of bank deposits and postal savings were essentially tax-exempt, and capital gains from stocks were also tax-exempt, provided the amounts were less than a certain limit that was considerably higher than the savings balance of an average citizen. The Nakasone-Takeshita tax reform changed many of these tax exemptions for savings. Details of these incentives, before and after, will be explained below.

6.3.1   Tax-exempt Savings before April 1988

Maruyu Accounts

A salient feature of the Japanese financial taxation system prior to 1988 was the prevalence of tax-exempt interest income from what were commonly known as *maruyu* accounts, and by other similar names. Interest income from those accounts, in which principal was beneath a ceiling and registered as such, were exempted from tax. Some kind of tax-exemption system for interest income can be traced back to 1920, but the modern system of tax exemption started in 1963 and was effectively abolished in 1988. At the time of the 1988 revision, interest income from the following assets, up to the specified principal amount, was tax-exempt.[2]

Interest income from a combined principal amount of up to 3 million yen,

---

2. Note that there had been several revisions of the maximum limits on tax-exempt savings. Limits for *maruyu* and *yucho* in 1963 were both 0.5 million yen and were both raised to 1 million yen in 1965. Special *maruyu* were introduced in 1968 with a limit of 0.5 million yen. In 1972, *maruyu* and *yucho* limits were raised to 1.5 million yen, while special *maruyu* limits were raised to 1 million yen. Also in 1972, *zaikei* were introduced with a limit of 1 million yen. In 1973, the *zaikei* limit was raised to 5 million yen and that for *yucho* to 3 million yen. In 1974, both *maruyu* and special *maruyu* limits were raised to 3 million yen. For the definitions of *maruyu*, *yucho*, special *maruyu*, and *zaikei*, see the text below.

in the form of bank deposits, securities, or mutual funds was tax-exempt. Each account that qualified for tax exemption must have been registered as such, with a specified ceiling amount, at the local branch of the tax revenue office. The system was known as *maruyu*. The *maruyu* accounts could be bank deposits, deposit accounts for employees within a company (*shanai yokin*), mutual trust funds (*kinsen shintaku, kashitsuke shintaku*) at trust banks, bonds (government bonds, municipal bonds, government guarantee bonds, corporate bonds, and yen-denominated bonds issues abroad, within five years of issuance), bank debentures (*kinyu sai*), bond mutual funds, and stock mutual funds (with a ratio of stocks in portfolio under 70 percent).

All interest income from postal savings (*yucho*) was tax-exempt. The principal in a postal savings account could not exceed 3 million yen per person. Hence, the ceiling for tax-exempt postal saving was 3 million yen. The most popular postal savings accounts were indefinite-maturity saving deposits (*teigaku yokin*), in which interest compounds up to 10 years, with increasing interest rate schedules over the years.

Government bonds and municipal bonds up to 3 million yen (face value), in addition to any bonds in *maruyu* accounts, could be registered as "special *maruyu*" accounts and yield tax-exempt interest income.

Interest income from housing (*jutaku*) *zaikei* accounts and pension (*nenkin*) *zaikei* accounts was tax free.[3] To qualify for tax exemption, the account holder had to be an employee under age 54, and monthly installments (deposits) had to be withheld at source and automatically transferred to the account at a financial institution. *Zaikei* accounts could be held as savings-type life insurance, as well as time deposits and other types of deposits in banks, mutual trust funds, and bonds. They had to be accumulated for more than 3 years, and pension *zaikei* accounts for 5 years. The combined principal of *zaikei* accounts could be up to 5 million yen. Housing *zaikei* accounts could be withdrawn only to purchase or improve housing (land, structure, or renovation), and pension *zaikei* could be withdrawn only after the saver reached age 55. The saver of these accounts also had access to preferential (housing) loans.

In addition to these accounts, postal installment savings (*juutaku tsumitate* postal savings) earmarked for housing, up to 500,000 yen, were tax-exempt. Interest income from savings for tax payment (tax payment preparation accounts) was also tax-exempt, as long as it was used for the said purpose.

In sum, the maximum amount of principal which could yield tax-exempt interest income (excluding the tax payment preparation account) can be tabulated as follows:

Bank deposits, bonds, and mutual funds
(*maruyu*)   3 million yen

---

3. *Zaikei*, an abbreviation for *kinrosha zaisan-keisei chochiku*, literally means employee property-formation savings.

Postal savings (*yucho*)	3 million yen
Government and municipal bonds (special *maruyu*)	3 million yen
Housing and pension savings (*zaikei*)	5 million yen
Earmarked savings for housing purchases (postal *zaikei*)	0.5 million yen
Total	14.5 million yen

All together, each individual in Japan was eligible for tax exemption on interest from savings of up to 14.5 million yen, which was far above average household savings. Moreover, a family of four could take advantage of four times of this limit using different family members' names for accounts and, if all were employees, qualifying for *zaikei*. Such use of different names did not prompt gift taxation. (Note that nonemployees could not take advantage of *zaikei* accounts.)

The Bank of Japan estimated that from 1973 to 1988, on average, 54.9 percent of household savings qualified for tax exemption. Table 6.3 shows that in 1988, assets of nearly 300 trillion yen, equal to half of all household savings, were tax-exempt. Since the maximum amount of exempt savings (14.5 million yen) far exceeded average household savings (6.8 million yen for all households in 1984), in practice, the interest earned on virtually all savings held by average (middle-income) savers was tax-exempt. Moreover, it was suspected that many wealthy savers evaded taxation by circumventing the limits on principal in tax-exempt accounts. Since there was no system of individual identification numbers (such as Social Security numbers in United States), it was relatively easy to open several accounts in different regions, each account under the limit, without being detected by the tax authority.[4] During the period between July 1985 and June 1986, the Tax Bureau estimated that over 12 trillion yen of household savings, held mainly by large-lot savers, were evading taxation by being kept accounts opened using fictitious names or the names of different family members (*Nihon Keizai Shinbun* [daily], October 5, 1986). The Tax Bureau took the view that the actual magnitude of tax evasion might have been larger than this estimate because the bureau did not examine postal savings, which comprised one-third of tax-exempt savings.

Individual utilization of tax incentives in the system of tax exemption is estimated in table 6.4. The results show that *maruyu* were the most popular form of tax-exempt accounts and that *yucho* (postal savings) came next. Special *maruyu* and *zaikei* were used by only a very small fraction. This was partly because exemptions for these accounts required certain application procedures, while *maruyu* and *yucho* qualified for exemption quite easily.

4. It was widely speculated that bank deposits and postal savings with false (phantom) names—names of those who had no assets—were not detected. Moreover, accounts opened by the same person but in different regions, i.e., tax districts, each account under the ceiling amount, tended to evade detection, because no national I.D. number for savers was used.

Table 6.3   Share of Tax-exempt Savings in Total Household Savings

Year	Tax-exempt Savings (billion yen)	Share of Tax-exempt Savings in Total Household Savings (%)
1973	38,946	43.1
1974	48,501	44.9
1975	64,699	50.3
1976	81,308	52.7
1977	98,629	54.7
1978	116,364	55.4
1979	136,547	56.5
1980	155,409	56.7
1981	179,892	58.5
1982	202,080	58.9
1983	225,906	59.4
1984	245,094	58.4
1985	268,113	61.3
1986	286,621	59.9
1987	294,537	55.9
1988	297,955	51.2
Average		54.9

Source: Bank of Japan, Economic Statistics Annual (Tokyo, 1988).

Table 6.4   Utilization Ratios for Tax-exempt Accounts in Household Savings (%)

Year	Maruyu	Special Maruyu	Zaikei	Yucho
1973	16.10	0.24	0.10	7.51
1974	19.65	0.31	0.07	4.63
1975	13.23	0.12	0.17	5.79
1976	16.27	0.22	0.30	7.24
1977	19.06	0.45	0.48	8.91
1978	21.54	0.66	0.72	10.92
1979	24.68	0.84	0.99	12.92
1980	27.28	1.20	1.28	14.78
1981	30.48	1.65	1.57	17.52
1982	33.67	2.07	1.91	19.54
1983	37.05	2.41	2.30	21.79
1984	39.32	2.66	2.65	23.92
1985	42.73	2.86	3.03	25.90
1986	44.69	2.93	3.48	28.22
1987	44.77	2.40	3.92	30.10
1988	44.01	1.95	3.92	31.87

Source: Bank of Japan database.
Note: Utilization ratio is calculated by actual amounts divided by legally eligible amounts.

Taxation on Dividends and Capital Gains from Stocks

Capital gains from stocks were tax-exempt prior to 1988. Small-lot dividends, that is less than 50,000 yen per semiannual payment, or 100,000 yen per annual payment, were taxed at 20 percent at source, separately from income from other sources (such as wages and salaries). For large-lot dividends (those other than small-lot dividends), the stockholder could elect either (1) to be subject to 20 percent withholding tax and later be taxed as a part of total taxable income for income taxation or (2) to be subject to 35 percent separate taxation at the time of dividend payment ("separate" means that the dividend is not to be aggregated with income from other sources for the purpose of income taxation).[5]

Taxation on Savings Other than Maruyu

Interest income from accounts other than *maruyu* were subject to taxation. Ordinary deposits, typically demand deposits in Japan, were subject to 20 percent separate taxation. For interest income from time deposits, mutual trust funds, and bonds and dividends from mutual funds, the saver could elect either (1) to be subject to 20 percent withholding tax and later be taxed as a part of total taxable income for income taxation or (2) to be subject to 35 percent separate taxation at the time of dividend payment, but not subject to income taxation. Discount income from discount bonds was taxed separately at 16 percent.

Income Deduction for Insurance Premium Payments

Some parts of premiums for social insurance, life insurance, and individual pension-type insurance could be income tax–deductible. Details will be explained in section 6.3.2.

"Green Card" Fiasco

As a part of tax reform intended to enhance revenues, the government proposed the introduction of value-added tax, called sales tax, in December 1978. However, public criticism mounted and demanded the closing of loopholes, including tax evasion using *maruyu* accounts and other provisions for interest income tax exemption. After intense debate, it was decided in the tax reform of 1980 that a "green card" would be introduced in January 1984 to identify all small-lot savers. According to the plan, one green card per person would be issued to prevent false accounts and other misuses of the system.

Strong opposition to green cards arose in 1981 and 1982 and resulted in the deferral of their introduction—originally scheduled for January 1984—to 1987. Then in 1985, the green card plan was abandoned altogether.

---

5. Those subject to a marginal income tax rate over 35 percent would elect to have dividends taxed at 35 percent separation taxation at source.

Table 6.5   **Summary of the Statutory Average/Top Tax Rates**

	1980	1985	1990	1992
Interest (non-*maruyu*)	20.0/35.0	20.0/35.0	20.0/20.0	20.0/20.0
Dividends	35.0/35.0	35.0/35.0	20.0/35.0	20.0/35.0
Capital gains from stocks	0.0/0.0	0.0/0.0	20.0/26.0	20.0/26.0

Source: Tax Bureau (various issues, b).

Interest income would be taxed via "separate taxation" (separate from income from other sources). In the process of the Nakasone-Takeshita tax reform (1988/89), not necessarily to combat large-scale tax evasion, but more fundamentally to achieve consistency and equality in the tax system, the system of tax exemption of interest income from household savings was effectively (although not completely) abolished in April 1988. The new system is a flat 20 percent tax—withheld at source, separately from income from other sources—on all interest income. A historical summary of the system of capital income taxation, including tax rates on dividends and capital gains, is given in table 6.5.

6.3.2   Taxation on Financial Savings in 1992

Many types of capital income in Japan are separately taxed—that is, not combined with other types of income, such as wages and salaries, and taxed at a flat rate at source, collected at the time of payment. This is withholding, but when taxes are filed on other income, capital income and taxes withheld at source are not reported (i.e., after collection of the 20 percent tax, individual names and other information are not reported by banks to the tax authority, and individuals are not asked about interest income at the time of tax filing). In the following, "taxed separately" should be interpreted as this practice. The system of capital income taxation now in effect (i.e., as of April 1, 1988) can be summarized as follows.

Interest Income

Interest income is taxed separately, at a flat 20 percent (15 percent national tax and 5 percent local tax). Note that this is still an incentive to save for those who are in a higher income-tax bracket (higher than 20 percent). In addition, some *maruyu* (tax-exempt savings) remain for the elderly (age 65 and over), widows (and widowers), the handicapped, and working students in special programs: these allow 3 million yen in bank deposits, securities, and mutual funds; another 3 million yen in postal savings; and 3 million yen in government and municipal bonds. Finally, there exist other tax-exempt financial instruments, available to all, including "employee's housing-formation saving account" (*jutaku zaikei*) and "employee's pension endowment–formation saving account" (*nenkin zaikei*). Interest income for these accounts is tax-exempt, up to a capital limit of 5 million yen total.

Dividends

The tax system for dividends to resident individuals varies with the size of the dividend:

Less than 50,000 yen. If the size of a semiannual dividend from holdings in one company is less than 50,000 yen (or an annual dividend of 100,000 yen), then a flat 20 percent tax is imposed, taxed separately at source (just as for interest income). This rule applies to holdings in *each* company. No individual tax filing is necessary, and no local "inhabitants" tax is imposed.[6]

Between 50,000 and 250,000 yen. If the size of a semiannual dividend from holdings in one company is more than 50,000 yen but less than 250,000 yen (or an annual dividend of 500,000 yen), then a taxpayer may elect one of the following:
1. A 35 percent tax, separately taxed at source. However, local inhabitants tax must be paid on total income (the aggregate of dividends and other income);
2. A 20 percent withholding tax, plus tax on total income at the time of tax filing. There is income deduction for dividend income when it is elected as tax filing with combined (total) income. At the time of tax filing, tax credit will be given. The tax credit is 10 percent of dividends for those with taxable income of 10 million yen or less, or 5 percent of dividends for the amount exceeding 10 million yen.[7] Local inhabitant's tax is also imposed.

More than 250,000 yen. If the size of a semiannual dividend from holdings in one company is more than 250,000 yen (or an annual dividend of 500,000 yen from one company), or if the dividend is from stock that constitutes more than 5 percent of issued stocks, then option (2), described for dividends between 50,000 and 250,000 yen, should be applied. Local inhabitant's tax is also imposed.

Note that an individual in a higher tax bracket will have an incentive to diversify his portfolio so that each dividend payment from any one company is less than 50,000 yen and so can avoid being reported at the time of tax filing. Also, dividend *rates* are much lower in Japan. The dividend/price ratio is about 1 percent. Therefore, in order to earn 100,000 yen as dividends, 10 million yen must be invested in one company. Finally, dividends in securities income trusts are taxed at 20 percent (15 percent national income tax and 5 percent inhabitant's tax), separately.

---

6. Inhabitant's tax is part of local (prefecture and municipal) tax. Local tax includes property tax, special land-holding tax, and real property acquisition tax, among others.

7. The personal and corporate income tax systems are not fully integrated. A partial shareholder relief scheme exists—that is, if income other than dividends is less than 10 million yen, but combined income of dividends and other income exceeds 10 million yen, then the 10 percent tax credit applies to part of dividends (10 million minus other income) and the 5 percent tax credit to the rest.

Capital Gains from Stocks

A taxpayer may elect one of the following treatments for capital gains from stocks:

1. Tax equals 1 percent of sales value (that is 20 percent capital gains tax on deemed capital gains of 5 percent), applicable to listed and over-the-counter stocks, separately taxed at the time of sales. No reporting at the time of tax filing is required.

2. Income tax of 20 percent and local inhabitant's tax of 6 percent on capital gains from all stock sales. If this option is elected, it is payable at the time of tax filing, but separately from taxes on other types of income.

Note that if capital losses are realized, option (2) should be chosen. Moreover, gains may be canceled against the loss. These options can be switched at any time during the year.

Real Estate Capital Gains

Capital gains from real estate will be treated separately in section 6.3.3.

Social Security Pensions

The social security pension program can be regarded as forced savings by the government for individuals. From a theoretical point of view (the life-cycle model to be explained later), there is no difference between social security benefits and individual savings toward retirement. With respect to social security, the following tax treatment is applicable:

1. Social security contributions (health insurance and others) are fully deductible from income.

2. Social security benefits (pension income) have special deductions: (i) a lump sum deduction of 1 million yen for persons age 65 and over (or 0.5 million yen for persons under age 65) is applied; (ii) after the 1 million yen deduction, the following deduction is applied: 25 percent of the first 3.6 million yen, 15 percent of the portion from 3.6 to 7.2 million yen, and 5 percent of the portion beyond 7.2 million yen (minimum guaranteed amount from deductions (i) and (ii) is 1.4 million yen); (iii) on top of these deductions, the elderly deduction of 500,000 is applicable.[8]

3. A special type of individual retirement (pension) account, called *kokumin nenkin kikin*, was introduced in April 1991 and became available only for nonemployees (between the ages of 20 and 59) and wives of nonemployees. Inter-

8. Before the September 1987 reform, social security benefits (pension income) were regarded as part of salary, and standard deductions for salaries were applicable. To replace these standard deductions, the new deductions illustrated in (2) were introduced. Combining these deductions with other basic deductions (350,000 yen), the spouse deduction (350,000 yen), and the special spouse deduction (350,000 yen), an elderly pension-income earner with a spouse, receiving pension income of less than 4.5 million yen, is not taxed. Considering the current level of benefits, most pension earners (with no additional source of income) are not taxed (for details, see Takayama [1992, app. 4C.5 and table 4C.2 of chap. 4]).

est income from this pension account is tax-exempt, and its contribution, up to 68,000 yen per month per person, is tax-deductible.

Retirement (Severance) Pay

It has been the custom that a Japanese corporation pays lump sum retirement severance pay, which amounts to three to five times annual salary at the time of retirement. The steep age-earning profile of Japanese workers, coupled with the practice of lifetime employment, makes this a sizable income (see Ito 1992, chap. 8). Lump sum severance pay can be regarded as a deferred payment of salary, or as forced saving by a corporation for a worker. Given the steep progressivity of the Japanese income tax, retirement pay would be taxed heavily at the payment of a retirement lump sum. Thus, special deductions and separate taxation apply to severance pay: (i) Deduct the lump sum (400,000 yen times the number of years worked for the company [up to 20 years] plus 700,000 yen times the number of years worked for the company exceeding 20 years). (ii) After deduction (i), divide the remaining amount in half. Apply the income tax table to this amount. This is taxed separately from other types of income, such as salaries.

Life Insurance

Some types of life insurance are also a form of savings—in Japan, savings-type life insurance, such as universal insurance, is more popular than term insurance. In particular, single-premium life insurance, which is essentially a saving instrument with tax advantage, became popular in the 1980s.

Before the 1988 tax reform, single-premium endowment (life) insurance enjoyed the following tax benefits:

1. Life insurance premium payments of more than 100,000 yen entitled the payer to a 50,000 yen deduction from (combined) income.[9]

2. Life insurance repayment at the maturity of the contract is considered occasional income (*ichiji shotoku*), which has a 500,000 yen lump sum deductible, and the amount after the lump sum deduction is halved and combined with other income. Note, however, that an employee whose other income is less than 200,000 yen did not have to file taxes. Considering this tax advantage, coupled with high dividends and with regulated bank deposit interest rates, many consumers shifted savings from bank deposits to single-premium life insurance policies in the 1980s. This prompted the following change. *After* the 1988 tax reform, (1) is still valid, and (2) is only applicable to life insurance premiums on a contract exceeding 5 years. For single-premium insurance policies with 5 years or less of maturity, the dividends are taxed at 20 percent, just like interest income.

9. Life insurance premiums up to 25,000 yen are fully deductible, half the amount between 25,000 and 50,000 yen is deductible, and one-fourth of the amount between 50,000 and 100,000 yen is deductible. The maximum deduction of 50,000 yen is reached at a premium payment of 100,000 yen.

3. Individual "pension" insurance policy premiums can be deducted from income, up to 50,000 yen per annum.[10]

4. Non–life insurance (such as fire insurance) premium payments are deductible, to a maximum of 15,000 yen.[11]

6.3.3 Housing-related Tax Treatment

As will be explained later, housing is one of the most important investment (or saving) decisions of one's life. There are special provisions related to land and structures for housing.

Tax Credit for a Home Owner

A portion of a mortgage can be applied as a tax credit for six years according to the schedule below, provided the following requirements are met: (i) housing is newly acquired and is inhabited by the owner within six months of purchase, (ii) housing has floor space of 220 square meters or less, (iii) home owner's annual income does not exceed 20 million yen, (iv) a special treatment in the carry-over of capital gains is not taken. The tax credit = (a) {1 percent of the mortgage balance at the end of year, up to 20 million yen} + (b) {0.5 percent of the mortgage balance between 20 million and 30 million yen}.

Requirement (ii) was added in 1991. The income limit in requirement (iii) was lowered from 30 million yen to 20 million yen in 1991, in exchange for the change in additional tax credit, part (b). The time limit of tax credit applicability was extended from 5 to 6 years in 1990. In 1986 and 1987, in the calculation of tax credit, part (a), the balance of a public (subsidized) mortgage was halved.

The ways in which owner-occupied housing is encouraged in the United States and in Japan are different. In the United States, the mortgage interest payment is *fully deductible from income,* as long as itemized deduction is chosen (this provision has been in place for a long time). In Japan, a similar tax incentive is provided through a *tax credit,* for only six years. This tax credit

10. The schedule of deductions for individual pension insurance premiums is the same that for single-premium insurance policies explained in item (1) and n. 9.

11. Premium payments on a non–life insurance policy with more than ten-year maturity and with end-of-contract dividends are deductible according to the following schedule: (i) if premium is 10,000 yen, fully deductible, (ii) for premium payments between 10,000 and 20,000 yen, the deductible amount is 5,000 yen plus half of premium payments, and (iii) for premium payments of more than 20,000 yen, the deductible amount is 15,000 yen. Premium payments on a non–life insurance policy with less-than-ten-year maturity are deductible according to the following schedule: (i) if premium payments are less than 2,000 yen, fully deductible, (ii) for premium payments between 2,000 and 4,000 yen, the deductible amount is 1,000 yen plus half of premium payments, and (iii) for premium payments of more than 4,000 yen, the deductible amount is 3,000 yen. Long-term and short-term policy premium payments can be combined to reach a deductible amount but such a deduction cannot exceed 15,000 yen.

Saving-type non–life insurance with maturity repayment is classified as saving (not as consumption). However, saving-type insurance usually contains a portion that is never paid back, which must be considered consumption. In this sense, official statistics have overestimated savings in the form of non–life insurance, although the total amount of overestimation must be very small.

schedule was introduced in 1986, and the details of this provision have been changing almost every year, as explained in the preceding paragraph. Before 1986, limited tax deductibility was available.

Capital Gains on Land and Housing Structures

Capital gains are divided into "long-term" gains on assets held more than five years and "short-term" gains on assets held under five years:[12]

Basic rule for long-term capital gains on land and housing. Capital gains *after deduction* are taxed, separately from other income, at 39 percent (i.e., 30 percent national tax and 9 percent local tax).

Basic rule for short-term capital gains on land and housing. Of the following, apply whichever leads to the larger tax: (1) capital gains *after deduction* are taxed, separately from other income, at 52 percent (i.e., 40 percent national tax and 12 percent local tax); (2) capital gains that are combined and taxed according to the income tax schedule are taxed at 110 percent of *additional* income tax.

Special rule for capital gains on owner-occupied housing in which an owner has lived for more than ten years. Capital gains after a 30 million yen deduction are taxed at 14 percent (10 percent national and 4 percent local) for the first 60 million yen, and at 20 percent (15 percent national and 5 percent local) thereafter. Note that this special rule does not apply to capital gains carried over due to the home replacement provision listed below.

Deductions on capital gains on land and housing applicable to basic rule. (i) owner-occupied housing—30 million yen (this provision cannot be invoked again for three years), (ii) forced sale to the government for public purposes— 50 million yen, (iii) forced sale for city planning—20 million yen, (iv) forced sale for housing development project—15 million yen.

Carry-over of capital gains. Because of the different needs associated with different stages of the life cycle, people tend to change housing. If capital gains can be carried over for life, this switch can be done smoothly. In fact, such a carry-over was created in 1952 and abolished in 1970; it was then revived in 1972 for long-term (more than ten-year) owner-occupied housing, but again

12. The definition of "long-term" housing is housing that has been owned for more than five years, on January 1 of the year in which the sale is made. Hence, a holding period of almost six years is required if the sale is made on December 31.

Separate taxation was introduced in 1969. The tax rate on long-term gains has been increased in recent years. It was 14 percent in 1970 and 1971, and it was 26 percent (on gains up to 40 million yen) and 32.5 percent (on gains exceeding 40 million yen) as recently as 1991. The definitions of "long-term" and "short-term" were changed in 1987, with the holding period changed from ten to five years.

abolished in 1985, when it was replaced by a very special rule: If a long-term (more than ten-year) owner-occupied house had been obtained by bequest from parents or grandparents and the current owner has lived in the same house for more than thirty years (presumably with parents or grandparents), then capital gains can be carried forward to the next house.

Land and housing when bequeathed is assessed at less than market value: this will be explained later.

Parents can help a child buy a house through a special provision in the gift tax: if the cash is used to purchase a house, parents can give an outright cash gift of 3 million yen to a child tax-free, and cash gifts between 3 and 5 million yen are taxed lightly.

Property Tax

This tax is imposed on owners of land, buildings, and tangible assets that are depreciable in individual and corporate income taxes (i.e., plant and machinery). The assessment of land and buildings is made every three years, and that of tangible business assets every year. Substantial underassessment, with regional variations, is more the general rule than the exception. Real property below a certain assessed value for each type of asset is tax-exempt. The standard tax rate is 1.4 percent, and the maximum rate is 2.1 percent.

It should be noted that there are many types of income which are sources of savings. Apart from labor, interest, and dividend income, there are retirement, timber, occasional, and miscellaneous income with separate deductible amounts. Japanese workers receive a sizable retirement severance payment. If it were subject to the usual income tax scheme, the typical retirement severance payment would put a worker in the top bracket of the progressive schedule. Hence, there is a special deduction for retirement income. Occasional income is formally defined as income deemed to be temporary and particular to one year; this may be considered a substitute for income averaging. Miscellaneous income includes all other types of income, such as honoraria. Household saving behavior is, in one way or another, bound by all these tax treatments. It should be noted, however, that interest payments for consumer loans are not tax deductible. The Nakasone-Takeshita tax reform reduced the progressivity and the level of total income tax rates at all levels of government, although the absolute levels are still high, compared with some other G5 countries. Figure 6.3 illustrates this dramatic change between 1986 and 1992.

6.3.4   Effective Marginal Personal Tax Rates

Mervyn King made an ingenious attempt to combine various tax rules into an index of effective marginal personal tax rates (this became known as the King-Fullerton method; for details, see King and Fullerton [1984]). Recently the OECD (1991a, 1991b) conducted an international comparison of capital income taxation for OECD countries employing the King-Fullerton method. The relevant results from the project are reported in table 6.6. The effect of the Nakasone-Takeshita tax reform does not show up clearly in the figures for 1985

Taxable Income
10 Thousand Yen

Taxable Income (10 Thousand Yen)	1986	1987	1988	1989	1990	1991	1992
8000	88%						
5000	83%	78%	76%				
4900	78%	73%					
3000	77%	72%	66%				
2900	72%	67%					
2000	71%	66%		65%	65%	65%	65%
1900	66%		56%				
1500	65%	65%		55%	55%	55%	55%
1200	60%	60%	55%				
1000	55%	55%					
950	50%	50%	45%				
800	49%	49%	44%	45%	45%	45%	45%
600	44%	44%					
570	39%	39%				35%	35%
550		38%	34%	35%	35%		
500	38%						
460		33%				30%	30%
400	34%		32%	30%	30%		
370							
300	33%	32%	22%				
260	29%	28%					
220						20%	20%
200	28%	27%	20%	20%	20%		
160	25%	23%					
150							
130	23%	19.5%					
120	20%	18.5%					
95	19%	17.5%	17%			15%	15%
70							
60	18%	16.5%		15%	15%		
50	16.5%		15%				
45	15.5%	15.5%					
20	15%	15%					
0							

Fig. 6.3   Statutory rates of personal income taxes, 1986–92
Source: Tax Bureau (various issues, b).
Note: Tax rates are combined at all levels of government (i.e., national, prefecture, and municipal).

and 1990. There are two explanations for this. First, as table 6.5 showed, under the reform average personal tax rates on interest remain the same, while average tax rates on dividends and capital gains move in opposite directions. On balance, the effective marginal personal tax rate remains at more or less the same level. Second, for the sake of comparison, the King-Fullerton method is

Table 6.6   **Effective Marginal Personal Tax Rates on Capital Income (%)**

	1980	1985	1990
United States	—	38.4	66.7
Japan	56.7	23.6	28.3
Germany	70.3	42.9	46.9
France	—	45.3	25.4
United Kingdom	—	67.8	63.2

Source: OECD (1991a).

Note: The King-Fullerton method is used with some modifications, using country-specific interest rates, inflation rates, and average personal tax rate.

based on hypothetical projections that do not necessarily capture reality. As reported earlier, average household savings were effectively tax-exempt before 1988, while, since 1988, a flat 20 percent withholding tax has been imposed on interest. Thus a calculation based on hypothetical projections using statutory tax rates might lead to a misleading conclusion. In fact, it is quite likely that effective marginal tax rates on capital income before 1988 were much lower than the figures in table 6.6 (see Shoven and Tachibanaki [1988] for similar results in the earlier period).

A drawback is that the above results are based only on domestic manufacturing investment. Without considering international portfolio investment, spillover effects of capital income taxation on international investors can not be fully captured. In terms of personal taxes, however, most household savings are liable to domestic personal taxation. In any case, during the period from 1980 to 1990, effective marginal personal tax rates on capital income in Japan were relatively low, compared with the other G5 countries. It is, however, an open question whether the high household saving rates in Japan can be explained, at least in part, by the low effective marginal personal tax rate on savings.

6.4   Asset Allocation

In this section, historical changes in portfolio selection are reviewed. An important question to ask is, What makes portfolio selection change over time? Possible reasons for portfolio shifts are: (i) a shift in real rates of return during the stock market boom in the 1980s, (ii) financial market liberalization (the introduction of new financial assets), (iii) tax reform (imposing 20 percent withholding tax on interest and dividends), and (iv) fiscal deficits (government bond issues).

Several characteristics of Japanese households can be identified from figure 6.4 and table 6.7. First, judging from figure 6.4, the Japanese are very risk-averse, in the sense that about 60 percent of the household portfolio is held in safe assets, as currency, time deposits, and government bonds (securities) are

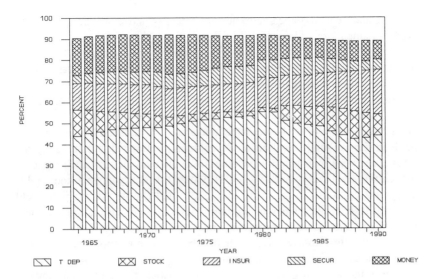

Fig. 6.4   Composition of household portfolio, 1964–90
Source: Bank of Japan, *Flow of Funds Accounts* (Tokyo, various issues).
Note: T DEP = time deposits; STOCK = stock; INSUR = life insurance; SECUR = securities
(mainly government and corporate bonds); MONEY = demand deposits and currencies.

considered to be in table 6.7. Horioka (1990, 56) estimates that during the
period from 1964 to 1984, the average annual rate of after-tax returns (including capital gains and dividends) on stockholdings in listed corporations was
about 17 percent, whereas the average annual deposit rate was about 5 percent.
The high degree of risk aversion among Japanese households may have contributed not only to skewing portfolio allocation toward safe assets but also to
raising the overall level of household savings. In addition, public opinion surveys find that preparation for unforeseen emergencies is by far the dominant
motive for saving in Japan. This implies that the level of precautionary savings
must be high and that such savings must be held in safe assets.

Second, cash holdings, including demand deposits declined constantly over
the 1964–90 period. This is partly because transactions between bank accounts

Table 6.7   **Correlation Matrix**

	Currency	Time Deposits	Insurance	Government Bonds	Stocks
Currency	1	0.13045	−0.76194	−0.73679	−0.36221
Time deposits	0.13045	1	−0.52664	0.48663	−0.91974
Insurance	−0.76194	−0.52664	1	0.20479	0.52276
Government bonds	−0.73679	0.48663	0.20479	1	−0.18827
Stocks	−0.36221	−0.91974	0.52276	−0.18827	1

Source: Bank of Japan, *Flow of Funds Accounts* (Tokyo, 1964–1990).

(current and deposits) became easier and cheaper and partly because credit cards became more widely used.

Third, the shares of life insurance (especially single-premium life insurance), stocks, and investment trusts have increased since 1982, particularly since 1985. This reflects the stock market boom during the 1982–1988 period. Japanese households might have increased their sensitivity to the "after-tax rate of return." Further investigations are required, at least on the following points: (1) because of the boom in the land and stock markets, Japanese households in general might have become wealthier and less risk-averse; (2) as the income and wealth distribution becomes more unequal, richer (usually older)[13] households hold risky assets, whereas poorer (usually younger) households keep their portfolios in relatively safe assets; and (3) the average household does not take the direct risk of holding stocks but goes through institutional investments, such as life insurance and investment trusts, to enjoy higher after-tax rates of return from savings (table 6.7 shows that households seem to consider insurance a risk-bearing investment).

Fourth, the share of government bonds (securities) has declined as new issues of government bonds became smaller during the process of reducing fiscal deficits in the 1980s.

The above observations indicate that changes in portfolio selection happened well before the Nakasone-Takeshita tax reform, and chiefly because of the stock market boom in the 1980s. But to identify how sensitive Japanese households are to tax incentives or "after-tax" interest rates, we have to use a microdata source, containing microeconomic characteristics and information on portfolio selection by the elderly and isolating tax factors from macroeconomic factors. This task will be taken up in future research.

6.5   Role of Intergenerational Transfers

6.5.1   Life-cycle Hypothesis and the Japanese Experience

In order to examine the effects of tax incentives on savings, we cannot ignore other factors that determine savings in society. The life-cycle hypothesis of saving and consumption is one of the most accepted principles in economics.

Although the budget constraint on individuals implies that they will save nothing over a lifetime, aggregate savings in a growing society will be positive. This is a basic observation of the life-cycle hypothesis. Japan, indeed, has ex-

---

13. Takayama and Arita (1992), using the 1989 NSFIE, report that rich elderly households hold a substantially higher proportion of risky assets than average households. See also Takayama (1992, table 2.13).

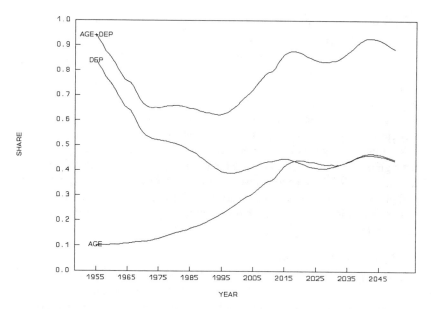

Fig. 6.5 **Aged and dependent population ratio to the population aged 20–64, 1955–2045**
Source: Horioka (1991).
Note: AGE = ratio of the population aged 65 and over to the population aged 20–64; DEP = ratio of the population aged 19 and under to the population aged 20–64.

perienced relatively rapid economic growth, accompanied by a high saving rate. This is supporting evidence for the life-cycle hypothesis. Could the life-cycle hypothesis be a dominant force? This is an important question because we have to evaluate how tax incentives work through saving decisions in the life-cycle framework (see Ito 1992, chap. 9, esp. 275–77).

At first glance, the Japanese experience is a strong case for the life-cycle hypothesis. The personal saving rate increased as the economic growth rate increased in postwar Japan, until both peaked around the first oil crisis of 1973–74 (see fig. 6.2). The correlation is strikingly high.

Suppose that life-cycle saving is a dominant force in Japan, then the rapid aging of Japanese society will have a profound implication for the saving rate. Currently, about 15 percent of the Japanese population is elderly (over age 65), and by the year 2015, the population share of the elderly will double (i.e., to about 30 percent, see fig. 6.5). As the population weight of the elderly—typical dissavers—rises, the saving rate will decline (see also Takayama 1992, fig. 2.3).

One test of the life-cycle hypothesis is an experiment of introducing (pay-as-you-go) social security pensions. The pension funds operated by the government enable people to save less from disposable income (net of pension fund contributions), so the personal saving rate should drop. The social security reform in the beginning of the 1970s in Japan came close to such a social experiment. However, there was no obvious drop in the personal saving rate among the generation who would benefit most from the reform (this was pointed out by Hayashi [1986]).

The validity of the (pure) life-cycle hypothesis is challenged on several grounds. First, if the elderly have a bequest motive, either purely altruistic or strategic, then they may not dissave even after retirement. That is, the aging of a society will not reduce the personal saving rate if the elderly do not spend down their life savings but instead hand down assets to their children, either through bequests or outright gifts. Second, if, for the elderly, personal savings are intended to build up enough wealth for contingencies—such as poor health and other unexpected expenses—during the retirement years, the introduction (the deterioration) of a social security health program would lower (raise) the saving rate.

6.5.2   Dissaving or Bequest

It is difficult to quantify how much the elderly save out of their labor and pension income, or dissave from their wealth. There are two kinds of measurement problems. First, when household surveys classify statistics by age, all surveys classify them by the age of the household head. In Japan, many elderly people live with their children. In such a "merged" family, the household head is usually defined to be the person who earns the most—that is, is most likely to be the elderly person's child, at the peak of life-cycle earning power. Therefore, statistics about the elderly contain a sample selection bias. A typical survey of this type is the FSS (see Ito 1992, table 9.2, 265).

One solution of the merged family problem is to look at a survey with age information on family members in the same household. Hayashi, Ando, and Ferris (1988) used the NSFIE to obtain such information, and estimated the degree of dissaving by the elderly. Their study attempts to extract as much information as possible on the behavior of older persons living with younger families, although it is not free from the data control problem. They find that, in the case of dependent older families (consisting of members of extended families), savings are somewhat larger than the savings of corresponding young nuclear families and that their total net worth increases less than the net worth of corresponding young nuclear families. These patterns are strong evidence that wealth is being transferred within extended families, and they are also consistent with the possibility that there may be additional intergenerational transfers from dependent old families to young nuclear families.

Another way to look at the question of whether the elderly dissave or not is to try measuring bequests directly. According to Barthold and Ito (1992), who use bequest tax filing information, about one-third to one-half of household assets are obtained by bequests in Japan, and the ratio is comparable for the United States. This is a significant proportion and supports the idea that the elderly do not dissave enough and leave sizable bequests, intended or not (see fig. 6.6 for a recent increase in intergenerational transfers in Japan).

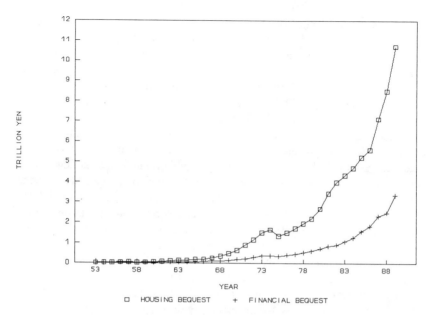

TRILLION YEN

YEAR

□ HOUSING BEQUEST   + FINANCIAL BEQUEST

Fig. 6.6   **Intergenerational transfers (nominal values), 1953–89**
Source: Tax Bureau, *Annual Statistics* (Tokyo, 1953–89).

6.5.3   How Tax Incentives Would Work

The most expensive purchase over the life cycle is usually housing. The treatment of housing was already touched upon in section 6.3.3. We will elaborate on this aspect from the particular viewpoint of life-cycle saving.

According to the pure life-cycle model (i.e., without the bequest motive), owner-occupied housing must be sold well in advance of death. Enough cash flow will be generated from home equity for lifetime financial support, and can be spent after moving into rental housing. However, in the statistics, there is no significant drop in the home-ownership rate after age 65.[14] There are three obvious reasons that elderly people are unwilling to sell their homes.

First, the quality of rental housing is quite low in Japan. House-lease law favors tenants, so that it is almost impossible to terminate a contract, even at its nominal end, without a tenant's consent. Hence, most rental housing is small and of low to medium quality, so that tenants will not stay forever (see Ito 1992, 423).

Second, high transactions costs coupled with a heavy capital gains tax (a flat 30 percent for nonfinancial assets) are disincentives for relocation. Even if the

---

14. The home-ownership rate of a cohort is defined as the ratio of the number of households with owner-occupied housing to the total number of households for a given cohort (age bracket). See, e.g., the Ministry of Construction, Housing Survey, for the aggregate statistics, cited in Ito (1992, 409, table 14.1) with cautionary remarks.

elderly prefer to live in housing more suitable to their stage in the life cycle, selling a house is a losing proposition in terms of one's portfolio.

Third, in the bequest tax code,[15] real estate is lightly assessed, as discussed in section 6.3.3. For example, the assessed value of land for bequest taxation (*rosen ka*) is at most 70 percent of the official survey price (*koji kakaku*), which, in turn, is about 70 percent of the market price. Hence, it is well known that assessed value is about 30–50 percent of market value. In addition, land up to 200 square meters (part of a large lot or an aggregate of smaller lots) is valued at 50 to 60 percent of *rosen ka*. In addition, the mortgage liability of the same asset is fully deductible from its taxable value. It does not take much calculation for an elderly person with bequest motive to figure out a scheme to lessen bequest (inheritance) tax liability: buy a house (or apartment building to become a landlord) and carry debt. This is exactly what happens among the Japanese elderly. About 60 percent of bequeathed asset values among Japanese decedents whose assets are subject to inheritance taxation is composed of real estate. On the other hand, only 25 percent of U.S. bequests subject to estate tax are composed of real estate (see Barthold and Ito [1992] for detailed institutional differences and simulation results). In sum, the bequest taxation code in Japan gives an incentive for the elderly with bequest motive to accumulate real estate after retirement, the opposite of the prediction of the pure life-cycle model. Evidence thus supports the existence of bequest motives.

Thus, for one reason or another, owner-occupied housing is not likely to be liquidated in Japan. Getting a reverse mortgage (borrowing money with a contract to pay off by bequeathing a house to the lender) is difficult, presumably because of asymmetric information problems and moral hazard in housing maintenance.[16]

6.6 Conclusion

This paper identifies government tax incentives for household saving and the historical changes in these incentives. Our findings can be summarized as follows.

1. Tax incentives for financial savings have been reduced since April 1988,

---

15. The bequest tax or inheritance tax is imposed when the total amount of inheritance exceeds 40 million yen plus 8 million yen times the number of statutory heirs, which is the basic deduction. Total tax liabilities are calculated in the following way: (1) assign the total tax base (property values after all deductions and exemptions) to each statutory heir by the statutory share, (2) apply the following tax schedule to the assigned amount for each heir to calculate a tax amount for each heir, (3) deduct any tax credit from this individual tax amount, and (4) sum up the individual tax amounts to arrive at the total inheritance tax liability. The schedule starts at 10 percent for the first 4 million yen. The marginal rate goes up to 70 percent at 500 million yen. For details, see Barthold and Ito (1992).

16. A particular form of reverse mortgage was introduced in Musashino City (a suburb of Tokyo). So such a contract is called the Musashino-type mortgage. However, not very many people have taken advantage of the system, and all contracts end with an option that the heirs buy back the contract, reclaiming the housing by paying off the debt, after the death of the contract holder.

while tax incentives for housing were strengthened in the tax reform. This reform might contribute to household wealth holdings skewed toward housing.

2. The reduction of tax incentives for financial savings did not seem to change household saving behavior by a significant magnitude.

3. The Japanese household sector is very risk-averse in general. This fact seems to explain the seeming insensitivity of Japanese households to the real rate of return from savings. If we remove the risk-aversion factor, Japanese households allocate their portfolios in a rational way.

4. To a certain extent, a household's portfolio selection might indicate its sensitivity to the real rate of return from savings during financial liberalization coupled with the stock market boom in the 1980s.

5. Intergenerational transfers have been made in substantial amounts in Japan. With institutional impediments and favorable tax treatments, the elderly tend to accumulate (rather than decumulate) wealth, especially in the form of housing, until the very end of their lives.

6. In the presence of large intergenerational transfers, the life-cycle theory of saving becomes dubious. The story of steady decline of Japanese household savings in a rapidly aging society, supported by the life-cycle theory, needs further testing to be validated.

The work that remains to be done is concerned mainly with microlevel data analysis. The saving behavior of the elderly is of particular interest. The test for a bequest motive on the part of the elderly may help to explain the high saving rate in Japan. This analysis may also give empirical support for the idea of generational accounting advocated by Kotlikoff (1992). Finally, and probably most important, the Japanese attitude toward risk must be analyzed and identified in the microdata. Portfolio selection by income class, by age, and by wealth may give important information about the degree of risk aversion. This may also supply an explanation for the high saving rate in Japan.

References

Barthold, T. A., and T. Ito. 1992. Bequest taxes and accumulation of household wealth: U.S.-Japan comparison. In *Political economy of tax reform*, ed. T. Ito and A. Krueger. Chicago: University of Chicago Press.

Bradford, D. F. 1991. Market value versus financial accounting measures of national saving. In *National saving and economic performance*, ed. B. D. Bernheim and J. B. Shoven. Chicago: University of Chicago Press.

Hayashi, F. 1986. Why is Japan's saving rate so apparently high? NBER *Macroeconomic Annual* 1:147–234.

———. 1992. Explaining Japan's saving: A review of recent literature. *Monetary and Economic Studies* (Bank of Japan) 10(2):63–78.

Hayashi, F., A. Ando, and R. Ferris. 1988. Life cycle and bequest savings. A study of Japanese and U.S. households: Based on data from the 1984 NSFIE and the 1983 survey of consumer finances. *Journal of the Japanese and International* Economies 2:450–91.

Horioka, C. Y. 1988. Saving for housing purchase in Japan. *Journal of the Japanese and International Economies* 2:351–84.

———. 1990. Why is Japan's saving rate so high? A literature survey. *Journal of the Japanese and International Economies* 4:49–92.

———. 1991. Future trends in Japan's saving rate and the implications thereof for Japan's external imbalance. *Japan and the World Economy* 3:307–30.

Ishi, H. 1989. *The Japanese tax system.* Oxford: Oxford University Press.

Ito, T. 1992. *The Japanese economy.* Cambridge: MIT Press.

King, M. A., and D. Fullerton. 1984. *The taxation of income from capital: A comparative study of the United States, the United Kingdom, Sweden and West Germany.* Chicago: University of Chicago Press.

Kotlikoff, L. J. 1992. *Generational accounting.* New York: Free Press.

OECD. 1991a. The future of capital income taxation in a liberalized financial environment. Working Party no. 1, Economic Policy Committee, OECD/CPE/ESD/WP1(91)8. Paris: Organisation for Economic Cooperation and Development.

———. 1991b. *Taxing profits in a global economy: Domestic and international issues.* Paris: Organisation for Economic Cooperation and Development.

Shoven, J. B., and T. Tachibanaki. 1988. The taxation of income from capital in Japan. In *Government policy towards industry in the United States and Japan,* ed. J. B. Shoven. Cambridge: Cambridge University Press.

Takayama, N. 1992. *The greying of Japan: An economic perspective on public pensions.* Tokyo: Kinokuniya, Oxford: Oxford University Press.

Takayama, N., and T. Arita. 1992. Income, consumption and wealth of the elderly couple (in Japanese). *Keizai Kenkyu* 43(2): 158–78.

Tax Bureau. Various issues, a. *The National Tax Office yearbook,* Tokyo: Ministry of Finance.

———. Various issues, b. *An outline of Japanese taxes,* Tokyo: Ministry of Finance.

7 Public Policies and Household Saving in France

Denis Fougère

7.1 Introduction

After relative stability at approximately 19 percent during the seventies, the household annual saving rate in France sharply decreased from 1980 to 1987 and then slightly increased over the period 1988–91 (see table 7.1). The evolution of the structure of household current financial assets (see table 7.2) sheds some light on this phenomenon. First of all, we observe a relative decrease of demand deposits, resulting from high real interest rates (which increase the opportunity cost of cash resources) and from the extension of the line of financial products during the eighties. After 1985, the proportion of investments in passbooks not subject to taxation diminishes with the decrease of the nominal rate of return. Moreover, the increase of the tax burden explains the decline of investments in passbooks subject to taxation.

In 1990, investments in securities became the major component of household financial assets. This is essentially due to the relative increase of shares and UCITS investments, which can be partly explained by the introduction of a tax deduction on bond interest and dividends (progressively raised to 8,000 francs for an individual and 16,000 francs for a married couple).[1] Finally,

Denis Fougère is researcher in the Centre National de la Recherche Scientifique (CNRS) at the University of Social Sciences, Toulouse.

The author is grateful to Luc Arrondel, Catherine Cazals, Jacqueline Lacroix, Stefan Lollivier, Jean-Jacques Malpot, Marie-Laure Morin, Véronique Paquel, and Lise Rochaix for their valuable help and advice. He is also indebted to Philippe Monard and Philippe Trainar (direction de la prévision, Finance Ministry), who gave him access to extremely useful information and thus contributed directly to this study. Finally, Marc Ivaldi, Jean-Charles Rochet, and especially James Poterba were kind enough to read carefully a first version of this text and make very constructive remarks. All remaining errors are the author's.

1. In France, mutual funds are collected by the so-called organismes de placement collectif en valeurs mobilières (OPCVM, or UCITS), which include sociétés d'investissement à capital variable (SICAV) and fonds communs de placement (FCP). At the end of 1990, UCITS deposits

Table 7.1   Household Saving Rate in France

	1981	1985	1987	1988	1989	1990	1991
Gross saving rate	18.0	14.0	10.8	11.0	11.7	12.2	12.6
Nonfinancial saving rate	11.3	9.2	9.2	9.0	9.6	9.3	8.8
Financial saving rate	6.7	4.8	1.6	2.0	2.1	2.9	3.8

Source: Comptes et indicateurs economiques: Rapport sur les comptes de la Nation (1988–91).
Note: The gross saving rate is defined as the ratio of gross savings to gross disposable income of households; nonfinancial savings include housing purchase and maintenance paid by households and investments made by sole company holders.

the proportion represented by life insurance has also increased, because of high rates of return and important tax deductions. (See *L'Allocation des flux d'épargne* 1991.)

7.2   Overview of the Household Balance Sheet

7.2.1   Share of Total Household Gross Worth in Various Assets

According to a recent Centre d'Etudes des Revenus et des Coûts (CERC; Center for the Study of Incomes and Costs) report (see Malpot and Paquel 1992), aggregate household gross worth (before the deduction of debt) in France was approximately 18,000 billion francs in 1988.[2] The mean household gross worth was 840,000 francs. But this mean varies highly across socio-professional groups: the mean gross worth of a professional is 3 million francs, while that of a worker is approximately 350,000 francs.

Different components of household gross wealth can be grouped in three categories: (1) *goods for domestic use* (38 percent)—liquidities (2.3 percent), primary home (31.2 percent), vacation home (4.3 percent); (2) *financial assets and rental goods* (51 percent)—savings-bank passbooks (6.4 percent), building-society passbooks and other bank deposits (5.7 percent), investments, bonds, and insurance policies (7.6 percent), quoted and nonquoted shares (12.5 percent), rental properties (14.9 percent), rented or nonrented lands and forests (4.5 percent); (3) *goods for professional use* (11 percent)—farmed land (1.9 percent), buildings (2 percent), equipment, cattle, and stock (4 percent), incorporeal assets (2.7 percent).[3] These proportions concern household gross wealth

---

amounted to approximately 2,000 billion francs, while bank deposit accounts amounted to approximately 6,000 billion francs.

2. These estimates do not include domestic durable goods (cars, furniture, consumer durables, gold, jewels, and works of art).

3. Wealth held by self-employed people for professional use does not include rented goods or any estimate of the "goodwill" associated with a professional reputation. It concerns equipment, machinery, buildings, farmed land, cattle, stock, and incorporeal assets (such as rights to a lease). It does not include shares, quoted or not.

Table 7.2   **Structure of Household Current Financial Assets (million francs)**

	1979		1985		1989	
	Amount	%	Amount	%	Amount	%
Liquidities:	1,580	62.2	2,697	50.9	3,456	36.0
Cash, demand deposits	468	18.4	764	14.4	1,123	11.7
Passbooks not subject to taxation	436	17.1	967.4	18.2	1,079	11.2
Passbooks subject to taxation	184	7.2	209.7	3.9	217	2.3
Savings plans	122	4.8	228.2	4.3	448	4.7
Others liquidities	370	14.6	527.7	10.0	589	6.1
Securities:	546	21.5	1,812	34.2	4,802	50.0
Shares	294	11.6	1,017	19.2	3,527	36.7
Bonds	204	8.0	380	7.2	283	3.0
UCITS	48	1.3	415	7.8	992	10.3
Insurance	168	6.6	443	8.4	959	10.0
Credits and accounting gaps	245	9.6	348	6.6	386	4.0
Total	2,539		5,300		9,603	100.0

Sources: Rapport sur les comptes de la Nation (1991); *Rapport annuel au conseil National du Crédit* (1992).

because available data do not permit any evaluation of the amount of debt incurred for the acquisition of each type of good.

The composition of household wealth varies across socioprofessional groups, as shown in table 7.3. Wealth of professionals represents more than half of farmers' total wealth, and between 20 and 30 percent of the total wealth of self-employed people (i.e., manufacturers, craftsmen, and merchants). The proportion of total household wealth marked for domestic use decreases with total wealth. The composition of "domestic use" wealth does not significantly vary across socioprofessional groups: the primary home represents its principal component (more than 70 percent). However, the primary home value for professional and senior executives is approximately twice that of workers and farmers.

The mean value of financial assets and rental goods held by households was around 430,000 francs in 1988. But, once again, this mean and the composition of this kind of wealth varies greatly across socioprofessional groups (see table 7.4). Socioprofessional groups whose mean value is high hold rental properties and shares proportionally more than the other groups. These goods represent about two-thirds of their whole wealth in financial assets and rental goods. On the other hand, more traditional liquid assets (savings-bank and building-society passbooks) represent a relatively higher proportion of the wealth of low-mean-value groups.

Moreover, farmers own proportionally less shares but more land and forest. By value, self-employed people (excluding farmers) and senior executives hold 57 percent of all shares, but 26 percent of all passbooks, while they represent

Table 7.3   Composition of Household Gross Wealth (%)

Socioprofessional group	Goods for Domestic Use	Financial Assets and Rental Goods	Goods for Professional Use
Farmers	17	29	54
Manufacturers, craftsmen, merchants	24	55	21
Professionals	25	43	32
Senior executives	41	56	3
Intermediate occupations	53	44	3
Employees	58	40	2
Workers	66	32	2
Nonparticipants	35	63	2
Total	38	51	11

Source: Malpot and Paquel (1992).

Table 7.4   Mean Value and Composition (%) of Financial Assets and Rental Goods Held by Households

Socioprofessional Group	Mean value (thousand francs)	Saving-Banks Passbook	Building-Society Passbooks	Investments, Bonds, and Insurance	Shares	Rental Properties	Lands and Forest
Retired self-employed (nonfarmers)	1,470	8	6	10	23	44	9
Professionals	1,250	6	8	17	25	35	9
Manufacturers, artisans, merchants	1,050	5	6	13	36	34	6
Senior executives	760	9	9	14	40	23	5
Farmers	590	11	13	16	7	19	34
Retired farmers	570	14	13	13	6	27	27
Retired wage earners	530	16	14	13	25	26	6
Intermediate occupations	290	17	15	17	20	26	5
Employees	150	22	14	18	11	27	8
Workers	110	24	18	25	8	20	5
Total	430	12	11	15	24	29	9

Source: Malpot and Paquel (1992).

only 17 percent of the whole population. The nonworking population, essentially retired people, holds 46 percent of the total value of financial assets and rental goods, while it represents 36 percent of the whole population.

Considering now total household wealth, self-employed people and wage earners own 27 and 36 percent of its total value, respectively, while they represent 11 and 53 percent of the whole population, respectively.

7.2.2   Importance of Debt on the Balance Sheet

Table 7.5 reports the evolution of the net outstanding financial assets and debts of households, at the end of each year, from 1982 to 1991. Because available data give no information on the yearly evolution of household gross (or net) wealth, it is impossible to appreciate precisely how the ratio between net (outstanding) debt and gross wealth has evolved during recent years in France. However, table 7.5 shows that:

- While the amount of household net outstanding debt has strongly increased during the past ten years, the ratio between this amount and the sum of net financial assets and net outstanding debts has remained approximately constant

- The share of medium- and long-term loans (for the most part mortgage loans) in household net outstanding debt has decreased: faced with the slackened growth of their purchasing power, households have increasingly used short-term loans to maintain their consumption levels during recent years.

These observations can be completed with the results of a study by Arrondel and Kessler (1989) using the 1986 Institut National de la Statistique et des Etudes Economiques (INSEE; French National Institute of Statistics and Economic Surveys) Survey on Financial Assets. According to this study, 45.6 percent of French households were indebted in 1986, while an earlier Centre de Recherches Economiques sur l'Epargne, Paris (CREP; Center of Economic Research on Savings) study estimated that this proportion was 39 percent in 1984. In 1986, 25.5 percent of all households were indebted to finance their primary home, 5.1 percent to finance other real estate, 5.2 percent to pay for construction work, and 17 percent to buy consumer durables. Finally, liquidity credits and other credits concerned only 2.6 and 5.6 percent of households, respectively.

Among indebted households, 27.5 percent were indebted for more than one reason: the most frequent combination is a real estate loan (frequently a long-term loan) together with a loan for the acquisition of consumer durables (usually a short-term loan).

The household rate of indebtedness is highest when the head of household is middle-aged at adult ages (73.2 percent for ages between 40 and 44 years old) and increases with household gross wealth and household current income. It is also higher for married couples with two or three children.

Table 7.5   **Household Net Outstanding Financial Assets and Debts (end of year; billion francs)**

	Net Outstanding Financial Assets							Net Outstanding Debts				Ratios (%)	
	Liquidities	Investment Securities	Bonds	Shares	Credits	Insurance Reserve	Total (1)	Liquidities	Short-term Loans	Medium- and Long-term Loans (2)	Total (3)	(3)/(1)+(3)	(2)/(3)
1982	2,212		385	455	338	267	3,656		514	1,022	1,536	29.6	66.5
1983	2,429		447	721	339	314	4,250	1	534	1,135	1,670	28.2	68.0
1984	2,579		424	1,006	340	374	4,723		684	1,275	1,959	29.3	65.1
1985	2,757		380	1,431	349	443	5,360	1	677	1,425	2,104	28.2	67.8
1986	2,918		491	2,347	412	532	6,701	1	820	1,505	2,236	25.0	67.3
1987	3,130	7	349	2,232	384	632	6,734	1	940	1,742	2,657	28.3	65.6
1988	3,365	14	384	3,292	334	771	8,160	1	1,217	1,903	3,122	27.7	60.9
1989	3,532	4	400	4,293	411	974	9,614	2	1,429	2,026	3,457	26.4	58.6
1990	3,652	8	382	3,683	504	1,145	9,373	2	1,422	2,166	3,590	27.7	60.3
1991	3,642	10	412	4,147	478	1,318	10,006	2	1,478	2,223	3,703	27.0	60.0

Source: Comptes et indicateurs economiques: Rapport sur les comptes de la Nation (1988–91).

Because the 1986 INSEE Survey on Financial Assets does not include any information on household debt incurred for professional reasons, the estimated rate of indebtedness for different socioprofessional groups is necessarily biased. However, Arrondel and Kessler (1989) found that this rate (excluding debt for professional reasons), and the rate for primary-home debt only, were respectively:

- Approximately 60 and 40 percent for those employed in intermediate occupations
- Approximately 55 and 35 percent for executives
- 55 and 28 percent for professionals
- Approximately 53 and 30 percent for the large-business self-employed
- Approximately 50 and 29 percent for qualified workers
- 45.6 and 25.8 percent for the small-business self-employed
- 29.1 and 13.9 percent for nonqualified workers
- 37.2 and 13.3 percent for farmers

7.2.3   Mean Net Worth of Households

Malpot and Paquel (1992) have estimated household mean gross wealth and mean debt (not including short-term indebtedness for nonprofessional reasons). On the basis of these two mean estimates, they have deduced an approximate evaluation of the mean net worth of French households in 1988. Their results are reported in table 7.6.

The rankings of socioprofessional groups according to their mean gross and net wealth are approximately the same. The mean net worths of some categories are very close—as for farmers and manufacturers, or for retired farmers and retired wage earners. However, (white-collar) employees and (blue-collar) workers, who hold approximately the same mean gross worth, have more differentiated mean net worths (because of unequal levels of mean indebtedness). Farmers, manufacturers, artisans, and merchants are relatively more indebted for professional reasons. Senior executives, incumbents of intermediate occupations, employees, and workers are relatively more indebted (in the medium and long terms) for nonprofessional reasons.

7.2.4   On the Concentration of Wealth

Using data from the 1986 INSEE Survey on Financial Assets, Lollivier and Verger (1990) have shown that, in France, wealth is much more concentrated than income. In fact, the less wealthy half of the population holds only 6 percent of overall gross wealth (including outstanding loans), while the wealthiest 10 percent holds 54 percent of overall gross wealth. However, when households are ranked according to activity income (which includes wages, profits, and pensions, but excludes Social Security benefits and income from personal

Table 7.6   Mean Net Worth of French Households, 1988 (thousand francs)

Socioprofessional Group	Mean Gross Worth	Mean Indebtedness			Mean Net Worth
		Professional	Nonprofessional	Total	
Professionals	2,880	191.5	150.3	341.8	2,538.2
Retired selfemployed (nonfarmers)	2,030	7.9	5.4	13.3	2,016.7
Farmers	2,020	315.3	41.4	356.7	1,663.3
Manufacturers, artisans, merchants	1,920	162.8	96.2	259	1661
Senior executives	1,360	6.2	138.5	144.7	1,215.3
Retired farmers	890	18.5	3.5	22	868
Retired wage earners	880	1.5	9.1	10.6	869.4
Intermediate occupations	660	6.1	122.5	128.6	531.4
Employees	370	2.8	61.8	64.6	315.4
Workers	350	2.8	77.4	80.2	269.8
Total	840	27.1	62.0	89.1	750.9

Source: Malpot and Paquel (1992).

assets), the top 10 percent earn only 28 percent of total income. Table 7.7 gives concentration curves for wealth and income in France during 1986.

This survey also shows that the concentration of wealth increases with the population density of the residence area. In rural districts, the wealthiest 10 percent hold 52 percent of the total wealth, while in Paris, they hold 74 percent of the total. Concentration is stronger at both extremes of the income distribution. Among households earning less than 30,000 francs per year, the 10 percent at the upper tail possess 58 percent of the subgroup's total wealth. The percentage held by the top 10 percent is close to 61 percent in the subgroup of households earning more than 300,000 francs per year. It is only equal to 38 percent for households earning between 200,000 and 300,000 francs per year.

Wealth concentration is also very strong among farmers and professionals, the opposite of the case for qualified workers and members of intermediate occupations. Wealth concentration is higher at extreme ages, and lowest for those between the ages of 30 and 40. Finally, wealth concentration is stronger among single individuals and among households receiving no gift or bequest after the death of parents.

7.3 The Taxation of Capital Income

First, note that any single individual with a yearly capital income of less than 8,000 francs is exempted from tax on this income; for married couples the amount is 16,000 francs or less. The tax revenue loss generated by this provision was equal to approximately 8.2 billion francs in 1991 (see *Project*

Table 7.7   **Concentration (Lorenz) Curves for Wealth and Income in France, 1986**

Quantile	Cumulated Wealth (%)	Cumulated Income (%)
0.05	0.03	0.81
0.10	0.12	2.18
0.15	0.25	3.90
0.20	0.44	6.01
0.25	0.75	8.34
0.30	1.21	10.95
0.35	1.87	13.82
0.40	2.77	16.97
0.45	4.11	20.39
0.50	6.04	24.17
0.55	8.74	28.36
0.60	11.94	32.96
0.65	15.71	37.99
0.70	20.15	43.52
0.75	25.25	49.52
0.80	31.13	56.15
0.85	37.98	63.61
0.90	46.21	72.28
0.95	57.28	82.74

Source: Lollivier and Verger (1990).

for the 1992 Finance Act 1992). This section describes tax legislation as of January 1, 1992.

7.3.1   Total Tax Burden on Interest Income

Interest income refers to household income received from fixed-yield or variable-yield investments, such as bonds and other marketable loan certificates, claims, deposits, current accounts, treasury bills, and short-term notes. Such income is subject to specific tax treatment, characterized by flat-rate withholding.

In fact, the beneficiary may require the debtor (or the institution or bank representing this debtor) to convert interest into a standard deduction at source. When this deduction is made, the beneficiary is discharged from the requirement to pay progressive income tax on the interest. This deduction involves two base rates: a 35 percent rate and a 15 percent rate (applied in particular to income from marketable bonds), which are increased to 38.1 and 18.1 percent, respectively, with the application of three additional taxes: (1) the social contribution (1 percent), (2) social withholding (1 percent), instituted in 1987, and (3) the generalized social contribution (1.1 percent), instituted in 1990.

The flat-rate withholding option is reserved for natural persons (as opposed to legal entities) and only allowed for claims and interest with no escalator clause; this includes convertible and profit-sharing bonds. Interest income paid to persons or corporations not residing in France must be subject to flat-rate withholding. In this case, maximum rates are 15 percent for bond income and 35 percent for other interest income.

Income from marketable bonds includes interest, redemption premiums, and lotteries. Interest yielded by marketable bonds issued before January 1, 1987, is subject to a 10 percent deduction at source made by the issuing legal entity. For redemption premiums and lotteries, the rate of the deduction at source is 12 percent (10 percent for redemption premiums on loans issued after January 1, 1986). When bond interest is subject to a deduction at source, the flat-rate withholding must be decreased by this previous deduction. For example, consider a 100 franc gross interest payment, subject to a 10 franc deduction at source; the theoretical amount of the 18.1 percent flat-rate withholding is 18.10 francs, but its effective amount is $18.10 - 10 = 8.10$ francs.

When the beneficiary does not choose the flat-rate withholding option, the bond interest is included in taxable income. The taxable amount is then the gross interest before deduction at source, but the amount of this deduction constitutes a tax credit which reduces the progressive tax.

The only short-term notes on which flat-rate withholding can be applied are the ones issued by banks. In this case, the rate, usually 38.1 percent (or 48.1 percent for short-term notes issued before January 1, 1990), is raised to 53.1 percent if the beneficiary does not communicate his identity and residence to the payer institution. Short-term notes issued by corporations other than banks are subject to the 10 percent deduction at source and then to the progressive tax.

For income yielded by investment growth bonds, capitalization, and life insurance contracts, the principle is the following:

• The tax takes the form of a 53.1 percent withholding when the beneficiary chooses a tax anonymity scheme.
• If the beneficiary does not choose a tax anonymity scheme, the tax is due only for contracts subscribed after a given date and may, on the beneficiary's request, take the form of a lower-rate withholding. For subscriptions taken before 1990, the tax concerns contracts with a maturity of less than six years: the withholding rate is 48.1 percent for a maturity of less than two years and 28.1 percent for a maturity between four and six years; for subscriptions taken after January 1, 1990, the exemption concerns contracts with a maturity of more than eight years, and there are only two withholding rates: 38.1 percent if the maturity is less than four years and 18.1 percent if it is between four and eight years.

Income from claims which are nonquoted but tradable in a regulated market (such as commercial paper issued by nonbanking corporations and certificates of deposit reserved for banks) may be subject only to 18.1 percent flat-rate withholding.

7.3.2   Tax Burden on Equity Income from Corporations

Dividend Income

It is interesting to recall that, until 1959, dividends distributed by corporations to shareholders were first subject to a proportional tax (deducted at source by the firm) and then the remaining net sum was included in the shareholder's total income for the calculation of the progressive surtax. For example, given that the proportional tax rate was 0.22 in 1959, if a corporation had to distribute a dividend of 100 francs that year, the shareholder received a net dividend of 78 francs. Then, if the shareholder was liable for a 45 percent progressive surtax, dividend income was subject to a withholding equal to $78 \times 0.45 = 35.10$ francs, so that the effective income was equal to

$$(1 - \tau_{div})(1 - \tau_{corp})100 = (1 - 0.45)(1 - 0.22)100 = 42.90 \text{ francs.}$$

The act issued on December 28, 1959, suppressed the proportional tax on dividends and kept up a deduction at source for investment income, which was finally suppressed for any natural or legal resident person by the act issued July 12, 1965. Moreover, this act allowed a 50 percent tax credit to beneficiaries of dividends. The principle of this tax credit is the following: whenever a firm liable for corporate tax distributes a dividend of 100 francs, the shareholder receives a total income of 150 francs, composed of the 100-franc coupon she cashes and the amount of 50 francs that is deducted from the tax on the 150 franc dividend income.

If, for example, the shareholder is subject to a 40 percent income tax rate, then her tax on a dividend income of 150 francs (including the tax credit of 50 francs) is calculated as follows: $(150 \text{ francs} \times 0.40) - (\text{tax credit of 50 francs}) = 10$ francs. So the effective income after tax is 90 francs. This example shows that the after-tax net income of a shareholder receiving a dividend income of 100 francs, accompanied by a tax credit of 50 francs, is exactly the same as the one resulting from a dividend of 150 francs without any tax credit. When the corporate tax rate was 50 percent (from 1958 to 1985), the distribution of a 100 franc dividend by a firm required a 200 franc profit; the distribution of a 150 franc dividend with the same profit could have been possible were the corporate tax rate 25 percent. Consequently, the tax credit for distributed dividends grants shareholders a kind of rebate on the corporate tax.

Reductions of the corporate tax rate to 45 percent in 1986 and 1987, then to 42 percent in 1988, have implied that the corporate tax rate effectively burdening distributed profits has been simultaneously lowered from 25 percent to 17.5 percent, and then to 13 percent. Successive reductions of the corporate tax rate to 39 percent in 1989, 37 percent in 1990, and 34 percent since 1991, have not changed the effective rate of 13 percent on distributed profits, because the distribution of a dividend is now accompanied by an additional tax intended to set the corporate tax rate at 42 percent.

To illustrate this point, let us assume that a firm has realized a 100,000-franc profit during fiscal year 1992. This profit implies a corporate tax of 34,000 francs and leaves an available profit of 66,000 francs. If the firm decides to distribute this whole amount to shareholders, it is subject to an additional tax of 8,000 francs, corresponding to the difference between the 42 percent tax rate and the 34 percent one. Note that this additional corporate tax represents 8/66ths of the available profit (after the 34 percent tax) and 8/58ths of the distributed dividends (equal to 66,000 − 8,000 = 58,000 francs). For this reason the legislation states that the additional corporate tax to be paid in the case of distributed dividends must be equal to "8/58 of the net distributed amount."

Capital Gains

1. Capital gains resulting from a transfer (for valuable consideration) of a shareholding representing more than 25 percent of the equity of a firm subject to corporate tax are subject to a 18.1 percent tax. Transfers without valuable consideration, via inheritance or donation to the spouse, a descendant, or an ascendant, are exempted from tax. However, this exemption can be annulled if, within five years, the transferee sells at least one of these shares to someone not a member of the transferor's family.

2. When the transfer concerns less than 25 percent of the equity of a firm subject to corporate tax, the tax rate is 18.1 percent if the total transfer during the fiscal year is greater than 316,900 francs (in 1991). This taxation scheme applies to quoted securities (shares, bonds, nonvoting preference shares, equity shares), application rights on such securities, mutual funds, but also to shares of nonquoted firms subject to corporate tax.

3. When a transfer for valuable consideration concerns shares of a non-quoted property development company, capital gains are taxable as ones yielded by the sale of private buildings.

4. When capital gains are made by one of the partners working in a partnership firm that is not subject to corporate tax, they are taxable as professional capital gains. Since September 1990, capital gains made by nonworking partners have also been taxable. The single tax rate is 18.1 percent.

7.3.3   Average Marginal Tax Rate on Capital Income

The marginal tax rate (MTR) and average marginal tax rate (AMTR) on capital income (interest income, dividends, capital gains) during 1989 are given in table 7.8. The calculation of MTR and AMTR are based on a 1 percent and a − 100 percent variation of capital income or dividends, respectively. In other words, AMTR is calculated by setting the corresponding income category to zero. The MTR and AMTR on dividends are lower than the corresponding ones on capital income excluding dividends. This is the direct consequence of the tax credit scheme applied to dividends.

7.3.4   Wealth Taxes

The 1989 Finance Act instituted a yearly wealth tax, called Impôt de Solidarité sur la Fortune (ISF), only slightly different from the previous wealth

Table 7.8   **Marginal and Average Marginal Tax Rates on Capital Income, 1989**

	MTR (%)	AMTR (%)
Capital income	16.1	8.8
Dividends	13.4	7.6
Other capital income	17.4	13.6

Source: Réponse au questionnaire O.C.D.E. sur la fiscalité de l'épargne (1992).

tax, called Impôt sur les Grandes Fortunes (IGF), which was applied from 1982 to 1986. The new yearly wealth tax has the following characteristics:

- It is exclusively a personal tax, with an application threshold of 4,390,000 francs since 1992
- It concerns all goods and assets making up the household net wealth, including any held by nonemancipated minor children
- The most important exemption concerns goods for professional use
- Its rate is progressive: the 1992 tax scale consists of five bands with progressive rates of 0.5, 0.7, 0.9, 1.2, and 1.5 percent
- The tax amount may be reduced according to the household income value;
- The ISF must be calculated by taxpayers themselves and paid when the yearly declaration of wealth is made.

Taxable wealth consists of all real estate (land, houses, etc.), business assets and goodwill, securities, claims, movables, and personal estate (cars, gold, cash, foreign currency, etc.). In addition to goods for professional use, exemption is given to works of art, rights of literary and artistic ownership, patent rights whenever these rights are included in the inventor's wealth, and rural goods on long leases. In 1992, the rates of the ISF are the following:

For the fraction of the taxable net wealth
- below 4,390,000 francs: 0 percent
- between 4,390,000 and 7,130,000 francs: 0.5 percent
- between 7,130,000 and 14,150,000 francs: 0.7 percent
- between 14,150,000 and 21,960,000 francs: 0.9 percent
- between 21,960,000 and 42,520,000 francs: 1.2 percent
- above 42,520,000 francs: 1.5 percent

Valuation of wealth subject to the ISF is made according to the following principles:

1. Real estate is appraised at its market value, defined as the price at which it could have been sold at the beginning of the fiscal year. The valuation must take into account real estate characteristics and maintenance, but also legal causes of depreciation, such as renting agreements.

2. Listed bonds and shares are appraised according to closing prices on the last day of the year preceding the tax declaration; their valuation may be alternatively calculated as the mean of the last 30 quotations of the previous year. The market value of unquoted shares is based simultaneously on their yield value, on the value of firm net assets, and on growth prospects of the firm.

3. Claims are valuated at their nominal value, increased with accrued interest.

4. Jewels cannot be appraised at a value lower than the one fixed in an insurance contract.

5. Movables may be valuated on an inclusive basis, set to 5 percent of the whole value of other nonexempted wealth components. Tangible property (including cars, boats, race horses, etc.) must be valuated at its market value.

Debts to be paid to banks and other credit institutions (including debts contracted for the acquisition of real estate) may be deducted from taxable wealth.

Total wealth and income taxes that must be paid in the same year cannot exceed 85 percent of income and interest (subject to withholding taxes) realized during the previous year. If a surplus is observed, it must be deducted from the ISF. For example, consider a person whose net wealth is evaluated at 40 million francs on January 1, 1992, and so, who owes under the ISF 353,420 francs. If his or her 1991 taxable income and interest consists of an income of 500,000 francs (subject to an income tax of 207,000 francs) and bond yields of 150,000 francs (subject to a withholding tax of 25,500 francs), the total wealth and income taxes amount to 353,420 + 232,500 = 585,920 francs. The upper limit under the 85 percent ceiling is 650,000 × 0.85 = 552,500 francs. Consequently, there is an excess of 585,920 − 552,500 = 33,420 francs, which must be deducted from the ISF, which finally amounts to 353,420 − 33,420 = 320,000 francs.

During 1990, 140,461 tax declarations were subject to the ISF, and the payment of this tax yielded a total of 6,061 million francs: from 1989 to 1990, the number of declarations and the amount of tax paid increased by 11.2 percent and 6.1 percent, respectively. (See Gambier and Mercier 1992.)

7.3.5 Inheritance Taxes

When an inheritance passes to a spouse or an individual in the direct lineage, the calculation of inheritance taxes is the following:

- Since January 1, 1992, a personal tax exemption of 330,000 francs applies to the spouse's share; an exemption of 300,000 francs applies to the share of each child or ascendant.

- After application tax exemptions, the share of any heir is subject to progressive rates, between 5 and 40 percent. Initially, the rates increase rapidly: for example, a 20 percent rate applies to any child on the part above 100,000 francs, and to the spouse on the part above 200,000 francs. Then the tax scale increases less progressively: higher rates apply only on the part above 3,400,000 francs for any heir. More precisely, the rate is 30 percent for the fraction between 3,400,000 and 5,600,000 francs, 35 percent for the fraction between 5,600,000 and 11,200,000 francs, and 40 percent for the fraction above this last amount.

- Any testamentary heir with three or more children is eligible for a reduction of 4,000 francs per child after the third one.

When inheritance concerns collaterals or nonrelatives, exemptions are very low and rates particularly high:

- For bequests between brothers and sisters, the rate is 35 percent and goes up to 45 percent for the fraction above 150,000 francs
- For bequests between uncles (or aunts) and nephews (or nieces), or between first cousins, it is uniformly equal to 55 percent,
- It is uniformly equal to 60 percent for relatives above the fourth degree of kinship (e.g., grandparents' grandparents) or for nonrelatives.

Goods to which inheritance taxes apply must be estimated at the date of death. This estimation concerns business and real estate, quoted and nonquoted shares, and movables. Among exclusions, the most notable are: (1) life insurance policies taken out by the decedent (however, the fraction above 200,000 francs of premiums paid after the age of 70 is subject to inheritance taxes), (2) woods and forests (up to three-quarters of their value), (3) rural goods long leases (up to half or three-quarters of their value, and when they are transferred free of charge for the first time), and (4) works of art donated to the state with its approval.

Inheritance taxes can be avoided to a certain extent through donations. Generally, donations are subject to the same tax rates as inheritances, but with the following particularities: (a) debts entailing donated goods cannot be deducted, and (b) the donor may pay taxes usually incumbent on the donee: thus, for the same total disbursement, the donor may increase the donee's wealth in this way.

In the case of a donation partition, taxes are reduced by 25 percent if donors are under age 65, and by 15 percent if they are between 65 and 75 years old. Donations of equity shares to the benefit of a firm's employees may give rise to a tax reduction of 100,000 francs for each beneficiary, if the Finance Ministry consents.

When a firm is transferred through inheritance or donation, tax payment may be deferred for five years from the date payable and then split into twenty-one installments over ten years (the interval between two successive installments being six months). This measure applies to individual industrial, commercial, craft, agricultural, or professional firms, but also to nonquoted shares of such firms, provided that the beneficiary receives at least 5 percent of the capital. Taking advantage of this deferral requires the payment of interest, whose basic rate is reduced proportionally as the heir's or donee's share increases. The rate of interest is reduced still more when beneficiaries are collaterals or nonrelatives. (See Gambier and Mercier 1992.)

7.3.6   Tax Treatment of Consumer Debt

Interest on consumer debt is generally not deductible from income tax, except for interest on debt contracted for the acquisition, building, repair, or amelioration of property.

7.4   Employment-linked Retirement Saving

7.4.1   Tax Treatment of Employer-provided Pensions

According to French social legislation, any wage earner must be affiliated with a basic pension (Social Security) plan and then to a complementary pension plan. Wage earners may be also obligated to support another complementary (called "overcomplementary") pension scheme, either within their firm or within their line of work.

Contributions to obligatory plans are deductible. However, deduction is allowed only below some fixed amount, which depends on the total yearly amount of employee's and employer's contributions to basic and complementary pension schemes and to complementary provident funds. The upper limit was 209,395 francs in 1991. Contributions to optimal or voluntary plans, however, are nondeductible.

Private or public retirement pensions are included in the calculation of the taxable income. They are subject, first, to a 10 percent tax reduction with a lower limit of 1,800 francs for each pensioner, and an upper limit of 29,300 francs for the total amount of retirement pensions received by household members; then, to a 20 percent tax reduction, with an upper limit of 125,200 francs for each pensioner. The net amount of public and private retirement pensions (calculated after the two successive tax reliefs) is added to the whole taxable income of the household.

The payment of capital within the framework of a private pension plan is not taxable. Tax legislation does not stipulate any penalty in the case of withdrawal from a private pension plan.

Life annuities in return for payment are subject to taxation only on a given proportion of their amount. This proportion is a function of the annuitants' age when they take possession of the annuities. It is fixed at: 70 percent under age 50, 50 percent between ages 50 and 59, 40 percent between ages 60 and 69, and 30 percent over age 69.

7.4.2   Private Pensions in Saving and Retirement Income

To complete individual retirement income resulting from obligatory pension plans (i.e., Social Security and complementary pension plans), insurance companies and banks offer "capitalization contracts" to firms and households, among which we can distinguish: (1) individual contracts, collective contracts, or collective contracts with individual adhesion; (2) contracts in which the contribution is payable by the employer, by the employee, or by both; (3) contracts with predefined contributions or with predefined benefits, and (4) contracts involving (obligatory or optional) life annuities.

Individual contracts include individual savings plans (called "PEPs") and life-insurance contracts, which will be presented in sections 7.5 and 7.6, respectively.

Among capitalization contracts signed inside the firm, two kinds of contracts may be distinguished. They are identified by the number of the corresponding article of the Internal Revenue Code (IRC). The first kind consists of contracts specified by article 83 of the IRC which may be signed in the framework of either a collective agreement or a firm agreement; they concern either the whole personnel of the firm or a homogeneous category only, such as executives; the retirement funds are supported by employer contributions, and eventually by employees' contributions. The second consists of contracts specified by article 82 of the IRC which are subscribed to and financed by the employer to the benefit of appointed employees.

These "article 82"–type contracts may involve either predefined contributions or predefined benefits. The predefined contributions comprise a given percentage of the employee's wage, the employee keeping the benefit of the accumulated capital if he or she leaves the firm. In the case of predefined benefits, the firm offers to all or part of its personnel an additional retirement pension whose level is equal to some percentage of the employee's last wage before retirement. The firm may also complement the amount of individual retirement income with "hat" insurance (*retraite "chapeau"*), such that the total amount equals some given percentage of the employee's last wage for each year of service in the firm (such contracts are sometimes called "article 39"–type contracts).

In this case, contributions are exclusively chargeable to the employer: the aim is to develop personnel loyalty, because eventual extra pensions are paid only to employees still occupied in the firm at the date of their retirement. The firm may also transfer its commitments to an insurance company; however, the insurance company may change substantially the level of contributions paid by the firm. In fact, the insurance company must achieve actuarial balance between contributions and returns on their investments on the receipt side, and pensions to be paid and charges on the expense side.

Funded pension plans are offered by life insurance companies but also by other bodies, such as institutions coming under the French Mutual Insurance Company (Mutualité Française) and distributing the "Mutex" contract to firms or to their members.

A firm savings plan (*plan d'epargne d'entreprise* [PEE]) may be set up inside a firm agreement; it is funded by the employee's contributions (eventually chosen to benefits from profit sharing) and by a lump sum paid by the firm.

This lump sum may be restricted to plan management charges, its ceiling value is 10,000 francs per year (15,000 francs in the event that the employee purchases the firm's shares), and it must be lower than three times the employee's contribution. The employee's contribution as set out in the agreement may reach 25 percent of wages. Devoted to the purchase of securities, stocks, and bonds, PEEs benefit from tax incentives: given that invested sums are held for at least five years, returns and capital gains from the plan are tax-exempt. The PEE may be converted into a life insurance contract allowing the payment of a taxable life annuity from the date of retirement (see section 7.4.1 for tax rates applied to life annuities).

Unfortunately, available statistics do not permit us to identify precisely (1) the amount of contributions paid by firms preparing complementary retirement pension plans for (some of) their employees and (2) banking investments corresponding to individual long-term savings, which will be withdrawn essentially during the retirement period.

7.4.3   Severance Bonuses for Retirement and Early Retirement

Several measures have been taken to ensure replacement income for wage earners who come to the end of their working lives or who resign, agree to cut back their working hours, or get laid off. These measures include:

- The special allowance of the French National Employment Fund (Fonds National pour l'Emploi [FNE]), which is provided to older workers when they are subject to economic redundancies or when they agree to change from full-time to part-time employment
- The Solidarity Contracts for progressive early retirement
- The progressive retirement system, which permits to workers over age 60 who have made 150 quarterly payments to the Social Security System, to receive part of their retirement pension while continuing to work part-time.

The FNE agreements are concluded between firms and the state. Older workers who are laid off by a firm that has concluded a FNE agreement are eligible for a special allowance equal to 65 percent of the reference daily wage, if this wage is lower than 390.25 francs (the threshold wage on January 1, 1992), and equal to 50 percent of the reference daily wage, if it is higher than 390.25 francs. The reference daily wage is calculated from wages earned during the past twelve months. The FNE special allowance is paid until the beneficiary is 65 years old, or until the beneficiary (if more than 60 years old) has made 150 quarterly payments to the Social Security system. To be eligible for the FNE special allowance, a laid-off worker must be more than 55 years old and must have been employed in the firm for at least twelve months prior to dismissal.

A firm that has reached an FNE agreement contributes to the special allowance according to a rate depending on its size: on average, 6 percent for firms with fewer than 500 employees, and 8 percent for firms with more than 500 employees or belonging to a trust.

A firm laying off a worker over age 50 must pay a contribution to the Association for Industrial and Commercial Employment (ASSEDIC) when an FNE agreement has not been previously reached.[4] The amount of this contribution varies from one to six months' gross wages, according to the age of the laid-off worker at the time of dismissal.[5] The rate of this contribution is reduced by half for firms that normally have fewer than twenty employees. For the firm, this contribution is deductible from its corporate tax.

Under an act issued July 30, 1987, any retirement is accompanied by the payment of compensation defined as follows. In the case of voluntary retirement of an employee over age 60, the employee receives either the indemnity fixed by the law or the indemnity fixed by the collective agreement or by the labor contract (if this amount is greater). The indemnity fixed by the law is equal to: half the monthly wage when the employee's seniority is greater than ten years; one month's wages when it is greater than 15 years; one-and-a-half month's wages when it is greater than 20 years; or two months' wages when it is greater than 30 years. In these cases, the monthly wage is calculated as the mean wage over the past twelve months, or as the mean wage over the past three months if this is greater.

In the case of retirement initiated by the employer, the law distinguishes between two situations:

- If conditions for compulsory retirement are fulfilled (i.e., if the employee is eligible for the full-rate pension and is older than the compulsory retirement age fixed by the collective agreement or the labor contract), then the employee is entitled either to the official redundancy payment or to the contractual redundancy payment, which may be higher. The official redundancy payment is equal to one-tenth for each year of seniority in the firm (if seniority is between two and ten years), or one-tenth per year plus one-fifth per year above the tenth year of seniority (this gives, e.g., 7.9 months for a seniority of 33 years).

- If the above conditions are not fulfilled, compulsory retirement is considered a redundancy. The employer then must respect the stipulated procedure, and the redundancy must be justified by a cause such as the reduction of professional abilities due to age. Otherwise, the employer may be ordered to pay damages to the employee.

4. The age limit at which such contributions are required was previously 55 years old: it was lowered to 50 years old on August 1, 1992.
The ASSEDIC is the institution that manages the payment of unemployment insurance.
5. The number of paid months increases with the age of a dismissed worker.

Beneficiaries of severance pay for (early) retirement may divide the taxable amount of this pay in four equal parts over the four successive years following the year of payment. In general, this option is attractive because taxable income during the years immediately after retirement is usually lower than in the last working year. The tax-exempted portion of severance pay is 20,000 francs. But in the case of retirement or early retirement initiated by the employer, the exemption may reach the level of the severance pay defined by collective, professional, or interprofessional agreements.

7.4.4   The Social Security Replacement Rate

The general Social Security pension scheme involves any wage earner in the trade, industrial, craft, or service sectors.[6] In return for contributions withdrawn from monthly wages at the rate of 15.80 percent, any wage earner receives a full-rate retirement income when he reaches age 65, or age 60 if he or she has made 150 quarterly payments to the Social Security System. The full rate is 50 percent of the mean yearly wage, which is calculated over the ten "best" years (after 1948). Deductions are applied to wage earners who are less than 65 years old and have contributed fewer than 150 quarterly payments. For example, the rate is 37.5 percent at ages 60, 61, or 62, when 140 quarterly (35 years) payments have been made. In fact, the amount of the basic Social Security pension (P) is calculated as:

$$P = \bar{W} \times T \times \frac{N}{150},$$

where $\bar{W}$ is the mean yearly wage calculated over the ten "best" years for the fraction below the stipulated upper limit,[7] T is the pension rate, and N is the number of quarterly payments made to the Social Security plan. In the previous example, $T = 0.375$ and $N = 140$. In the normal case, $T = 0.50$ and $N = 150$.

Generally, given the adjustment rates and the upper limits used for the calculation of $\bar{W}$, the Social Security retirement income is frequently lower than half of the effective mean wage resulting from the ten "best" years. It is particularly true for people who earned more than the Social Security ceiling wage: the replacement rate of their Social Security retirement pension can be much lower than 50 percent of the last wage they earned.

Such replacement rates have been recently calculated for a sample of individuals born in October 1922 and surveyed in 1988 (see Lacroix 1991; and table 7.9 below). Estimates show, for example, that women whose last monthly

6. Administration officials and salaried farm employees are insured by special pension plans. However, the Social Security regime is extended to nonsalaried categories, such as students, artists, and actors.

7. Wages of the ten "best" years and their corresponding upper limit are adjusted according to yearly varying rates. On July 1, 1991, e.g., these rates were 1.721, 5.843, and 15.942 for the years 1980, 1970, and 1960, respectively. The corresponding upper limits of $\bar{W}$ are 103, 466, 105, 174, and 109,043 francs, respectively (the Social Security monthly wage ceiling was 11,620 francs).

Table 7.9   **Mean Replacement Rates of Retirement Pensions for Individuals Born in 1922 and Surveyed in 1988**

Last Monthly Wage (francs)	Men			Women		
	Global	Social Security Pension	Complementary Pension	Global	Social Security Pension	Complementary Pension
<5,000	1.13	0.86	0.27	0.95	0.72	0.23
5,000–6,000	1.02	0.75	0.27	0.79	0.60	0.19
6,000–8,000	0.93	0.63	0.30	0.79	0.57	0.22
8,000–10,000	0.84	0.52	0.32	0.75	0.49	0.26
10,000–12,000	0.83	0.43	0.40	0.74	0.41	0.33
12,000–16,000	0.77	0.34	0.43	0.69	0.34	0.35
>16,000	0.66	0.20	0.46	—	—	—

Source: Lacroix (1991).
Note: The last monthly wage and the retirement income are net of social contributions.

wage was less than 5,000 francs have a global replacement rate equal to 95 percent and a Social Security replacement rate equal to 72 percent; for men whose last monthly wage was greater than 16,000 francs, these two replacement rates are equal to 66 and 20 percent, respectively.

7.4.5   Health Expenses[8]

The French health-care system of social insurance (the so-called Sécurité Sociale) was set up in 1945 with the objective of guaranteeing health care for all, especially children, mothers, and retired workers. The legislators' concern was clearly equality of access. Thus the 1958 hospital reform defines the notion of public duty (*mission de service public*) which mandates access to hospital care for all. The system is based on both the notions of insurance and of solidarity. Risk sharing applies, as in insurance, but contributions are compulsory, are related to income rather than risk, and entitle the insured and family to open-ended benefits. The system is based on a three-tier solidarity principle: between the sick and the healthy, the young and the elderly, and the poor and the wealthy. It is divided into three main branches: Assurance Maladie (health insurance), Assurance Vieillesse (pension fund), and the Branche Famille (family benefits).

In 1990, the total share of GDP allocated to health-care spending rose to 8.9 percent, or 538 billion francs. Its rather rapid growth over the past decade has been of growing concern to policymakers.

Today, more than 98 percent of the population is covered under three main national health insurance funds: salaried workers (75 percent) under the

---

8. This subsection is largely based on a paper written by Lise Rochaix (1992). I wish to thank her for giving me permission to use some parts of her text.

CNAMTS (Caisse Nationale d'Assurance Maladie des Travailleurs Salariés) also called the Régime Général, agricultural workers (8 percent) under the MSA (Mutualité Sociale Agricole), and the self-employed (7 percent) and the remaining 10 percent of the population under about fifteen different special funds.

Contributions to the Régime Général are compulsory and paid by the employees and employers: their shares are, respectively, 30 percent and 70 percent, although these rates may vary across occupational regimes. In 1990, up to 73.6 percent of health-care expenditures were financed by Sécurité Sociale. The state and local authorities contributed 1.1 percent through earmarked taxes on households and 19.2 percent through earmarked taxes on private insurance. The remaining 6.1 percent was paid by the "*mutuelles*" (a kind of nonprofit insurance society). Originally, the *mutuelles* offered insurance to those not covered by Sécurité Sociale. With the extension of Social Security to the vast majority of the population, they now tend to restrict themselves to refunding the cost-sharing element.

For ambulatory care and drugs, the insured generally pays the service charge in full and receives a refund at a fixed rate, depending on the occupational regime. It is usually 75 percent for medical services and 70 percent for pharmaceuticals. The remaining copayment, the so-called *ticket modérateur*, can be partly or totally refunded by private complementary insurance schemes (including *mutuelles*). However, at least 10 percent of the insured suffering from long-term serious illness (such as cancer) are totally or partially exempted from copayment. But the *ticket modérateur* can rise to 40 percent for some pharmaceuticals that are considered nonessential. A small but increasing proportion of pharmaceuticals are actually nonrefundable.

For hospital expenditure, Sécurité Sociale acts as a third-party payer, and patients make only the copayment, which cannot exceed 20 percent of the total bill, exclusive of expensive services. The same principle applies to diagnostic hospital services provided on an outpatient basis and to costly drugs and laboratory tests. In fact, only 4 percent of hospital resources are actually directly financed by households, and only 10 percent of hospital days bear a copayment.

A survey (Bocognano et al. 1992) conducted in 1991 by the Centre de Recherche, d'Etude et de Documentation en Economie de la Santé (CREDES; Center of Research Studies and Documentation on Health Economics) on a sample of households including at least one person covered by Sécurité Sociale shows that:

- 7.8 percent of surveyed individuals are partly or totally exempted from copayment (*Ticket modérateur*); this percentage increases with age (see table 7.10)

- 84 percent are covered by complementary health insurance; as shown in table 7.10, this share decreases with age; among these individuals, 61 per-

Table 7.10   **Individuals Exempted from Copayment and Covered by**
                       Complementary Health Insurance, 1991 (% of age group)

Age	Exempted from Copayment (%)	Covered by Complementary Health Insurance (%)
<16	1	84
16–39	4	82
40–64	11	87
65–79	26	85
≥80	41	67

Source: Bocognano et al. (1992).

cent are complementarily covered by *mutuelles,* 24 percent by insurance companies, and 15 percent by *caisses de prévoyance* (provident societies)[9]

- The mean monthly expenses paid by an individual for ambulatory care and drugs are strictly increasing with age (see table 7.11)

- 3.2 percent of the sample has been hospitalized at least once in the three months before the survey; this rate increases with age (2.4 percent for people less than 16 years old, 3.3 percent for those between 16 and 39 years old, 3.1 percent for those between 40 and 64 years old, and 4.7 percent for those more than 65 years old)

7.5   Targeted Saving Incentives

During the past ten years, several measures have been taken to stimulate household saving. New products have been successively offered, such as the individual savings passbook (*livret d'épargne populaire*), the industrial development savings account (*compte pour le développement industriel* [CODEVI]), long-term savings commitments (*engagements d'épargne à long terme*) up to 1982, the savings plan provided within the framework of the law promulgated by then Finance Minister Monory (in effect up to 1982), the stock market investment savings account (*compte d'epargne en actions* [CEA]) from 1983 to 1988, the individual retirement plan (*plan d'epargne retraite* [PER]) in 1988 and 1989, the individual savings plan (*plan d'epargne populaire* [PEP]) since January 1, 1990, and finally the stock market investment savings plan (*plan d'epargne en actions* [PEA]) since September 1992.

Common characteristics of these products are the nontaxation of their interest payments below some ceiling value and a deduction of the invested amount from taxable income or a limited tax cut.

9. The percentages covered by mutuelles, insurance companies, and caisses de prévoyance are respectively 59, 26, and 15 percent for people less than 65 years old and 72, 10, and 18 percent for people more than 65 years old.

Table 7.11   Mean Monthly Expense (in francs) Paid by an Individual for Ambulatory Care and Drugs, 1991

| | Mean Monthly Expenses for: | |
Age	Ambulatory Care	Drugs
<16	80	21
16–39	87	31
40–64	136	47
>65	210	97

Source: Bocognano et al. (1992).

Interest yielded by deposits in savings passbooks, CODEVIs, and building society savings accounts and plans are exempted from income tax.

The two main saving incentive schemes, which are associated with a premium assigned by the state, are (1) the building society savings account (*compte d'epargne logement* [CEL]) and the building society savings plan (*plan d'epargne logement* [PEL]) and (2) the individual savings plan (PEP). We will discuss these in detail.

7.5.1   Building Society Savings Accounts and Plans

The main characteristic of these plans and accounts is that they can be borrowed against (usually for home acquisition).

Building Society Savings Account (CEL)

The rate of return on deposits is 2.75 percent. The premium rate is 1.25 percent in the case of mobilization of loan rights: the upper limit of the premium is 7,500 francs. The ceilings for deposits and loans are 100,000 and 150,000 francs, respectively. The lending rate is 4.25 percent, and the minimum duration of deposits required for the granting of a loan is eighteen months. At the end of December 1991, the number of accounts opened was 8,550,000, and total deposits and loans were 123 and 63 billion francs, respectively.

Building Society Savings Plan (PEL)

The rate of return on deposits is 6 percent, including the premium rate of 1.5 percent, the upper limit of the premium being fixed at 10,000 francs. The ceilings for deposits and loans are 400,000 and 600,000 francs, respectively. The lending rate is 6.32 percent. The minimum and maximum lengths of this plan are four and ten years, respectively. At the end of December 1991, 10,550,000 PELs were currently subscribed, and total deposits in and loans on these plans were 471 and 170 billion francs, respectively.

Table 7.12 gives the evolution of total deposits and distributed premiums (i.e., the income paid) on such accounts and plans from 1989 to 1991. In this

Table 7.12   **Evolution of CEL and PEL Deposits and Premiums (billion francs)**

	1989		1990		1991	
	CEL	PEL	CEL	PEL	CEL	PEL
Total deposits at the end of December	120	448	119	459	123	471
Distributed premiums	0.90	7.6	0.96	9.2	0.91	7.9

Source: Rapport annuel au Conseil National du Crédit (1992).

table, distributed premiums concern rights relative to accounts or plans that come to maturity and are closed within a given year, and from which deposits have been withdrawn.

In fact, after steps taken in 1982 and 1983 to raise ceiling values and rates of return, the growth of deposits in CELs and PELs was particularly strong up to 1989 and then slackened. This slackening may be explained by the low return rates of CELs and PELs relative to those of more recent products (such as short-term UCITSs and PEPs), but also by the extension of the tax-exemption scheme to such alternative products. However, 33 percent of households participated in a CEL or a PEL in 1992 (see Arrondel et al. 1992).

7.5.2   Individual Savings Plan (PEP)

Individual savings plans (PEPs), offered since 1990 by banks and insurance companies, have replaced individual retirement plans (PERs). The number of PEPs opened in 1990 (nearly 7 million) and the total deposits during the same year (112 billion francs on December 31, 1990) testify to the success of this new product.

The authorized upper limit on saved capital is 600,000 francs for a single taxpayer or 1,200,000 francs for a household, which may open two plans. Interest is tax-free capitalized inside the PEP, if there is no withdrawal during the first eight years. At the end of a PEP, the subscriber can choose either the use of the tax-free saved capital or the payment of an annuity exempted from any income tax. If the plan takes the form of a life insurance contract, the subscriber benefits from the corresponding tax exemption.

The duration of a PEP is at least eight years but usually ten; the plan is contractually renewable up to ten years. After the tenth year, the plan is no longer provisioned but still runs tax-free: partial withdrawals are possible and do not induce the closure of the plan.

In fact, withdrawals are possible at any date, but returns from the plan are taxed if the withdrawal takes place during the first eight years. In this case, returns may eventually be subject to flat-rate withholding of 38.1 percent if the duration of the plan is less than four years and 18 percent if the duration is between four and eight years. Any withdrawal before the tenth year implies the closure of the plan.

However, a tax-exempt withdrawal is possible at any time in the following cases: death, disability, end of eligibility for the unemployment insurance system, liquidation subject to court supervision (the event may concern either the plan holder or his spouse if either subject to common taxation). Except in the case of death, which implies immediate plan closure, the tax-free withdrawal may occur during the two years following the event.

Deposits made during the first ten years by persons domiciled in France who are not subject to income tax are entitled to a state premium equal to 25 percent of the annual payment; the upper limit of the yearly premium is 1,500 francs per year. The premium is capitalized with the official rate of interest. The sum of yearly premiums and of their capitalized interests is paid by the state either ten years after the opening of the plan or at the date of closure (if this closure happens between the eighth and tenth years of the plan). The premium is not paid when a withdrawal is made before the eighth year (except in the cases listed above).

At the end of December 1990, total current deposits in PEPs and corresponding yearly premium entitlements were, respectively, 112 and 2.3 billion francs. One year later, they were, respectively, 199 and 2.5 billion francs. The rates of return announced for 1990 and 1991 were between 8 and 9 percent.

Characteristics of PEPs vary among the institutions that offer them to the public. The structure of investments, eventual penalties for withdrawal or transformation before the deadline, terms of payments or withdrawal, management charges, and performances (which may be guaranteed or not, indexed or not) make the PEP a differentiated product.

Contractual savings (mainly PELs and CELs) and PEPs opened in banks amounted to 649.3 billion francs in 1992. Their share of household financial assets (excluding UCITS investments and insurance reserve) was 12.6 percent in 1988, 13.5 percent in 1989, 16.3 percent in 1990, and 19.1 percent in 1991.

7.5.3   Stock Market Investment Savings Plan (PEA)

Since September 1992, a new product has been offered to the public by banking institutions: the stock market investment savings plan (PEA). This type of savings plan, oriented toward stock market investments, benefits from tax exemptions after the sixth year.

More precisely, returns of savings invested in a PEA are capitalized totally tax-free (exempted from taxation on income and capital gains) and the tax credit (see section 7.3.2) is refunded in the plan after the sixth year. The minimum length of the plan is eight years. Complete or partial withdrawal before this deadline implies plan closure. Any withdrawal made before the sixth year results in taxation at a flat 18.1 percent on returns and capital gains (including the tax credit) above the yearly threshold of 316,900 francs. Before the sixth year, returns are exempted. There is no ceiling for yearly deposits, but there is a global upper limit of 600,000 francs for a single holder, or 1,200,000 francs for a married couple.

A PEA consists of essentially two kinds of products: shares of French companies listed on the Paris Bourse and mutual funds (*Sociétés d'investissement à capital variable* [SICAV] and *fonds communs de placement* [FCP]) invested primarily in French shares. Holders can modify the structure of their PEAs: they may transfer some shares to buy others or prefer one SICAV to another.

Many PEA plans offered by banking institutions make a capital guarantee. The holder is then assured of keeping the invested amount. Moreover, some plans allow an investor to benefit from the upward movement of stock prices without being affected by downward movement. It is still too early to evaluate the success of this new product.

7.6   Insurance as a Saving Vehicle

7.6.1   Life Insurance and Capitalization Contracts

In addition to life insurance contracts, capitalization contracts are the main saving vehicle offered to households by insurance companies. Life insurance contracts for natural persons may be subdivided into two types of agreements. The first is insurance coverage "in case of decease," which implies the payment of capital to assignees when the insured person dies before contract termination. The second is insurance coverage "in case of life," which involves the payment of accumulated savings to the insured person if he or she is still alive at contract termination; the payment may be realized either as the payment of capital or as the payment of a life annuity that complements, for example, individual retirement pensions.

Capitalization contracts are similar to this second type of life insurance contract. The subscriber pays a premium capitalized by the insurance company with a guaranteed minimum rate. At contract termination, the company pays the capital back to subscribers, or eventually to their assignees. Today, capitalization contracts are often used as complements to retirement pension plans (see section 7.4.2).

Although the growth rate of life insurance turnover slackened slightly in 1990,[10] this turnover reached a particularly high level at the end of the eighties (167.5 billion francs in 1990). The mean contribution per resident was 3,100 francs in 1990.[11] Total contributions to life insurance contracts "in case of life" amounted to 124.5 billion francs in 1990 (up 19.0 percent over the previous year): because of the continuous growth of their contributions, such contracts represented 74 percent of total life insurance turnover in 1990 (they represented 26 percent of this turnover in 1980). Among all contributions paid for such contracts, the amounts corresponding to individual, "open group," and

10. The growth rate of life insurance turnover was + 20 percent (approximately) in 1988 and 1989, and + 15.4 percent in 1990 (see L'assurance française en 1990 1991).
11. The same year, it was equal to 7,000 francs in Switzerland, 4,700 francs in Finland, and 4,400 francs in Great Britain.

collective contracts were equal to 41.4, 67.2, and 15.9 billion francs, respectively, in 1990.[12] In the same year, contributions to life insurance contracts "in case of decease" amounted to 37.2 billion francs. They can be divided into parts of 6.8, 9.0, 1.9, and 19.5 billion francs, corresponding to complementary guarantee, individual, "open group," and collective contracts, respectively.

After a sharp increase from 1984 to 1989, capitalization contract turnover fell drastically in 1990: it was then equal to only 39.0 billion francs (down 29.6 percent from the previous year). This decrease may be explained primarily by the reassignment of savings to individual savings plans (PEPs).

Table 7.5 (section 7.2) gave the evolution of insurance reserves in household net current financial assets: over the past decade, their share of these assets grew from 7.3 percent in 1982 to 13.2 percent in 1991.

7.6.2   Tax Treatment of Accumulations through Insurance Policies

Premiums provided by life insurance contracts with a maturity greater than six years are eligible for a 25 percent tax reduction before their incorporation into taxable income. However, this reduction can be applied only on the fraction of the premium under 4,000 francs (plus 1,000 francs for each dependent child).

Life annuities in return for payment are taxable only on a given proportion of their amount (see section 7.4.1).

Returns provided by capitalization contracts are subject to income tax at contract termination. Taxable returns are equal to the difference between the amount refunded and the premiums paid. The beneficiary may choose the flat-rate withholding scheme: for contracts subscribed after January 1, 1990, the rate is 35 percent when the contract maturity is strictly less than four years, and 15 percent when the contract maturity is greater than four years. These rates are raised by 3.1 percent for persons domiciled in France. Returns are tax-exempt when contract maturity is greater than eight years.

References

L'Allocation des flux d'épargne. 1991. Paris: Conseil National du Crédit.
Arrondel, L., F. Dumontier, H. Valdelièvre, and D. Verger. 1992. Le patrimoine des ménages en 1992. INSEE Première, no. 210. Paris: Institut National de la Statistique et des Etudes Economiques.
Arrondel, L., and D. Kessler. 1989. Endettement, revenu et structure patrimoniale des ménages. Rapport technique. Paris: CEREPI.
L'assurance française en 1990. 1991. Paris: Fédération Française des Sociétés d'Assurances.

12. Collective contracts include the ones subscribed by firms to provide their employees with complementary retirement pension plans.

Bocognano, A., N. Grandfils, Th. Lecomte, An. Mizrahi, and Ar. Mizrahi. 1992. Enquête sur la Santé et la Protection Sociale en 1991: Premiers résultats. Paris: Centre de Recherche, d'Etude et de Documentation en Economie de la Santé.

Comptes et indicateurs économiques: Rapport sur les Comptes de la Nation. Economie Générale, nos. 1–2, 14–15–16, 36–37, 54–55–56. Paris: Collections de l'INSEE.

Gambier, C., and J. Y. Mercier. 1992. *Les impôts en France.* Paris: Editions Francis Lefebvre.

Lacroix, J. 1991. Les retraites remplacent 80% du salaire. Informations Rapides, no. 1. Paris: Ministère des Affaires Sociales et de la Solidarité.

Lollivier, S., and D. Verger. 1990. Le patrimoine aujourd'hui: beaucoup entre les mains de quelques-uns. Données Sociales, 167–170. Paris: Institut National de la Statistique et des Etudes Economiques.

Malpot, J. J., and V. Paquel. 1992. Que possèdent les diverses catégories sociales? Notes et graphiques, no. 19. Paris: Centre d'Etudes des Revenues et des Coûts.

Project for the 1992 Finance Act. 1992. Paris: Ministère de l'Economie, des Finances et du Budget.

Rapport annuel au Conseil National du Crédit. 1992. Paris: Conseil National du Crédit.

Rapport sur les Comptes de la Nation . 1991. Une année en demi-teinte. Série "Etudes." Paris: Institut National de la Statistique et des Etudes Economiques.

Réponse au questionnaire O.C.D.E. sur la fiscalité de l'épargne. 1992. Paris: Ministère de l'Economie, des Finances et du Budget, D.P., S.L.F., D.G.I.

Rochaix, Lise. 1992. Towards regulated competition in the french health care system. Paris: Direction de la Prévision, Ministère de l'Economie et des Finances.

Contributors

James Banks
Institute for Fiscal Studies
7 Ridgmount Street
London WC1E 7AE
U.K.

Richard Blundell
Institute for Fiscal Studies
7 Ridgmount Street
London WC1E 7AE
U.K.

Axel Börsch-Supan
Department of Economics
University of Mannheim
P.O.B. 10 34 62
D-68131 Mannheim 1
Germany

John B. Burbidge
Department of Economics
McMaster University
Hamilton, Ontario
L8S 4M4
Canada

James B. Davies
Department of Economics
Social Science Centre
University of Western Ontario
London N6A 5C2
Canada

Denis Fougère
CNRS and CREST
15 Boulevard Gabriel Péri
92245 Malakoff cedex
France

Takatoshi Ito
Institute of Economic Research
Hitotsubashi University
Kunitachi, Tokyo 186
Japan

Tullio Jappelli
Istituto Di Studi Economici
Istituto Universitario Navale-Via
    Acton 38
80133 Napoli
Italy

Yukinobu Kitamura
Institute for Monetary and Economic
    Studies
The Bank of Japan, 2-1-1 Hongoku-Cho
Nihonbashi, Chuo-ku
Tokyo
Japan

Marco Pagano
Universita Commerciale Luigi Bocconi
Via Sargartti 25
20136 Milano
Italy

James Poterba
Department of Economics
Room E52-350
Massachusetts Institute of Technology
50 Memorial Drive
Cambridge, MA 02139

Author Index

Subject Index